Invalid Women

The
University
of North
Carolina
Press
Chapel Hill
and
London

Figuring Feminine

Illness in American

Fiction and Culture,

1840–1940

Invalid Women

Diane Price Herndl

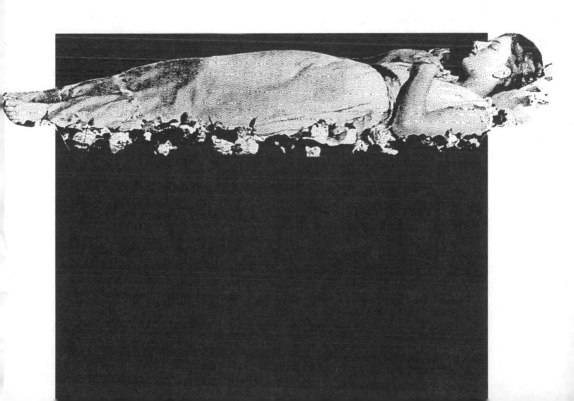

© 1993 The University of
North Carolina Press
All rights reserved
Manufactured in the United States of
America

Library of Congress Cataloging-in-
Publication Data
Price Herndl, Diane, 1959–
    Invalid women : figuring feminine
illness in American fiction and culture,
1840–1940 / by Diane Price Herndl.
        p.   cm.
    Includes bibliographical references and
index.
    ISBN 0-8078-2103-9 (alk. paper). —
ISBN 0-8078-4406-3 (pbk.: alk. paper)
    1. American fiction—19th century—
History and criticism.   2. Women and
literature—United States—History—19th
century.   3. Women and literature—
United States—History—20th
century.   4. American fiction—20th
century—History and criticism.
5. Physically handicapped women—
United States—History.   6. Physically
handicapped women in literature.
7. Invalids in literature.   8. Diseases in
literature.   9. Sick in literature.   I. Title.
PS374.W6P74   1993
813.009′352042—dc20   92-21433
                          CIP

97   96   95   94   93   5   4   3   2   1

The paper in this book meets the
guidelines for permanence and durability
of the Committee on Production
Guidelines for Book Longevity of the
Council on Library Resources.

For Carl

and for my parents,

Cooper and Roberta Price

Contents

Illustrations

Nancy and I are sorry to learn
about your illness. Our thoughts
and prayers are with you. God
bless you.
  —Ronald Reagan, letter to
    Augusta Lockridge, a fictional
    character who was blinded in
    the soap opera "Santa
    Barbara," Newsweek,
    30 April 1990

Preface

There will not be much in this book that is funny, and little
from contemporary popular culture with no pretensions to being "literature," but two popular and comic renderings of women's illnesses
strike me as suitable examples with which to begin this study.

In the "Kudzu" cartoon of 21 June 1989, the title character confers
with his minister about the attachment his mother enforces with illness,
complaining that when he "assert[s his] independence she gets sick"
and that he believes she can even sense his "betrayal" in speaking to the
minister about her. At that moment, she faxes in a response: "Cough,
cough. Wheeze."

In a 1990 episode of the television situation comedy "Roseanne,"
Roseanne, her sister, and their husbands discuss what kind of film they
want to see. Roseanne's husband says any kind of movie is fine, as long
as it is not one of those "women's movies." Acting out his definition, he
slumps in the recliner, claiming to be dying of "one of those women's
diseases." The brother-in-law joins him, and both collapse on the floor
after feigning romantic deaths.

Neither of these texts actually represents a woman's disease; instead,
each represents men reacting to a representation of female disease (a
fax, a film). They represent the interpretation—the male interpreta-

tion—of women's disease as, in one case, manipulative, and, in the other, not a serious subject, not something men care about. While it certainly would be overstating the case to claim that our culture treats women's diseases as a joke, it would not overstate it to say that these perceptions of female illness—that it is used for manipulation or to achieve a sentimental reaction—are strongly negative. They are so strong, in fact, that many women have to prove that they are not feigning illness before they can be taken seriously.

If this dubious attitude toward women and illness were found only in cartoons and situation comedies, there would be no need for this book. But all around us is evidence that women's illnesses are not taken seriously. The most damning is the June 1990 study by the U.S. Congress General Accounting Office that found that the National Institute of Health's (NIH) medical studies regularly focus on only men, leaving questions of how new medical treatments affect women completely unaddressed. According to this study, even scientific studies of rats regularly use only male rats, leaving questions of gender-based differences completely unaddressed. In some cases, when the studies do focus exclusively on women, their funding is more tenuous than the funding for other studies; only 13 percent of NIH funding goes to research on women's health issues.[1] In the 25 July 1991 issue of the *New England Journal of Medicine*, there is yet more evidence that such attitudes have real effects in the world: two different studies found that women's complaints of chest pain are not taken as seriously by physicians as are men's.

Of the many pressing health problems in the United States in the 1990s, women's health issues are among the most urgent. High infant mortality is an issue of women's health because babies suffer from their mothers' lack of prenatal care. The crisis in care for the elderly is a women's issue because the majority of elderly people are women.[2] Poverty, too, can be a cause of illness, and more and more in the last decade, poverty has become a women's issue.[3] Women's health should be a high priority for all feminists, but it is not. The health issue we tend to be most concerned with is abortion, which, although important, is nonetheless a healthy woman's issue, an issue for those who are well enough to make decisions about their own bodies.

Some of the reasons for our attitudes toward and interpretations of ill women and the representations of them will become apparent through this study. Illness has been and, one hopes, will continue to be an issue that affects only a few at any given time. The well always outnumber the sick, and the sick have too much to worry about to make illness a political issue. Illness isolates; it separates us from one another. Our experience of illness is individual; our experience of pain is solitary. Modern medical treatment further isolates illness; hospitals, nursing homes, and mental institutions keep ill people out of sight and out of mind.[4] Illness never seems the result of ideology.[5] Perhaps more important, however, are two attitudes that are deeply ingrained in American culture and fiction. First, Americans, the celebrants of robust heartiness and self-sufficiency, are suspicious of illness as a manifestation of laziness or willful attention seeking. Further, as the inheritors of a Protestant, Calvinist tradition, Americans often view (consciously or unconsciously) illness as a deserved punishment. These attitudes are apparent in public policies. Take, for example, the message of policies on elderly people's illnesses: had they taken proper care of their bodies and their finances, the American system seems to assert, they would not now be suffering.

American rhetoric and public policies are so clearly paradoxical that they invite a look at the discourse of illness. This book will examine that discourse primarily as it appears in literary texts, partly because of the power of literature to define and shape discourses through its ability to represent, and partly because of my own training and interests. I examine both how representations assumed the forms they have and how those representations have been—and are—received. This means looking at the cultural situations in which the figures appeared and the responses to those representations, both historical and contemporary.

The fact that every day women are dying of those "women's diseases" and every day their illnesses are being *interpreted* forms the cultural context that lies behind my analysis of fictions produced between 1840 and 1940. This is a study not of women's health but of the literary representations of it. As the penetration of these figures into contemporary popular culture texts like "Kudzu" and "Roseanne" suggests, this is a representational form that is not accidental. In fact, the figure of the invalid woman has a specific history that is at least 150 years old. This work analyzes the history of that literary figure and the responses to it, which are materially connected to how women's illnesses are interpreted through legitimating, or de-legitimating, reactions to those illnesses. While I do not suggest specific remedies to the problem of how our culture views women's sicknesses, I do hope that this study can help us to take them seriously, to refuse the joke that invalidates female illness.

During the five years I have been at work on this project, I have accumulated a number of debts I would like to gratefully acknowledge. The University of North Carolina Department of Social Medicine provided me with a two-year teaching fellowship in literature and medicine, during which I first taught this material, discussed it with colleagues, and participated in a genuinely interdisciplinary program. My students in "Gender and Medicine" during the 1986 and 1987 fall terms were often my teachers as well.

Linda Kauffman was instrumental in all stages of this study; her guidance, encouragement, and prodding kept me on track and challenged. Without her continuing support, this study would never have been written. Joy Kasson read drafts with care and attention; her suggestions often cut to the core of the issues here. Jane Tompkins offered me provocative criticism and challenged me to understand what was invested in this study; Townsend Ludington and Iris Tillman Hill were especially helpful and supportive at early, crucial stages in convincing me that this could be, and should be, written. Amy Koritz and Ann Folwell Stanford offered helpful advice, suggested strategies, and listened to interminable discussions of my rhetorical problems; they both helped me to work through some of my thorniest theoretical dilemmas. Dale Bauer supported my work long distance, offering encouragement, enthusiasm, and a much-needed sense that my work was valuable. In later stages of revision, Robyn Warhol and Roxanne Lin offered useful advice and support.

The interlibrary loan offices at the University of Vermont and New Mexico State University were extremely helpful in locating some hard-to-find materials, and the Emory University library was most generous in loaning a rare edition of *Christine*. Many thanks go to my research assistant at New Mexico State University, Michelle Holland, who helped me track down illustrations.

I would also like to thank Gillian Brown and Cynthia Jordan, who read the entire manuscript and offered much needed, helpful advice about revisions. Their suggestions made this a much better book.

The debts to my parents, Cooper and Roberta Price, are innumerable; to them I owe the chance and the confidence to ever try this in the first place. To Carl Herndl, besides apologies for the months during which I was obsessed with this project, I offer thanks for his support (material and emotional), for his patience, for his good ideas, and for being my first, and best, reader.

Invalid Women

An invalid, one who has been invalidated.
  —*Margaret Atwood,* The Handmaid's Tale *(1985)*

I choose not to suffer uselessly
to detect primordial pain as it stalks toward me
flashing its bleak torch in my eyes.
  —*Adrienne Rich, "Splittings" (1974)*

Infection in the sentence breeds
We may inhale Despair
At distances of Centuries
From the Malaria.
  —*Emily Dickinson (ca. 1873)*

Figures take shape insofar
as we can recognize, in passing
discourse, something that has
been read, heard, felt. The figure
is outlined (like a sign) and
memorable (like an image or a
tale). A figure is established if at
least someone can say: "That's so
true! I recognize that scene of
language."
—Roland Barthes,
    A Lover's Discourse
    (1978)

Introduction

Defining invalidism is a function of history. We usually re-
serve the term "invalid" for someone who is bedridden, but in the
nineteenth century it meant a state of weakness or a predisposition to
illness. Invalidism therefore referred to a lack of power as well as a
tendency toward illness. It is for this reason that I choose to discuss the
invalid woman rather than just the *ill* one. "Invalid" further carries
traces of its etymology and suggests the not-valid. Invalidism is therefore the term that best describes the cultural definition of women in the
nineteenth century (and perhaps in the twentieth) and the ill woman's
relation to power and her culture. But it also describes the historical
status accorded to ill women's (and maybe all women's) desires: not
valid.

Looking at the *figure* of the invalid woman involves a number of
specific issues. First, it involves gazing at the empty space, form, or
shape into which the woman is placed to understand the origin of the
figure's meaning. The figure, a signifier, though maintaining the same
shape and outward appearance, represents different signifieds in different narrative or cultural contexts. Nevertheless, each new appearance carries with it the "ghosts" of the others. Studying the figure of the
invalid therefore involves considering not just the particular case but

that case in the context of other appearances of the figure. Like a musical figure that structures the composition and is repeated with variations, the literary figure becomes recognizable and effective through its repetitions. Focusing on these variations, we can unpack the representation to analyze its form, content, and ideological influences.[1]

These are the issues that will shape my study of the figure of the invalid woman in American fiction and culture. This analysis will focus on the dialogue between literary representations and the cultural situations out of which these representations of women's illnesses come and into which they enter. In so doing, it will move back and forth between cultural and literary discourses, and between cultural and literary history; that is, it will examine both the situations that shaped the figure and those that have shaped its reception.

It is difficult for the feminist critic to approach the subject of the invalid woman because invalidism, which could be described as the extreme of patriarchal definitions of woman, is one of the roles against which feminism historically has had to struggle. Whereas women in general are characterized as weak and lacking power, better off staying quiet at home, the invalid is specifically recognized as even weaker and more powerless than most women and is required to stay at home. Whereas women have been discouraged from involving themselves in productive work, the invalid has been absolutely forbidden it. For a latter twentieth-century feminist, working toward equality of the sexes in the workplace and the home, this powerlessness seems antithetical to feminist goals. A woman's manipulation of that powerlessness is an act that we may understand but that we have learned to distrust and to disapprove of. Further, it can be painful to sort out which strategies of defining or using invalidism subvert norms (illness as a resistance to patriarchal definitions) and which collude (illness as an acceptance of patriarchal definitions). Whereas the nineteenth-century woman may have seen refuge, solace, purpose, and even empowerment in illness, we may see accession to patriarchal definitions and limitations. Why then write about representations of women as sickly? Why not focus on the positive roles women have chosen for themselves?

There is much for us as feminists to learn from historical and literary representations of illness that will prove vital in understanding our own attitudes toward women's health and their bodies, our own attitudes toward sick women and representations of women in general. These representations are now so familiar, so natural, we no longer see them as ideological positions. We need to do some "archaeological" work on such attitudes to better understand them, which we cannot do by focusing only on the happy moments in women's history and literature. But my study *is* specifically political. It is "feminist" according to the definition offered by Rosalind Delmar in "What Is Feminism?": it reveals "an active desire to change women's position in society" (13). This book is, further, motivated by anger at the injustice of the invalid's position.

In "Women's Rage," film critic Julia Lesage argues that we need to articulate our rage against women's oppression in order to "understand the different structures behind different women's rage" (420). Women's relations toward their own bodies are often marked by anger; their relations to medical institutions are frequently hostile. This study recognizes that anger, but it is marked by a double vision and a double attitude. As I look at the body of the invalid woman, aesthetically arranged on her deathbed to teach the male world a lesson, I see a woman who had something important to say, but I also see a woman who died trying. Sympathetic I may be, but I do not want to follow in her footsteps. When women are taught that illness and death offer them the best route to power, we all suffer the loss of possibilities.[2] There is nothing empowering about victimage.

For the feminist reader, studying the figure of the invalid woman necessitates assuming several paradoxical stances. She must be both sympathetic and distant. To refuse the sympathy is to re-inscribe the cultural isolation of the ill woman—to refuse kinship, involvement, and perhaps even implication. But to lose distance is to miss the opportunity to observe illness as an outsider, that is, *not* as an "objective" viewer (I make no claims to objectivity) but as someone who can watch the operations of power without the specific attitude of those directly involved. A certain amount of anger is necessary for any feminist undertaking; too much anger may blind us to our own participation in patriarchal systems, our own acquiescence in the isolation of invalid women. Too much anger may also cause us to blur important distinctions. Not all women are "invalid women," nor are we all threatened in the same way by the cultural forces that define invalidism. We must be able to recognize when invalidism is a useful or necessary strategy of subversion and when it is a sign of defeat and despair. But while we are not all marked by physical invalidism, we are all marked by cultural invalidity; we may not be invalid women, but we do have a certain solidarity with them.

The figure of the invalid woman insists on a reading that focuses on the play of power and desire in the narrative, the family, and the culture. The woman who becomes sick is portrayed as a figure with no power, subject to the whims of her body or mind, or as a figure with enormous power, able to achieve her desires through the threat of her imminent death or her disability. Sometimes she is both powerful and powerless. The woman whose illness becomes a focal point for a narrative lives on the boundaries of power; one minute she is in the grips of her own body, which has turned against her and put her at the mercy of doctor, family, and friends, the next minute she is dominating her family and friends in ways that a healthy woman could achieve only in fantasy.[3] Reading the narrative of the invalid demands that one examine the attraction and the repulsion of this figure for readers and for writers and analyze how the narrative power of the invalid translates into cultural power or the lack of it. One must recognize the anger at powerlessness but also the uses of (apparent) powerlessness.

In this study, therefore, I attempt to mediate between sympathy and distance, praise and criticism, for figures of invalid women and their creators. All of the writers I discuss created their invalid women as a response to a situation that seemed threatening. I agree here with Kenneth Burke's claim in *The Philosophy of Literary Form* that literature "is produced for purposes of comfort. . . . It is undertaken as *equipment for living*, as a ritualistic way of arming us to confront complexities and risks. It would *protect* us. Let us remind ourselves, however, that implicit in the idea of protection is the idea of something to be *protected against*. . . . [Literature] is 'medicine,' therapeutic or prophylactic" (61). From the vantage point of the 1990s, some of those responses seem more successful than others. Unlike the patriarchal critic who disguises his ideological evaluations as purely aesthetic ones, I do not keep my ideological and aesthetic criticisms separate. Textual strategies that seek to find power through submission, for example, were the nineteenth-century woman writer's best line of defense against a patriarchal system of value that threatened to diminish the woman's worth. For late twentieth-century readers, however, such strategies leave us dissatisfied, even if we recognize and admire their efficacy for their own times. For the maker of the 1939 film *Dark Victory*, a rich woman's moral improvement because of illness was an effective response to Depression-era realities, an attempt to reconcile the audience's own profound sense of loss with a promise of character building. But for the contemporary viewer, such a representation only seems to reinforce class stereotypes in which rich women's illnesses are more beautiful and tragic than other people's. I will pursue here, then, a doubled criticism that will recognize the simultaneity of oppression and resistance and will acknowledge the double position women occupy as both victims and agents of their own oppression.

Reading Illness

In the last several years, feminist historians, psychoanalysts, and literary critics have written much about women's illnesses during the mid- and late nineteenth century. As with all histories, their work has been history *for,* not just history *of;* as Hayden White explains in his essay "Historicism, History, and the Figurative Imagination" in *Tropics of Discourse*, all histories are for something. "It is not only history *for* in the sense of being written with some ideological aim in view, but also history *for* in the sense of being written for a specific social group or public" (104). These texts, in addressing a difficult period in the history of women's emancipation, have aimed at interpreting that illness as much as describing it or exposing it.

Presenting an outline of those earlier interpretations of illness will inevitably be an oversimplification. Still, this schematic view will allow us to understand the relation between interpretation and the understanding of women's illnesses. To this point, women's illness has been seen largely as a result of the oppressive use of male power, as the resistance to oppressive power, or as the means to a kind of power of its own (artistic, political, or "sentimental"). These three views of illness sometimes overlap and are sometimes mutually exclusive; they sometimes focus on only one kind of illness and are sometimes more wide-ranging. What I want to investigate in this book is how women's illness can stand in all three relations to power at the same time, how it can be both redemptive and destructive, resistant and dominated, liberatory and oppressive. This is, of course, yet another interpretation of the representations of illness, but it is also—and perhaps more so—an interpretation of the *discourse* on illness that questions whether illness per se means anything at all.

By far the most influential school of thought about women's illness holds that nineteenth-century women's illnesses were most often the result of "cultural conditioning," patriarchal oppression, and the masculine power to define and control women's bodies. These arguments usually take two forms—maintaining either that oppression actually caused the illness or that oppressive norms caused women to be defined as ill. ("Illness" in this study refers to both physical and mental illnesses. There is no easily made distinction between the two today, and there certainly was none in the mid-nineteenth century. Physical and mental illnesses exist along a continuum.) Sandra Gilbert and Susan Gubar argue in *Madwoman in the Attic* that nineteenth-century norms for women's behavior—selflessness and submissiveness—were themselves the causes of ill health (54).[4] In a parallel argument, historian Carroll Smith-Rosenberg argues in *Disorderly Conduct* that much nineteenth-century illness can be understood as an exaggeration of Victorian feminine norms. Historians and literary critics—from Barbara Ehrenreich and Deirdre English to Elaine Showalter and Mary Poovey—have focused on how medical thought was able to solidify masculine privilege by defining women as ill and enforcing that definition.

There have been, however, other voices who speak of illness not as the *result* of oppression but as the resistance to it. Certainly this group of writers is not always entirely separate from the first. Carroll Smith-Rosenberg discusses at length how hysteria could have been the woman's only means to redefine her social and familial position during the cultural changes of the mid-nineteenth century; and Elaine Showalter in *Female Malady* raises the question of whether hysteria was a mode of protest, concluding that "hysteria and feminism do exist on a kind of continuum" (147, 161). In "Escaping the Sentence," Paula Treichler argues that the heroine's madness at the end of Charlotte Perkins Gilman's "The Yellow Wallpaper" is the beginning of a language of resistance. These analysts see illness not as a fulfillment of sexist stereotypes but as a way to resist them.

Some writers—especially those involved in or influenced by the antipsychiatry movements in France (led by Gilles Deleuze, Felix Guattari, and Jacques Lacan) and in England (led by R. D. Laing and David Cooper)—see women's mental illness as not only a kind of resistance to oppressive power but itself a form of artistic expression and feminine power.[5] Like Phyllis Chesler in *Women and Madness*, these writers (who most often focus specifically on mental rather than physical illness) see insanity as a label applied to the woman who rebels. Hélène

Cixous, in her critical play "Portrait of Dora," sees the ill or mad woman as a courageous figure refusing to accept masculine norms, while Luce Irigaray in *Speculum of the Other Woman* sees her as a woman whose artistic and self-expressive attempts to redefine her relation to language and its (negative) definitions of her are, because different, defined as mad.

The third approach to women's illness is, again, not always precisely separate from the second (although it can be distinguished from the first); here illness is seen expressly as a form of power gained either through exploitation and manipulation or through a sacrifice modeled on Christian values. In "'The Fashionable Diseases,'" Ann Douglas Wood argues that in the nineteenth century illness became a matter of being "fashionable" and that women often exploited their position as invalids, an argument that had been developed during the nineteenth century by the writer Abba Goold Woolson in *Woman in American Society*. Douglas further argues that texts which depicted illness and death became the means for "ministers and women" to assert the significance of those previously thought insignificant. Their motive for this, she argues in *Feminization of American Culture*, was to "establish a new balance of power in the free-for-all, intensely competitive democracy of American culture," a balance of power that would favor them and their political ideals (202). In a reading of illness completely opposed to Douglas's, Jane Tompkins argues in *Sensational Designs* that illness in the nineteenth century often was read as a mark of one's genuine election by God and became a chance to demonstrate, or use, the power of the deathbed to propagate Christian morals and values. In these interpretations, the representation of illness, whether as a sign of ruthless exploitation or ultimate goodness, is understood as a means to an end.

Except for in the last of these three approaches to illness, feminist historians tend often to look primarily at the illness itself rather than its representation. This book will focus specifically on the representation and on the political work of that representation. Like Gilbert and Gubar, Smith-Rosenberg, Ehrenreich and English, Showalter, and Poovey, I see patriarchal culture as potentially sickening for women and as defining women as inherently sick, especially when they resist its norms. Guided by Chesler, Irigaray, and Cixous, I understand that illness can often be simply the label given to women's moves toward artistic expression or the manifestation of repressed artistic impulses.

And, like Douglas and Tompkins, I see that illness and its representations can have a real, material effect on the world.

To hold all these views of illness at once is not necessarily contradictory; it is to insist that to read any one representation of an illness, one must situate that representation not just within a specific historical moment but also within a specific discursive and literary moment. It would be a mistake to generalize from any one of these writers about "illness." Illness itself is not discursive; it is not a story or a narrative. We have access to that illness, however, only through its narrative, through the discourse on illness. The woman who is experiencing an illness, who is living it, also can communicate that experience to others only through story, only through the discourse that is available to her to express what she is feeling. While the sufferer's experience of illness itself is rarely only a matter of language (as it can be in some forms of paranoia and in hysterical language disturbances), any communication about that illness is always discursive. So *our* experience of, or access to, another person's illness is always through language and usually through narrative.

Invalid Ideology

The figure of the invalid woman is a significant focus for the study of literature and culture because invalidism, of all the other roles offered to women, appears to be the role that is most "obviously natural," the least likely to be influenced by cultural constructions. Illness, beyond childhood claims of stomachache to avoid school, does not appear to be a role that one would choose to assume, at least not for long. It is significant for a feminist study because the invalid, defined by her body and her weakness, represents an exaggeration of one of the "natural" definitions of all women. This study will call into question the "obvious naturalness" of feminine illness in fiction. Such obviousnesses are the points at which Roland Barthes situates the figure and at which Louis Althusser locates the workings of ideology: "It is indeed a peculiarity of ideology that it imposes (without appearing to do so, since these are 'obviousnesses') obviousnesses as obviousnesses, which we cannot *fail to recognize* and before which we have the inevitable and natural reaction of crying out . . . 'That's obvious! That's right! That's true!' " (*Lenin and Philosophy*, 172, emphasis added). Ideology makes its appearance in representations, then. In *Feminist Criticism and Social Change*, Judith Newton and Deborah Rosenfelt identify ideology with representation: ideology is "a complex and contradictory system of representations (discourse, images, myths) through which we experience ourselves in relation to each other and to the social structures in which we live" (xix).

An illness, most would argue, is a real thing, not a representation. Because feminine illness has always seemed so "natural" in literature, it has never been questioned as a working of ideology through the text. People *do* get sick and many of those people are women; women getting sick in narratives must therefore be natural, true to life, "realistic." But "illness" is a defining term, especially when it involves the categorization of someone as an "invalid"; it is a figure for explaining one's place in society. Representing one's self as an invalid puts into play a whole structure of care, attention, responsibility, and privilege. Defining what counts as illness, setting boundaries around who can and cannot be considered an invalid, however "natural" these definitions may seem, are functions of ideology, influenced by representation.

The invalid woman, then, can serve as the focus for questioning the history and the ideological power of representation. Looking at her figure can help us understand how knowledge and perception—more specifically, self-knowledge and self-perception—are shaped by representation. When is one sick enough to be classified an invalid? When does an illness become severe enough that it warrants "taking to bed"? When does it warrant a complaint? The answer is made clear by the culture. As Clifford Geertz explains in *Interpretation of Cultures*, "Culture patterns . . . are 'programs'; they provide a template or blueprint for the organization of social and psychological processes" (216). The private experience of pain therefore becomes a public phenomenon when it is declared to be "illness." However "natural" the experience of illness seems, we can only define it according to socially constructed categories. Using the work of anthropologist Mary Douglas, Carroll Smith-Rosenberg argues in *Disorderly Conduct* that "there is no natural way to experience the human body. Our mind, shaped by its social experiences . . . interprets the physical body's impulses, requirements, and sensations, shaping them into culturally anticipated categories" (48). She points out that "the human body, known only through the social body's conceptual categories, has never existed as a 'natural' entity. Always experienced as a cultural construct, its carnal realities are easily transformed into a cloak for political and economic forces" (51). We are taught by familial and social norms what kinds and amounts of pain count as being sick. This study focuses on the *embodiment* of ideologies, on a "politics of the body," particularly a politics of the female body, because, as Michel Foucault argues in *Power/Knowledge*, power over the body "produces effects at the level of desire—and also at the level of knowledge" (59).

The figure of the invalid woman at once unites the romantic ideology of woman as "body" (as opposed to man as "mind"), the Victorian stereotype of woman as weak and delicate, and the bourgeois ideal of woman as "conspicuous consumer" (who passively consumes since as invalid she must be served at all times). She therefore stands in a specific relation to money and productive labor; she is expected to consume (by the turn of the century, "consumption" had moved from describing a disease to describing a cure),[6] and yet she can do no labor at all. The ill woman becomes the ultimate consumer in the process of being herself consumed by disease. She also stands in a specific relation to sexist definitions of women; she embodies the negative discourses about women.

Invalidism has historically offered women a way to resolve seriously conflicting definitions of woman to achieve a kind of power when no other means opened up. Invalidism, therefore, can offer women a coherent and simple role in a world where multiple and conflicting roles are threatening or disappointing.[7] But erasing conflict can be another function of ideology, according to Michael Ryan in "The Politics of Film": "Ideology in this sense is forced closure, the imposition of harmony on the ever-open possibility of conflict. . . . Ideology, as the suturing of difference or the representation of unity where there is conflict, is a symptom of an attempt to reduce differences of force that are a necessary structural part of an inegalitarian society to a spurious identity of interests or common desire" (484). The invalid woman can be an important site of the working of ideology to cover up or disguise sexual inequality under the mask of "nature." This study will attempt to reopen those lines of conflict and difference which illness has been used to suture.

What I address in this book is the history of one century's discourses about women and illness; I trace the changes in the medical discourses, the relations between medical and other social/political discourses, and how literary figurations of illness are part of medical parlance and how they resist it. Implicit in this argument, then, is a notion of resistance. But resistance to what and by whom?

Culture, Dialogue, and Discourse

The central tenet of my study of the representations of illness is that literary representations take place among a plethora of other representations, that literary discourse occurs in a world of other discourses. The relationship among all those representations and discourses, and between them and someone's "lived experience" of illness, is therefore, not surprisingly, complex. I argued earlier that a woman's sense of whether she is sick comes from categories set out by the culture. But where do those categories originate? What does it mean for a "culture" to determine them? What is the individual woman's relation to those models and definitions of illness?

To ask these questions is to enter into two of the most central debates in contemporary literary scholarship, which I cannot hope—and do not pretend—to resolve here. *Invalid Women* is just one *essai* in the ongoing attempt to understand and frame the questions. I can, however, sketch out what the debates look like and situate this study within them. The first two of the three questions, on "culture" and the issue of categories ("templates," "patterns," or "models"), as well as the subtitle of this work (*Figuring Feminine Illness in American Fiction and Culture, 1840–1940*), place this study in the debate over "cultural studies," a field that is still in the process of defining itself, or, as Richard Johnson would have it in "What Is Cultural Studies Anyway?," resisting definition. In this study, what counts as "culture" consists of texts, discourses, and "cultural products," in the broadest sense of those terms—books (fiction and nonfiction), pamphlets and journals, art (high and popular), advertising, speeches, and other ways that human beings communicate ideas with each other. In other words, representations count as "culture" here. In choosing this definition, I am placing myself in the "structuralist" paradigm of cultural studies rather than the "culturalist" one, in the terms that Stuart Hall identifies in "Cultural Studies: Two Paradigms."[8] The answers to the questions with which I began this discussion of "culture," then, are that "templates" come from the representations through which people understand their relations to each other and to the world they live in.

Another way to ask the third of my questions (on the woman's relation to the definition of illness) would be to phrase it in terms of the current debate between humanists and post-structuralists: what relation does the speaking subject bear to discourse? Is that subject, as the post-structuralist would argue, determined or structured by the discourse? Or, as the humanist would have it, is the subject in control of discourse, capable of free agency, acting entirely from her own experience of the world? This study will mediate between these two positions and offer itself as a dialogue between them.[9] Certainly one is limited in what one can think or represent by what has been thought and represented before; but that history of thought and representation is rich and ever varied.[10]

In this study, the subject will be seen neither as an entirely passive construct nor as an entirely active agent. Neither the woman experiencing an illness nor the author writing a story about a woman's illness is free of the ways that illness has been represented before, but neither one is entirely constrained either. When Edith Wharton began *The House of Mirth*, she certainly was drawing on her "lived experience" as a member of New York's high culture, but she drew equally on earlier depictions of women's illnesses in both sentimental and realist novels and on the paintings of dying women that were so popular at the turn of the century.

The theoretical difficulty here is to understand what motivates change, where it comes from, and what the subject's—or agent's—role is in that change. If this study is, as I claimed at the outset, motivated by the desire for change, where is that change to come from, and, for that matter, where is the desire for that change to come from? Am I to constitute myself, as critic, as some kind of free agent opposed to the subjects I critique here whom I see as being constrained by their discourses? I hope not. But to address those issues, it will be necessary to rephrase my questions again: what is the relation between subject, discourse, and lived experience?

Post-structuralism has come under attack for being formalist, too removed from "real life," and apolitical. To this end, critics drag up the political history of Paul de Man to argue for the apoliticism of deconstruction. A number of feminist critics, however, anticipated and answered this critique even as it was being formulated. As early as 1980, Barbara Johnson argued in *Critical Difference* that one of the insights of post-structuralist thought was that "the text is not constative but performative. . . . The reader is in fact one of its effects" (143); that is, language is never "only" language because it creates real effects in the world. More recently, in *A World of Difference*, she returns explicitly to this question, problematizing specifically the sense that deconstruction has nothing to do with the "real world," trying, in her words, to "recontextualize a certain way of reading." She works from what she describes as "de Man's central insight: that language, since it is (to use Raymond Williams' term) *constitutive* of the human, cannot itself be entirely 'human.' It is neither inside nor outside the subject, but both at once" (6). From this insight, that language is neither entirely human nor inhuman, neither entirely inside nor outside the subject, she argues that the goal of criticism is to explore "not whether or not language is problematic as a medium of understanding, but rather what use we can make of the perception that it is" (6–7).[11] This study tries to use this insight into the problematic nature of representation, while keeping squarely within the context of the material world. When an author writes to resist the current construction of illness, as did Charlotte Perkins Gilman, in what ways is she constrained by that very construction? In what ways does the power of discourse itself keep an author, like E. D. E. N. Southworth or Nathaniel Hawthorne, from being able to represent transparently a particular viewpoint of women's bodies? And, further, what kind of relation does the discourse establish between real women and their ill bodies?

Social change here is centered in an understanding of resistance and in the conflict between differing discourses. My use of difference in this book takes two forms: first, the essential difference that exists within any individual, and second, the difference that exists within discourse. I maintain a view of the subject in which the individual is radically split and in which it is inappropriate even to speak of the "individual," as such, because the term assumes a certain kind of autonomy, identity, and, well, "individuality" that precludes the sense of the power that a cultural discourse can have in shaping that subject. On the other hand, because the subject is split, there is never an individual "identity" even within that discourse, partially because of the nature of subjectivity but also because of the resistance inherent in discourse.[12]

This "resistance" in discourse appears in several forms in this study, most often as a resistance or a conflict within a given discourse about women's illnesses; medical theories are often internally divided, conflicted, and at odds with themselves. Despite the pervasive popular notion that there is such a thing as "medicine," which is a monolithic, monologic institution with a clear theoretical bent and a single methodology, "medicine" is a hotbed of contention—there are virtually no uncontested medical "truths," even at the end of the twentieth century—and the period between 1840 and 1940 was a time of intense change within the medical profession, change that came amid fierce battles about which theory, which discourse, would hold sway. But even though medicine often defined the parameters of the debate over the body and illness during the period this text covers, it was never the only discourse about the body or femininity at work in any given period, nor always the most powerful. Medical theorists often sought or forged alliances with other kinds of thought—religious, political, social, or economic—to bolster their own effectiveness and were just as often met with resistance from those same discourses. The power to define—and therefore to stand a chance to control—the body was and continues to be immeasurable. Medical and literary "institutions" can present illness as the most coherent role for women by denying and disguising those conflicts. Exploring the political and economic conditions out of which representations come and through which they are comprehensible reveals their constructedness, removes the disguise; such societal conditions provide the ground on which figures are drawn.[13]

This theory of discourse has its origins in the work of Mikhail Bakhtin. In *The Dialogic Imagination*, Bakhtin sets out the fundamentals of his theory of novelistic discourse, the model for my own sense of how all discourse works. Such a discourse resists identity and definability because it is "double-voiced," "dialogic," and "polyphonic." So while the American Medical Association presents a public front of unity, in fact the medical discourse is at odds with itself and with other discourses. Meaning is not created through a single voice but in the interaction of voices, in dialogue. It is always discourse-in-progress. "Discourse lives, as it were, on the boundary between its own and another, alien, context" (284). What I see happening in novels, in medical texts, and in writings about the place of women is the dialogue not only between these texts but within them. "Alien" forces and contexts create the possibilities for change, and the differences already existing within the individual can motivate that change.

Those same alien forces can also interfere with an author's own ideological purposes. Bakhtin defines heteroglossia as "*another's speech in another's language*, serving to express authorial intentions but in a refracted way. Such speech constitutes a special type of *double-voiced discourse*. It serves two speakers at the same time and expresses simultaneously two different intentions. . . . In such discourse, there are two voices, two meanings and two expressions" (324, emphasis in original). I see no simple discourses in this text, no representation of illness that is entirely clear in its ideological purposes. In every case, when an author sets out with a clear agenda of change, that agenda is at some point undercut, at some point problematic. I want to see what use can be made of that problematic representation.[14] Even when Tillie Olsen describes the plight of the poor laborer's wife in *Yonnondio* as a problem created by society, she opens the door for placing the blame on the poor themselves.

I set this understanding of dialogue within the context of "fiction and culture" because I want to emphasize the various dialogues that exist— between fiction and other cultural discourses, between the discourses, and among fictional representations themselves. This latter dialogue, what Bakhtin calls "intertextuality," is specifically tied to my reading of figuration—the repetition of figures in different texts and contexts is a testament to the power of intertextuality and to the dialogue among different authors. The context against which I read the figures of illness is the complex interaction of forces that has been illustrated diagrammatically by Richard Johnson in "What Is Cultural Studies Anyway?" as "the circuit of the production, circulation and consumption of cultural products" (46). Each representation, its readings, and misreadings become, along with changes in lived experience, part of the *conditions* for the production and reception of the next representation. The process is dynamic and ongoing. Every contribution, whether of "production" or "reception," has an effect on the discourse, and every change in the discourse affects both production and reception as well as the "forms" the cultural products will take.

The traditional figure of the invalid becomes an interesting focus for a study of culture, dialogue, and discourse because the narrative constraints on any story about a sick person are so tight. There are essentially only three outcomes: she can die, go mad, or get well.[15] Such constraints allow the critic to examine the repetitions enacted by the narratives and to look at the various ways the figure has been filled. When Henry James, in 1902, picks up the figure of the invalid woman that E. D. E. N. Southworth used in 1849, he is responding not only to Southworth and to his own sister's journal but to other representations of ill women in his own time in medical journals and the popular press. The meaning of Milly Theale's illness in *The Wings of the Dove* is to be found "on the boundary" of those contexts. The "natural" assumption that there are only two stories for the invalid, and that we know what counts as a happy or an unhappy ending, then, can be questioned and understood in its rhetorical relation to specific historical and ideological contexts.

To call this interaction among discourses a "dialogue" may be too gentle a term, though. "Battle" may be the more appropriate term for what I discuss here. The stakes are no less than the dominance of women's bodies and, therefore, of women themselves. To call the interaction recorded here a conversation, or even a dialogue, is to cast that interaction in an altogether too civil light. It is a battle, a struggle that may exist under the imprimatur of polite conversation but is never to be seen as less than a fight over life and health.

Invalid Women

The kind of feminist criticism influenced by cultural studies that I do in this book cannot be "gynocriticism," the study of works written only by women, because it must examine the ideology upheld by the dominant culture as well as individual reactions to, revisions of, and rebellions against that ideology. For the same reason, it cannot study only canonical works. It must focus, instead, on the differences and similarities of texts produced inside and outside conventional power structures—be they sexual, literary, or political.

Although such a study ideally would also look at texts from different socioeconomic and racial groups, mine will not. All of the writers and central characters of the texts in this study are white and middle class. My decision is meant both to give consistency to the study and to focus on the figure of the invalid woman as a specifically class-oriented representation. Because of her historical relation to money and labor, the invalid woman has almost always been a woman of leisure; working-class women's illnesses have been relatively obscure in literary representations.[16] Analyzing these representations allows me to focus on writers' and critics' aesthetic valuations and their ideological roots as well as historical attitudes toward leisure and work.[17]

My study encompasses the century between 1840 and 1940. These dates mark important changes in American literature, medicine, and culture. In literary terms, the 1840s mark the beginning of the ascendancy of American literature in the United States. The decades of the 1830s and 1840s were the first in which more books by domestic writers were sold in America than by British authors. Circulating libraries were started, and reading became a major part of popular culture. For the first time, an American literature seemed to be emerging, written to fulfill the domestic, economic, political, and philosophical needs of people in the United States.

In medical terms, the decade between 1840 and 1850 marks the beginning of the professionalization of American medicine. The rise of the medical profession is important in the depiction of the ill woman for a number of reasons, but the most significant is that women provided the easiest entry into American households. Through appropriation of birthing from midwives, the establishment of gynecology as a specialty, the burgeoning of the patent medicine business, and home health guides that stressed the necessity of calling in the doctor for most illnesses, physicians moved into the American household by means of the woman of the house. One of the requirements for this move was to convince women that they were sick enough to need a doctor.[18] There is no question that this strategy was successful; from the 1840s until the 1890s, women were increasingly defined as sickly and weak.

Politically and economically, the 1840s were a time of real change in America. During the first half of the nineteenth century, there was a marked shift in the American economy from an agricultural to an industrial base, a change from a predominantly rural to an increasingly urban population, and a move toward a more definite capitalist class structure. By the 1840s, it was clear that the old social order that was established in the colonies was gone, but it was not clear exactly what the new social order would look like. Patterns established in the 1840s would shape the rest of the century and, arguably, much of our own century. Those patterns were industrial, urban, and capitalist.[19]

The 1840s also mark the emergence of two critically important discourses on women in the United States: feminism (the Seneca Falls women's rights convention was held in 1848) and domesticity (in large part shaped by the "women's novels" of that decade). The two movements based on these political ideologies—both led by women—would shape the thinking and writing on women's social and political roles for decades (if not to the present day). Sometimes complementary, sometimes opposed, both movements militated against a definition of woman as invalid; whether she is to be man's equal in the workplace and government or the moral and physical protector of her family, woman has to be strong. And yet writers in each of these movements seem fascinated with the kind of power that the invalid could wield, even while frequently associating woman's failure to fulfill her appointed role with invalidism.

This study ends at 1940 because World War II occasioned revolutionary changes in the figure of the invalid. While many of the same tropes of female invalidism can be traced even to the present—especially in works like Sylvia Plath's *The Bell Jar* (1962), John Barth's *End of the Road* (1967), Walker Percy's *The Second Coming* (1980), and Margaret Atwood's *Bodily Harm* (1983) and *The Handmaid's Tale* (1985)—gender roles and illness roles were greatly altered during the second world war. Advances in medical technology, too, have further removed illness from our view and made our experience of it and its treatment particularly alien.

In literature, representations of illness since about 1940 have become pervasive. Just before and after the war, illness came to represent the metaphysical condition of men facing an existential crisis; Jean-Paul Sartre described this condition in *La Nausée* (1938), as did Albert Camus in *La Peste* (*The Plague*, 1947). And in American literature, the "illness story" became the dominant mode of postmodern American fiction; according to Richard Ohmann in "The Shaping of an American Canon," "For the people who wrote, read, promoted, and preserved fiction, social contradictions were easily displaced into images of personal illness" (83). Describing this phenomenon, Ohmann points not only to Sylvia Plath's *Bell Jar*, but also to J. D. Salinger's *Franny and Zooey* (1961), Ken Kesey's *One Flew Over the Cuckoo's Nest* (1962), Philip Roth's *Portnoy's Complaint* (1969), and novels by Saul Bellow and John Updike, among others. A study of the continuing representation of the invalid after 1940 will therefore have to take into account enormous social, medical, and literary changes, a project that must be left for another volume.

The first three chapters of *Invalid Women* deal with the middle of the nineteenth century, the period during which the figure was established as a feature of American fiction and culture. Chapter 1 focuses on the medical formulation of women as invalids, and chapters 2 and 3 examine how literary texts written by Harriet Beecher Stowe, E. D. E. N. Southworth, Laura Curtis Bullard, Washington Irving, Edgar Allan Poe, and Nathaniel Hawthorne about ill women both used and resisted this formulation. All of the discourses I examine in this section—medicine, domesticity, feminism, and romanticism—are marked by a contradictory attitude toward and formulation of the ill woman, but all four end up figuring women as, to some degree, invalid.

Chapters 4 and 5 examine changes in the figure as it appeared in the writing of Charlotte Perkins Gilman, Edith Wharton, and Ellen Glasgow during the late nineteenth and early twentieth centuries. As theories of cure changed and as women were granted more rights within the culture, one would expect that the figure of the invalid would go through corresponding changes, but the changes were not as dramatic as might be expected. Chapter 4 examines variations in the figure associated with the shift from somatic to psychic cures, and chapter 5 investigates changes associated with the advent of germ theory.

Chapter 6 addresses the explicit associations between illness, money, work, and value in novels by Henry James and F. Scott Fitzgerald. Although these associations are implicit throughout this study, chapter 6 specifically questions the variety of ways that illness can "pay": for the character who is figured as sick, for the culture that needs a system of retribution and reward, and for the male author who creates that ill woman. The conclusion returns to theories of representation, illness, and culture in its examination of two dramatically different invalid figures from a novel by Tillie Olsen and a "golden age" Hollywood film.

Chapter **1**

Defining the Feminine/ Defining the Invalid: Women and Medicine in the Mid-Nineteenth Century

In 1855, Catharine Beecher (sister of Harriet Beecher Stowe and an advocate of female health reforms) declared in *Letters to the People on Health and Happiness* that female illness was increasing so rapidly that "ere long, there will be no healthy women in the country" (9). In an informal survey that she conducted in 1866, respondents from across the United States reported such numbers of ill women that Beecher concluded, "The more I traveled, and the more I resided in health establishments, the more the conviction was pressed on my attention that there was a terrible decay of female health all over the land, and that this evil was . . . increasing in a most alarming ratio" (quoted in Gail Parker, *The Oven Birds*, 165). William Dean Howells remarked in 1872 that American society "seems little better than a hospital for invalid women" (quoted in William Wasserstrom, *Heiress of All the Ages*, 135). Another writer, reviewing *The Effect on Women of Imperfect Hygiene of the Sexual Function* (1882), wrote, "Three of every four married women suffer from sexual ill-health due to ignorance before and after marriage" (ibid., 12). Today many historians recognize the epidemic proportions of nineteenth-century women's "illnesses"; Robin Haller and John Haller have dubbed it the "nervous century," and medical historians Vern Bullough, Martha Voght, Martha Verbrugge, Carroll Smith-Rosenberg, and Charles Rosenberg have all pointed to the widespread cultural acceptance of women's innate unhealthiness.

The causes of such alarming reports of ill health are not only uncertain today but were the subject of heated debate at the time. The theories put forward by nineteenth-century doctors to explain illness among women were more than inconsistent; they were downright contradictory. Even when physicians practiced the same kind of medicine (and there was much more heterogeneity of medical care than there is today), they often disagreed as to what was causing the widespread collapse of feminine health. Some physicians saw illness as the result of moral and sexual decay; some held that sex education increased sickliness, while others saw sexual ignorance as the root of much illness. Some doctors, like Edward H. Clarke, contended that women's increasing education weakened their bodies by strengthening their minds, but others maintained that the boredom of too little education left women prey to disease. Illness was believed to be both woman's lot because of her feminine role as a mother and her lot when she violated the feminine role and refused motherhood. Today we are still unsure of the exact causes of women's ill health during the nineteenth century and unsure how widespread this "illness" was; many of the diseases diagnosed then are no longer recognized as "real" diseases today or are recognized as psychosomatic or psychological afflictions about which the nineteenth-century physician would have been ignorant. In her controversial article " 'The Fashionable Diseases': Women's Complaints and Their Treatment in Nineteenth-Century America," Ann Douglas Wood argues that women of the nineteenth century may have been no more unhealthy than their eighteenth-century mothers and grandmothers but learned to think of themselves as unhealthy (27).

The sickly woman emerged as a figure in American society just as the sickly woman became a predominant literary figure. There have, of course, always been ill, suffering, and dying characters in literature, and many of them have been women, but in the mid-nineteenth century, the female invalid became a standard feature of much American fiction.[1] In fact, one of the first novels published in America by an American author, Susanna Rowson's *Charlotte Temple* (1794), features a woman who is betrayed by her lover, falls ill, and dies. In the 1840s, however, in magazine fiction, novels, biographies, and religious tracts,[2] the figure of the sickly woman gained new prominence. One could argue that such fiction merely reflected the reality of the times, but such a view assumes that there is an easily recoverable "reality" with which to compare the fiction. Instead, we have contradictory and polemical accounts of the nineteenth-century "realities" of women's health. Some recent studies, like Martha Verbrugge's *Able-Bodied Womanhood* and Frances B. Cogan's *All-American Girl*, even question whether invalidism was ever the widespread phenomenon that other historians have claimed it was. Whatever the "true" statistics on real women, however, their literary counterparts dropped like flies. Given the power of literary representation, such cultural figures may well have, in part at least, *caused* such alarms.

There are a number of reasons why women might have been genuinely more sickly in the nineteenth century than in other centuries; social and sexual conventions, dress styles, dietary and exercise regimes had changed in ways that left women repressed, confined, sedentary, and often malnourished. These changes in life-style, however, were not drastic enough to explain entirely the emergence of sickliness as a cultural and literary figure at mid-century. Nor do they address Ann Douglas Wood's supposition that women were suffering from diseases that were as much fashionable as pathological. If we understand that many women's illnesses of the late nineteenth century could have been "fashionable diseases," that is, culturally accepted, expected, and even culturally induced, then we begin to understand how language and literature can have shaped women's experiences of their bodies.

The figure of women's failing health arises from a specific conflict over women's "proper role" in the 1840s. At the same time that women—guided by the tenets of domestic ideology—were asserting their increasing importance in the household and feminists were beginning to argue for their rights as political and social equals, physicians, seeking to improve their economic and professional standing, were asserting women's weakness and innate unhealthiness. Meanwhile, the urbanization of the United States and the shift to industrial capitalism were changing the relationships between men and women and between people and their work. Men were increasingly expected to leave the household to earn their living and to depend on women to run the household amid the changing technologies of housework. The result was a dynamic struggle among competing ideologies to define gender roles (for both sexes) and to gain control of people's bodies. Increasingly, this conflict became a struggle to define *women's* bodies as sickly; even so, not all definitions of woman as invalid meant the same thing, nor did they come from the same motivation. To better understand this conflict, we must first examine the history of women's health and health care in the nineteenth century.

Women's Health in the Mid-Nineteenth Century

Late twentieth-century physicians and historians understand nineteenth-century women's ill health better than did contemporary physicians. Even though we cannot know the causes and exact nature of the diseases with certainty, we recognize today that American society was peculiarly equipped to encourage sickness. The cultural norms for women encouraged frailty and delicacy; robust health was thought to be the working woman's mark, not the leisured lady's. The middle-class woman was encouraged from childhood to view herself as weaker and less healthy than her brothers. When she entered adolescence, if she was taught about her monthly cycle at all, she was taught that it would be debilitating and leave her prone to nervous attacks. As an adult, she was to be the symbol of her husband's status, to do no work, and to be beautiful and feminine, that is, frail and delicate. The working-class woman, no matter the real state of her health, had no choice in the matter; she had to continue working, despite illness, to feed her family. As Lorna Duffin explains in "The Conspicuous Consumptive," "Middle-class women in the home were pure but sick; working-class women outside the home were able-bodied but contaminated and sickening. This classification further reinforced the boundary between home and work within the context of sex" (31). But even modern historians of women's health have had some difficulty explaining and accepting the power of the nineteenth-century stereotype. For every theory we come up with, there is a corresponding countertheory. In many ways, our understanding of the history of women's health is just as conflicted and contradictory as were nineteenth-century theories.

Twentieth-century people tend to think of the history of health and health care in terms of progress, assuming that there has been a steady arc upward since the Dark Ages in terms of medical treatments. When confronted with a claim that antebellum American women were, or saw themselves as, unhealthier than their eighteenth-century counterparts, we do not accept it easily. One response is to follow Ann Douglas Wood's argument in " 'The Fashionable Diseases' " that such diseases were just "fashionable" and that women were not really more ill. Illness was not just a fad, she argues, but "was exploited by its victims and practitioners as an advertisement of genteel sensibility and an escape from the too pressing demands of bedroom and kitchen" (27).[3] Another response to the dilemma of explaining women's declining health is to argue, as do Carroll Smith-Rosenberg and Martha Verbrugge, that female illness may well have been a response to the overwhelming social and political changes of the mid-nineteenth century, a somaticization of the "disease" of the anxiety, stress, and unhappiness women felt about the restrictions on their lives.

There are few reliable statistics about public health before about 1890, so evaluations of women's health must be based on less reliable documents like individual case studies, diaries, letters, and published contemporary assessments. There may not have been more ill women in the nineteenth century than in other times, but only more women who were willing to think of themselves as ill and to accept the role of invalid. The statistics that do exist suggest that men's health was just as bad as (and, based on death rates, possibly worse than) women's. The public perception, however, was that women were truly at risk, and both popular and professional reforms of health care began to address that perception.

In colonial America, sickness had been understood as inevitable and was expected, but by the mid-nineteenth century, public attitudes toward sickness and health had changed. Martha Verbrugge documents this change during the years between 1820 and 1860 in New England and finds that people began, during those years, to believe that good health, rather than bad, should be seen as the normal condition. A new model of womanhood emerged (which Frances Cogan calls "Real Womanhood") in which women were seen as strong, capable, and healthy.

Yet another way to understand the new emphasis on feminine illness, then, would be to see it as a reaction to the ideology of "able-bodied womanhood" that was emerging; in the same way that Twiggy and other very thin models made normal women of the 1960s feel fat, the new healthy model of womanhood at mid-century may have made the average woman, by comparison, feel sickly.

The contradictory models of womanhood—the "Cult of True Womanhood" (described by Barbara Welter), the "cult of female frailty" and the necessity of "Able-Bodied Womanhood" (both described by Martha Verbrugge), and the model of "Real Womanhood" (described by Cogan)—coexisted. One need only think of Louisa May Alcott's *Little Women* (1868–69) to understand that they need not be exclusive (although a historian is often inclined to argue that her own model was the chief one). Did nineteenth-century girls follow the model of the pious but doomed invalid, Beth; the strong, capable, and domestic Meg; or the rebellious, high-spirited, and robust Jo? Despite the often polemical claims of historians, no one model of womanhood fit every woman. Every nineteenth-century woman may not have believed herself an "invalid woman," but the "cult of female frailty" was one of the dominant models of womanhood in mid-century fiction. It was, absolutely, the model adopted in mid-century writing about female health, even in texts that were written to promote reforms in health care.

There are several reasons why women's health might have been genuinely worse in the nineteenth century than in the twentieth century and possibly even the eighteenth. First, women were very poorly informed about their bodies. Doctors knew very little about the female body or how to treat its ailments; women knew even less. The modesty encouraged by nineteenth-century social mores kept many from expressing any interest in bodily functioning and even made it difficult for physicians to find out much about the female body, since women would often refuse physical examination (Douglas Wood, " 'The Fashionable Diseases,' " 32–33). This modesty was in some cases so extreme that when physicians were taught how to deliver babies (which was not until mid-century), they were taught to do so without looking at the woman, even if they were using forceps, according to Judith Leavitt in " 'Science' Enters the Birthing Room" (285). Peter Gay, in *The Education of the Senses*, disputes the widely held notion that this Victorian prudishness was established by women and argues that the standards of modesty for examining female patients may well have been imposed more by the doctors than by their clients. Gay claims that "there is good evidence that nineteenth-century women were often less squeamish than men, and that when men were squeamish in their behalf, they were protecting an ideal in their minds, suiting their own needs" (347). No matter who imposed such standards of modesty, though, there is little disagreement that they led to ignorance, on the part of both doctors and patients, and poorer standards of health care.

Pregnancy and menses had been accepted in the eighteenth century as natural, if unpleasant, events, but in the nineteenth century they came to be considered pathological conditions (Jane Donegan, " 'Safe-Delivered' but by Whom?," and Judith Leavitt, *Brought to Bed*). When women were taught about their bodies or their monthly cycles, often they were told to expect weakness, pain, and illness. S. Weir Mitchell, the doctor who treated Charlotte Perkins Gilman and William Dean Howells's daughter Winifred and supervised the treatment of Edith Wharton, wrote in the 1880s, "We may be sure that our daughters will be more likely to have to face at some time the grim question of pain than the lads who grow up beside them. . . . To most women . . . pain is a grim presence in their lives" (*Doctor and Patient*, 84). Carroll Smith-Rosenberg and Charles Rosenberg, describing Victorian medical theories of women's health in "The Female Animal," show that many were not based on "scientific fact" but were mirrors of cultural stereotypes that assumed a woman's health was controlled by her reproductive system: "The image granted women in these hypothetical designs was remarkably consistent with the social role traditionally allotted them. The instincts connected with ovulation made her by nature gentle, affectionate, and nurturing. Weaker in body, confined by menstruation and pregnancy, she was both physically and economically dependent upon the stronger, more forceful male, whom she necessarily looked up to with admiration and devotion" (14). Although there were a number of medical tracts to the contrary, the most widely accepted theories were those which corresponded to the cultural norms, despite the fact that there was a great variety of health and sexual information available to the Victorian reader, as Carl N. Degler explains in "What Ought to Be and What Was: Women's Sexuality in the Nineteenth Century." Degler provides evidence that women had access to more accurate information about sexuality than is commonly believed and reports evidence from an ongoing survey of women that shows that the numbers of "sexually ignorant" women were greatly exaggerated. But Degler does not deal with the question of why such a powerful stereotype was and has been able to co-opt the "facts." (And though it is outside the scope of this study to answer such a question directly, my argument indirectly addresses it through the power of representations to shape reality.) Whatever possibilities were offered by alternative medical theories,[4] mainstream medical theories did not change substantially until the culture did. As we shall see in a closer examination of one of these medical tracts, when women were provided with medical information, it was often wrong, ideologically motivated, or more frightening than informative.

A second reason for women's poor health lies in nineteenth-century clothing styles. Almost all middle-class women wore corsets, some even into the seventh month of pregnancy. In the eighteenth century, this practice had been limited almost exclusively to wealthy women, but by the mid-nineteenth century, even serving girls who did heavy manual labor, in an attempt to elevate their apparent status, wore corsets on the job. On average, corsets reduced women's waists by 2 to 10 inches and put from 35 to 88 pounds of pressure on the abdomen (Helen Ecob, *The Well-Dressed Woman*, 28, 35). One study showed that the average woman's waist measurement was 20 inches in the 1890s and that the long, heavy, sweeping skirts that women wore with several petticoats restricted their ability to move freely.[5] In addition, these skirts and petticoats often meant more than 15 pounds of clothing hanging from a restricted waist (Vern Bullough and Martha Voght, *Women, Menstruation, and Nineteenth-Century Medicine*, 35). Helen Ecob's *The Well-Dressed Woman* (1892) provides convincing evidence that women's internal organs were deformed by these practices, that their breathing was constricted, and that exercise was made all but impossible. The dress reform movement caught on slowly (feminists and physicians, in a rare alliance, argued for dress reform as early as the 1840s), but improvements in women's clothing did not occur until the early 1900s.

Third, women's diet, exercise, and basic hygiene were sometimes neglected. As industrialization and urbanization increased, middle-class women were given more freedom from physical labor than women had ever experienced and their lives became sedentary as a result. Further, working under the theory that spicy, rich foods and exercise excited girls to masturbation and other sexual infelicities, doctors and parents sometimes deprived girls of protein and physical activity, which resulted in anemia and emotional disturbances that lasted well into their adult years (Bullough and Voght, *Women, Menstruation, and Nineteenth-Century Medicine*, 34). In *Women and Economics* (1899), Charlotte Perkins Gilman devotes much energy to diet and exercise reform, as did many other feminist reformers in the late nineteenth century, especially women physicians.[6] After a number of years, the reformers were finally persuasive; in the early decades of the twentieth century, there was an enormous upsurge of interest in exercise for girls and women's health improved dramatically. A study of "water cure" establishments, Susan Cayleff's *Wash and Be Healed*, also suggests that chronic dehydration and uncleanliness might have been a cause of headaches, malaise, fatigue, kidney stones, and several gynecological ailments. The very success of "water cure" advocates in moving their techniques—daily baths, therapeutic soaking, douches, and drinking more water—into the realm of basic public health may have been the cause of the decline of "water cure" as a profession (as Joanne Brown suggests in her review of Cayleff's book).

In addition to the many physical causes of sickness, ill health in the nineteenth century had a number of psychological causes. For one thing, illness had many positive effects for women. It entailed sexual abstinence and was therefore often the only means of birth control available or understood in a world where multiple childbirths were both common and life threatening. Despite the fact that America was "a notoriously unhealthy place" where "fevers, agues, rheumatism, dyspepsia, [and] flux were chronic national complaints . . . the fecundity rate was the highest ever recorded, and thus doubly burdened many wives died long before their husbands" (Helen Papashvily, *All the Happy Endings*, 127). In a growing country where many children meant many hands to help in the fields or with the family business, large families were not only common but economically necessary. And in a time when even doctors misunderstood women's menstrual cycles and birth control was associated with the suspect patent medicine business (Linda Gordon, "Voluntary Motherhood," 106, and James Reed, "Doctors, Birth Control, and Social Values," 127), pleading illness was often the only means available to avoid pregnancy.

Illness was also one of the few opportunities for real rest for the mother and housewife; for the woman who felt ignored or unappreciated, it was a clear way to get the attention, ministration, and affection that were expected of her but not for her.[7] It also offered one way that women could demonstrate their courage and piety: a woman who bore a debilitating illness quietly and stoically could be looked toward as a model of courageous and Christian womanhood. In *Sensational Designs*, Jane Tompkins cites a number of religious tracts that describe scenes in which illness provides the setting for a woman to prove her piety and exhibit saintly behavior (chapter 6, especially 150–56). In these religious tracts, and the fictional accounts that echo them, illness is one way women can prove their religious commitment. While I do not mean to suggest that such illnesses were "staged" merely to provide an opportunity for piety, illnesses might nevertheless be exaggerated by women who otherwise had no outlet for creative energy, no chance to be fully appreciated.

Social expectations in the decades of the first half of the nineteenth century encouraged a kind of selflessness that could have resulted in a woman's thinking of herself as nothing, or less than nothing. Some medical treatments bore out such self-evaluations; treatment—ranging from complete confinement to leeches and electricity applied to the genitals—was sometimes more a matter of torture than cure. Such treatment either reinforced the cultural inference that women were not really valuable or confirmed the suspicion that they were sexually promiscuous; rest cures ensured that women would do no useful work, and treatments aimed at the genitals could easily have been perceived as specific punishments.[8] Domesticity and domestic fiction were in part a reaction to this denigration of women, as was feminism. Neither, however, could counteract this attitude entirely because domestic ideology still subordinated women to their husbands' or sons' ends and because feminism urged changes that were too drastic for most women to embrace. (Chapter 2 will take up the domestic and feminist resistance to medical definitions of women.)

In *Disorderly Conduct*, Carroll Smith-Rosenberg argues that one of the most often diagnosed diseases, hysteria, must be seen as a cultural phenomenon.[9] The enormous social, economic, and demographic changes occurring in the nineteenth century—urbanization, industrialization, and a move toward bourgeois values—must have been psychologically difficult for all members of society, but they would have been especially trying for women because "the family and gender role socialization remained relatively inflexible. It is quite possible that many women experienced a significant level of anxiety when forced to confront or adapt in one way or another to these changes. Thus hysteria may have served as one option or tactic offering particular women otherwise unable to respond to these changes a chance to redefine or restructure their place within the family" (200). In a culture that encouraged their passivity, most women would not have thought to protest their newly restricted place in society. Those who did resent the domination of fathers, husbands, and brothers would not have found outright protest a viable or effective option. Thus, illness can be seen as one of the only methods of resistance open to many women (208).[10]

Hysteria (and by extension all culturally induced illnesses) can be seen as a cultural phenomenon because "in a very literal sense [the] characteristics of the hysteric were merely hypertrophied versions of traits and behavior commonly reinforced in female children and adolescents. . . . The effect of [their] socialization was to teach women to have a low evaluation of themselves, . . . to depend on others and to altruistically wish not for their own worldly success, but for that of their male supporters" (212). Similarly, the characteristics of the invalid exaggerated socially accepted roles. For the woman who lacked any other feasible way to express her dissatisfaction and who was, in fact, taught not to value or even recognize that dissatisfaction, an illness that was merely an extension of socially acceptable traits may have presented itself as the easiest outlet for expressing her problems.

Whether or not such illness was a real technique of resistance, it was, at the least, a symptom of social "dis-ease." The concern with physical health, Martha Verbrugge argues in *Able-Bodied Womanhood*, displaced a concern with the health of the body politic: "By diagnosing their bodily ills, ante-bellum Americans also formulated a moral and social pathology of their times. By promoting physical health, they sought to mitigate less tangible disorders in their lives" (12). As we shall see, the concern for women's physical health may well have masked a much deeper concern for women's place in a changing society.

Physicians and Women

Before the second half of the nineteenth century, health care in the United States was considered to be women's domain, conducted in the home and disseminated by an oral tradition. This was most often the case because of necessity; few doctors came to the fledgling country, even fewer moved west with the pioneers. It was also the case, however, because it was thought proper; as the one who nurtured and tended to the needs of the family, the wife and mother assumed medical care as a matter of course. With information gleaned from oral tradition and popular medical tracts like William Buchan's *Domestic Medicine*, women took care of most minor ills and aches and quite often most major ones, too. In *The Social Transformation of American Medicine*, Paul Starr argues that American culture before 1850, with its egalitarian insistence on equality and independence, was not ready to accept the claims of superior knowledge made by physicians. For that matter, physicians, often with little or no professional training, were hardly in a position to make good on those claims. Women—from herbalists and midwives to mothers—seemed not only the proper ones to provide medical treatment but also the most effective.

Medicine was hardly the homogeneous profession that it is today. As Benjamin Rush (one of the most important "regular" physicians in the early nineteenth century and an advocate of "heroic" dosing and blooding) once commented, "A Mahometan and a Jew might as well attempt to worship the Supreme Being in the same temple and through the medium of the same ceremonies, as two physicians of opposite principles and practice, attempt to confer about the life of the same patient" (quoted in ibid., 93). The comparison is apt. Increasingly throughout the nineteenth century, medicine became a matter for belief and sometimes a substitute for religion. As traditional religious belief declined over the century, medicine increasingly became the arbiter of life-style and even morality. As the faith in science grew and the faith in God weakened, "Doctors found themselves the spokespersons for the affirmation of traditional cultural verities" (Regina Morantz-Sanchez, *Sympathy and Science*, 207). But before they could assume such high cultural power, physicians had to quell the "sectarian" threat of alternative medical practices.

"Regular" physicians, who held to the allopathic medical theory that would become modern medicine (that disease can be cured by a drug that induces effects opposite to the patient's symptoms in a healthy person), were threatened not only by female nonprofessional practitioners but by physicians who held opposing medical views.[11] Chief among these was homeopathy (which is still practiced somewhat today); it opposed the heroic dosing common in regular treatment—the giving of large doses of drugs—by advocating the administration of tiny amounts of a drug that, in a healthy person, would bring on symptoms identical to those the patient was suffering. Homeopathy was a double threat in that homeopathic medical schools often admitted a relatively large number of women. Nor were allopathy and homeopathy the only medical theories. "Botanics," later called "Eclectics," advocated the use of traditional herbal cures; hydropaths used water exclusively to offer cures in the form of drinks, baths, and compresses. There were numerous dietary cures, as well; among the most popular was "Grahamism," a vegetarian and hygienic regime advocated by Sylvester Graham and remembered now for the crackers named after it. These latter cures appealed particularly to women who were frustrated with the heroic dosing and bleeding of regular physicians and to those who, in a Jacksonian resistance to authority, believed in their own abilities to cure themselves.

The regular physician found his practice, social standing, and livelihood threatened, then, by competing medical sects and found his patients sometimes threatened by the quackery that such eclecticism made more likely. In 1846, the American Medical Association was formed, in part to quell the threat to doctors' standing by consolidating professional, social, and legal power and in part to improve the standards for medical care and medical training.[12]

Physicians at mid-century who wanted to improve the standing of their profession—economic as well as social—had two tasks, then. First, in order to convince the public that they were needed, they had to convince women of doctors' abilities. As is still largely true today, it was the wife or mother who decided when a member of the family needed more care than she could provide. The best way for physicians to convince women of the value of professional care was to convince them that women could not provide adequate health care. To solidify this position, physicians also needed to convince women that they themselves needed to receive medical care, that women were weak and sickly.

According to medical historian Judith Walzer Leavitt, the first major inroads American physicians made into the previously female world of healing was in birthing. For centuries a woman-dominated and woman-centered activity, birthing gradually came under the control of male obstetricians in the mid-nineteenth century. The novelty and promised safety of new birthing instruments (like forceps) along with newly discovered anesthetics made obstetricians popular with rich women in large cities.[13] Soon reliance on male obstetricians, even though their safety record was no better than that of midwives (and in some cases worse), became a status symbol (Leavitt, *Brought to Bed*). Only working-class and rural women used midwives. (The move to hospital birthing followed the same pattern in the twentieth century [ibid.].) After having turned a medical event as common as birthing over to a "professional," a woman was much more easily convinced that other medical events needed professional attention, too.

The move toward professionalizing and extending the domain of medicine was concurrent with new threats to male domination. Although the faith in men's superiority was still strong at mid-century, it was being challenged by some groups of women. At the 1848 Seneca Falls Convention, women declared themselves capable of voting, obtaining education, and practicing professions; they rejected traditional Christianity in favor of a revised, woman-centered Bible, and they even threatened to start wearing pants. One growing religious sect, the Shaker faith, had been founded by a woman, Ann Lee, and held that God was equally male and female. Even domesticity, though it maintained women's place in the home, nonetheless challenged some tenets of male superiority by implicitly asserting women's higher moral achievements. Conservatives felt that the stability of the culture depended on finding a new position from which one could argue for women's innate inferiority.

Science and medicine proved a convenient base for such claims. Already employed in the business of "proving" blacks, Asians, Native Americans, and other people of color to be innately inferior to the white race, scientific research was a natural place to look for proof of feminine deficiency.[14] Women's smaller brains and bodies and their lesser physical strength offered an obvious basis for such claims. The faith in empirical research born in the eighteenth century reached new heights in the nineteenth and, as the century wore on and the religious fervor of the 1830s and 1840s waned, would become the ideal focus for the faith of the American people.[15]

We can see that for two reasons regular medical men had a vested interest in maintaining the doctrine of women's innate physical inferiority. First, it was an important basis for their own increasing revenues and status; it guaranteed more patients and more reliance on the physician's "expertise." (Nor were regular physicians alone in this; all medical practitioners stood to gain financially from being able to convince the laity of the need for medical intervention.) Second, it was a basis for men's—and therefore their own—claims to biological and intellectual superiority. By the 1880s, male physicians would have another, even more pressing reason to maintain the weakness and sickliness of women—the threat posed by female physicians. But at midcentury, the first two reasons were powerful enough to initiate the "medical reformulation of the Cult of True Womanhood" (Carroll Smith-Rosenberg, *Disorderly Conduct,* 179), which, revealing its origin in religion, argued that "God and nature would punish women [who refused to take their proper social and biological place] with cancer, insanity and a wasting death" (23). The assumption of the power to arbitrate decisions about health also gave physicians the power to arbitrate culture and life-style, to judge, and to decree. Their own increasing financial and social standing, as well as the needs of professionalization, made theirs a conservative position, dedicated to the preservation and extension of the ideology of "separate spheres."[16]

The medical formulation of woman's inferiority took two contradictory directions. On the one hand, it argued that women were biologically inferior; nature had made a mistake in organizing the female constitution. Female organs were just not very strong and were, by nature, given to disease and pain. On the other hand, it held that women were personally responsible for the ills they suffered because they intentionally overtaxed these already weak organs. Menstruation, childbirth, and lactation—the exclusive purposes for which the female body was intended—sapped all the energy a woman had; anything that distracted "vital energy" from her reproductive organs damaged her health and that of her unborn children. Operating under the "closed energy" model of medical treatment—in which the body only has so much energy that must be hoarded and carefully spent in a proper way—physicians forbade activities such as reading, dancing, or eating strong foods because they sent energy to the wrong parts of a woman's body (her brain, her legs, her stomach).[17] Proper activities, like light housework (even for the wealthy woman with many servants) and taking care of children, on the other hand, were guaranteed to produce just the right amount of exercise needed to keep a woman's body fit and to provide enough stimulation to keep her mind off distressing events.

Most of the medical "discoveries" of women's deficiencies were disseminated to the public through popular medical books about women's health. These were usually written in the same vein as the domestic medical tracts, that is, as "self-help" books for women who had little access to physicians. However, except for occasional information about personal hygiene, these books consisted primarily of warnings and descriptions of symptoms and diseases that only one's doctor could diagnose and treat exactly. Typical of this genre is E. H. Dixon's *Woman and Her Diseases, from the Cradle to the Grave: Adapted Exclusively to Her Instruction in the Physiology of her System, and All the Diseases of Her Critical Periods* (1855).[18]

Dixon's professed goal in writing the book was to instruct the American woman about the functioning and malfunctioning of her body, with emphasis on her reproductive organs. While it purports to offer information on her diseases "from the Cradle to the Grave," it nonetheless concentrates almost exclusively on the "critical period" of her child-bearing years. In the chapter entitled "Puberty to Menopause: The Cycle of Femininity in Nineteenth-Century America" in *Disorderly Conduct*, Carroll Smith-Rosenberg argues that after the middle of the century, physicians believed that a woman's whole system was governed by her reproductive organs and that she was only truly "a woman" during her reproductive years. Her conclusion seems to be borne out by books like Dixon's. While Dixon's title may be accounted for by considering that the field of gynecology was only just then being formulated and had not, perhaps, found an adequate nomenclature, Smith-Rosenberg is nevertheless right in calculating the rhetorical effect. Dixon does not make the disclaimer that his book only covers women's diseases peculiar to reproduction; he claims to cover "All the Diseases of Her Critical Periods," thereby defining only the reproductive years as "critical." Further, at several points Dixon explicitly argues that a woman is ruled and defined by her uterus; he agrees with "the ancients" that the uterus is "an animal within an animal" because a woman's "whole organism [will] respond to its slightest affectations" (195–96) and explains that a whole range of disorders from "irregularity of feeling" to "sudden startings" are "almost invariably" rooted in some "uterine derangement" (197).

Like other books in the genre, Dixon's reveals the conflicting messages of medical thought mentioned above: woman is both innately sick and responsible for her poor health. The uterus has a life of its own, but the woman should do whatever she can to avoid upsetting it. In the "Introductory," Dixon argues that instruction of the kind he offers is not only proper but necessary because from her position on the social scale, [a woman] is subjected to so many causes of physical degeneration from the evident design of nature . . . that it seems but an act of humanity to make an effort for her instruction in some of the more common evils that so constantly beset her; but more especially from the time when her organism asserts the distinctive peculiarity of her sex, to its eventful close, when she drops prematurely into the grave, the victim of some of those numerous ills incident to that period in which she is fulfilling the great end of her existence. (5)

Dixon makes it clear that women's illnesses are from "the evident design of nature," but if the medical world accepted the notion that nature was flawed and could not be repaired, there would be nothing for physicians to do for women and therefore no need for the profession. So Dixon hastily adds, "I claim no sympathy from him who can day after day approach the bedside of the invalid, and console himself that she who has failed to receive at his hands the anticipated benefit, is beyond the reach of his skill from vices inherent in her organism." Those "vices" may be "inherent in her organism," but the skillful doctor can overcome the insufficiencies of nature. The doctor is thus pitted against the "vices" of nature in the struggle for a woman's health. The doctor takes on the role of the romantic hero here; he finds himself in a contest with the forces of nature itself—a trope we will see again (in chapter 3) in Nathaniel Hawthorne's "The Birthmark." The last thing the heroic doctor needs is for the woman to complicate her already delicate condition with foolish behavior.

Like that of modern health experts, much of Dixon's advice pertains to everyday, commonsense matters of life-style. He argues that proper exercise, dress, and diet are necessary components of good health. He recommends dancing and games, but only as long as one can maintain a "constantly equable state of warmth of the skin" and as long as it is before dark (67).[19] Corsets and swathing children, he believes, restrict natural movement and are to be avoided. Strong foods—including meat more than once a day, spicy foods, tea, coffee, and alcohol of any kind—are also sure to cause health problems.

The two most insidious causes of bad health, according to Dixon, are luxurious living and city dwelling. Early in the book, he promotes the life of poor children over that of wealthy children; "pampering" is the surest route to later health problems, premature old age, and "mental feebleness" (13). He repeatedly warns against the evils of featherbeds and "luxurious education" (44). He quotes a Doctor Columbat at length, warning against life in large cities, where "idleness, effeminacy, or sedentary life, the constant contact of the two sexes, and the frequenting of places where everything inspires pleasure; prolonged watching, excessive dancing, frivolous occupations, and the study of the arts that give too great activity to the imagination; erotic reading; the pernicious establishment of artificial puberty . . . [will keep] the genital system in a state of constant excitation" (115).

Dixon's prudery is likely to place his bourgeois reader at odds with her culture. The ideology informing his medical theory is agrarian and is suspicious of pleasure and education, frivolity and laziness. He sees women in a newly urbanized industrial world—relieved of many of the household duties attendant on their rural counterparts, indulging in unrestrained education, reading, and entertainment, and bearing fewer children—as a threat to the social order. Native American women and farming women in Pennsylvania, he points out, never suffer from the diseases common to white women in the city (89, 154). But Dixon's reader was not likely to be a farm woman or a Native American. She was most likely a middle-class city woman with little choice about her life-style, which would have been dictated by a husband or father. Nevertheless, it was she who would pay for their social position with illness and invalidism.

Dixon's book therefore leaves the woman little choice. Since she cannot escape city life and will not be able to avoid the evils it brings, she is condemned by nature and her life-style to disease. In such a case, the only thing for her to do is to turn herself over to the physician. In raising her daughter, "she must make the physician her friend and with his aid and friendly suggestion" inform her daughter of the "legitimate functioning of her uterine system" so that the young girl will avoid "improper practices" (58). Dixon emphasizes this point with an anecdote of a mother who took her daughter's care into her own hands, after he had refused to give her a drug to bring on menses, and killed the daughter with a patent medicine (44). If she develops "uterine ailments," "the female is to yield implicit obedience to her physician, in assuming the horizontal position" (196). In his discussion of pregnancy, Dixon tells his reader that four missed periods, nausea in the morning, swollen breasts, and a fluttering feeling in her stomach may be symptoms of cancer and not pregnancy and that she should see her doctor to be sure (247). When she is pregnant, he asserts, the woman should place herself under complete medical supervision because even if pregnancy is not designed by nature to be a disease, "yet it would seem, from the great variety of ailment to which it subjects them, that women have a right to consider themselves a legitimate subject for constant medical supervision" (265). If she wants birth control, she should consult a doctor because "the enlightened physician will always be able to judge who are its proper recipients" (317).

The rhetorical impact of Dixon's book, which continually lists symptoms that only the physician will be able to interpret accurately, is to convince his reader that she is in constant peril of mortal disease and must consult her physician over every bodily vicissitude.[20] In short, the doctor is to be her constant confidant and trusted adviser. She is to consider herself always in danger of illness, if not actually ill. And should she become ill, undoubtedly it will be due both to her inherent weakness and to her neglect of the good doctor's advice and instruction.[21] Since in the nineteenth century liability to illness *was* invalidism, in Dixon's view every woman was an invalid.

The discourses of nineteenth-century American culture and medicine offered the woman contradictory definitions on all but one point. She was pure and sexual, innocent and guilty, capable of running a large household but incapable of professional work, meant to live in the country but forced to live in the city, encouraged by social mores to bear fewer children but condemned for using birth control or abortion, expected to maintain her social standing but risking her health by seeking too much pleasure and luxury. American culture and medicine made it clear, however, that she was in constant danger of illness and sure to experience much pain during her life.

Medical Discourse, Cultural Definition

The woman of the nineteenth century had to negotiate her sense of self from among a number of seriously conflicting and contradictory discourses. She had to reject hopes for her own worldly success, even against her own self-interest; at the same time, as a member of the rising bourgeois culture, she was encouraged to think constantly of her own position. Charles Rosenberg explains in "Sexuality, Class, and Role in Nineteenth-Century America" that sexuality was extremely difficult for nineteenth-century women because they were expected to be both pure and maternal, which meant both rejecting and encouraging sexuality (150). In a world of increasing urbanization, medical advice books often encouraged women to avoid the "unhealthful" world of the cities. Faced with a plethora of conflicting discourses from which to construct the unified self that was upheld by romantic and bourgeois ideology, women may well have found invalidism to be the most coherent figure to fill.

Illness became the condition that could best accommodate the contradictory cultural and medical expectations of womanhood. Discussing contradictions in modern discourses about women, Catherine Belsey asserts in "Constructing the Subject, Deconstructing the Text" that "the attempt to locate a single and coherent subject-position within . . . contradictory discourses, and in consequence to find a non-contradictory pattern of behaviour, can create intolerable pressures. One way of responding to this situation is to retreat from the contradictions and from discourse itself, to become 'sick'" (50). Unlike the modern woman, for whom sickness becomes a retreat, the nineteenth-century woman would have found that becoming "sick" was a way to reconcile and affirm the cultural discourse. As she did so, she came to *embody* that discourse and to consolidate the standing of the medical profession.

A woman's acceptance of this definition may have been a way to affirm the dominant discourse, but it was not a simple matter. It may have been her destiny, but, as Dixon makes clear, it was also her fault or, at the least, her mother's fault. Whereas a twentieth-century observer can clearly isolate the causes in the patriarchal culture's definitions of womanhood, the nineteenth-century observer would see both the individual and the larger social system of propriety and responsibility. Dixon's own attitude is often paradoxical; while he repeatedly expresses sympathy for women's real sufferings (for example, he states that "nothing can be more heartless than a want of sympathy" for women who suffer from premenstrual symptoms [23]), he also frequently suggests that women fake their symptoms or bring their suffering on themselves: "It is certainly a mortifying discovery (but there is no doubt of the truth), that certain females will pretend hysteric attacks, in order to excite sympathy and obtain some desired luxury, avoid disagreeable visitors, or compel a guardian's or parents' consent to a disagreeable union" (140). The same man, then, who earlier had written that an "invalid should . . . never suffer a visitor to detain her" because "it [should] be distinctly understood that she is an invalid and no well-bred person will be annoyed with her departure" (68–69) also argues that illness should not be faked to avoid visitors.

Of course, such statements are not really contradictory as long as the difference between "real" and "faked" illness is clear; the same person who would not hold it against a woman for excusing herself from visits when she is ill does not have to excuse a woman for faking illness to get her way. But in the system Dixon has set up—where only a doctor can tell for sure when a woman is really ill—the layperson would be unable to make such a discrimination. Any woman excusing herself from tiresome tasks because of illness becomes, to a degree, suspicious.

This suspiciousness is intensified when one factors in what were often understood to be causes of illness: the woman's bad behavior. Natural weakness is, as we saw, at the root of her illness, but behavior is the trigger. "Hysteria," Dixon writes, "is undoubtedly mostly due to an indolent, luxurious, and enervating mode of life" (142), and painful menses come about because of "an erroneous movement of the forces, brought about in early life by the constraint of dress and the effect of an unnatural diet" (89). We certainly understand these issues differently today, but for Dixon they were in part a matter for blame—a woman's blame. If the woman herself were not directly at fault, then her mother, in not teaching her better habits, was.

A twentieth-century understanding of nineteenth-century women's diseases only takes us a little way toward understanding the antebellum discourse on illness. We can easily characterize such illnesses as the result of urbanization, sexual repression, patriarchal oppression, and physical ignorance, but the mid-nineteenth-century person would have used an entirely different vocabulary. The medical/social system, the ideology of illness, would have placed the blame for illness elsewhere: in nature, in the woman's own behavior, and in the training she received from her mother. We see the distinction of separate spheres as sickening; Dixon saw the violation of the "natural" division into separate spheres as sickening. We can easily see women's illnesses as the result of the world of men; if the antebellum physician saw blame outside the "obvious design of nature," it was with the women themselves.

There are a lot of reasons why the "regular" medical position finally became the dominant one. As we will see in chapter 5, the allopathic discovery of germ theory would finally consolidate medical power. But as medical historians Paul Starr and Jeffrey Berlant argue, the political savvy of the American Medical Association and its adoption of monopolistic strategies would also crush most competition. Another factor that contributed to the power of the allopathic physician as the century wore on was the increasing reliance on "experts" and "professionals" that gripped American society during the second half of the nineteenth century; sectarian physicians could lay little claim to such professionalism (and sometimes outright denied it). Some treatments, such as hydropathy, dietary programs, and hygiene regimes, that had been cures became part of daily routine, with no need for a professional's intervention.

It also seems likely that the allopathic theory of medicine came to dominate because it was so clearly interwoven with contemporary social theory and even contradictory at the same points as the society. It is impossible to say which came first; separate spheres ideology was as dependent on the physician's claim that male and female bodies were constituted differently (that biology was destiny) as medical ideology was dependent on women's acceptance of their own "inferiority." When one part of this sociomedical theory fell, so did the other. The discovery of germs, which finally replaced the "closed energy" model, was coincident with the success of the suffragist campaign and a dramatic increase in the number of women entering the public workplace.[22]

Before we discuss the crumbling of the closed energy model, the adoption of germ theory, and the rise of the female professional, however, the next two chapters will examine in detail literary texts from mid-century that reveal the power of allopathic medical theories during the 1840s and 1850s. Even when authors seem to be explicitly challenging these theories, as do all of the authors we shall examine, the medical model proves too strong to be overturned. What we shall see is that the literary discourses of domesticity, feminism, and romanticism may well have only further complicated the contradictory definitions of womanhood rather than maintaining any particularly clear position.

The nineteenth-century *imagination* of female invalidism was itself contradictory, even though it set itself in opposition to several points in other strong mid-century cultural discourses. This opposition will be the focus of the next two chapters—the conflicts between the medical discourse on women and domestic, feminist, and romantic discourses.

Central to these conflicts will be the question of responsibility and blame that Dixon leaves so doubled and confused. As we will see, though, the point of contact for all four discourses is a sense that women, if not already invalids, are continually threatened by invalidism, and that female invalidism threatens the opposing discourses themselves with their own invalidity.

Chapter **2**

The Threat of Invalidism: Responsibility and Reward in Domestic and Feminist Fiction

Charlotte Temple's death makes a kind of poetic and sentimental sense that could only work in a novel. As readers of her fate, we sympathize, recognize the unfairness of the world, and resolve within ourselves to treat other unfortunate young women better. Her death therefore provides her with a kind of power over us to make us kinder. Within her own world, though, Charlotte Temple has no power, or only the limited power to achieve a reconciliation with her father. Her death does not really do her or anyone else any good and in fact is harmful, since she leaves her child a motherless orphan. While her death is exemplary, it is hardly an example to follow. But what of other women's fictional illnesses? Can illness ever offer a pattern for readers to follow? Can illness ever *work*?

Before such a question can even be addressed, much less answered, one must explore what it would mean for illness to work, what kind of goals could be achieved through illness. My assertion that Charlotte Temple's death gives her (or her creator, Susanna Rowson) power over us as readers already suggests one formulation of power, that described by Jane Tompkins in *Sensational Designs*—"sentimental power." As a figure who can evoke our feelings of sympathy, love, and forgiveness, Charlotte Temple has the power to encourage us to be more humane. As Tompkins acknowledges, such a power exists primarily within the Christian ideology of self-sacrifice. But that Christian realm is not the only one in which women writers of the nineteenth century were interested.

Self-sacrifice and self-interest exist in women's fiction and ideologies in a dynamic tension. While domesticity taught the sacrifice of personal ambitions for the good of the family, it also advocated a kind of personal domination. The "sentimental power" that Tompkins describes places one's "reward" in the next world, but it also works toward political change in this one. And while feminism, the other major women's movement of the nineteenth century, fought for individual political rights, it also advocated a kind of communal good.

To understand how illness figures into this dynamic of power, self-sacrifice, and self-interest, we will have to explore the ways in which illness as a tool can make sense. Up to this point, readings of nineteenth-century American women's fiction have tended to focus on one version of "reward" or the other, to define it only in terms of earthly gain or in terms of a Christian conception of the afterlife. The figure of the invalid in these texts, however, shows how vital the interaction between those two models was. The conflicts and convergences among medical, domestic, and feminist discourses of reward and responsibility shape that figure.

Reward, however, is not the only issue in the use of illness as a tool. Responsibility, too, is in question. The responsibility for women's illnesses and deaths becomes central in understanding women's fiction. Often centered on descents into "brain fever" or deathbed scenes of great pathos, these novels constructed a discourse on women's illnesses that was at times aligned with the dominant medical model and at times in direct conflict with it. Domesticity and feminism had in common a

view of strong, able-bodied womanhood that denied E. H. Dixon's contention in *Woman and Her Diseases* that all women were invalids (see
chapter 1). Nevertheless, the fictions that appeared under the auspices
of these movements often represent the same invalid women that Dixon
described. Ultimately, the two female discourses are interpolated by the
stronger medical discourse, in part because of their lack of a coherent
rhetoric of resistance and in part because of the generic demands of
mid-nineteenth-century women's fiction.

"Woman's fiction," as it is called by Nina Baym, or fiction written by
and for women, is marked by strong emotional, political, and cultural
agendas for change. As *Literary World* observed in 1850, "The novel is
now almost recognized with the newspaper and the pamphlet as a
legitimate mode of influencing public opinion" (quoted in Baym, *Novels,
Readers, and Reviewers,* 214). The texts this chapter focuses on—
Harriet Beecher Stowe's *Uncle Tom's Cabin,* E. D. E. N. Southworth's
Retribution, and Laura Curtis Bullard's *Christine*—were all written to
make a point; Stowe wrote to end slavery, Southworth to challenge
adultery and the dissolution of the family, and Bullard to advocate
women's rights. But in all three novels, female illness is central to and
decisive in the plot structure. The figure of the invalid in these texts
reveals the contradictory attitude that even these women writers held
toward the possibilities of women's power that they offer; all three
reveal the difficulties of maintaining an ideology of women's strength
and importance in a culture that increasingly encouraged sickliness and
invalidism. All three further reveal the complexities of reward, responsibility, and blame caused by resisting medical definitions of women as
"natural" invalids.

Fiction Figuring Women

The male-dominated medical discourse was not, of course, the only
discourse seeking to define feminine roles. Women were themselves
taking charge of such definitions in several forums—popular magazines, lecture halls, political pamphlets, conduct books, guides to domestic management, and novels. Their goals were not always identical;
as do women today, nineteenth-century women differed in their conceptions of what kinds of roles women should fill and how they should fill
them. But they quite often strongly resisted the medical construction of

women as naturally helpless and ill. Two female discourses, in particular, were important in shaping and reshaping conceptions of womanhood—domesticity and feminism. Although they were quite often at odds with one another on issues of what kind of power women should wield, domesticity and feminism each offered a vision of a world at least in part dominated by strong, capable, and healthy women.

By far the most influential discourse of the two at the time, domesticity urged women to take control of their households, to be moral exemplars for their families, and to establish the home as not just a separate sphere but a superior one. Obviously, the woman who could do all this, in an age before modern housekeeping technologies, would have trouble taking to bed at the slightest whim. The "domestic woman," as Nancy Armstrong calls her in *Desire and Domestic Fiction*, was recognizable precisely in her difference from the aristocratic lady whose only function was to be an object of display. The middle-class woman who ran a household was a manager, an organizer, and a worker, even if her work was just to supervise servants (see Armstrong's second chapter, "The Rise of the Domestic Woman").

The woman in the domestic model is nonetheless threatened by illness. Underneath assertions that women can be powerful and strong in their management of the household are worries that women might not be able to do so. For every woman in a domestic novel who ends up in the center of her own happy home, there is another who fails. In one sense, their vision prefigures much feminist utopian fiction because it represents a dream of feminine community that could change the world for the better. But, as is true for most utopian fiction, there is a dark, dystopian world that underlies the women writers' vision. As Mary Kelley argues in "The Sentimentalists: Promise and Betrayal in the Home," "The domestic dream proffered, it vanishes in due course. Prescription runs aground in the protest of the fiction. . . . The glorified, heroic role envisioned for the wife is frequently seen as confining and stultifying. Social and economic disaster, sickness and death plague the performance of her roles" (442). What the fiction reveals, she claims, is a world where men betray women and where women have no material power to fight back. However strong their moral power, they are nonetheless subject to male control in the physical world. When women become invalids in domestic fiction, it is most often not from "natural" weakness but the result of men's behavior and a system that leaves no other practical alternative. Theirs is a world in which, as Harriet

Beecher Stowe once wrote, it is "the mothers and wives who suffer and must suffer to the end of time to bear the sins of the beloved in their own bodies" (letter to Henry Ward Beecher, quoted in Kelley, "The Sentimentalists," 440).

It is telling that Stowe describes this suffering as taking place in women's *bodies*. Throughout domestic novels, women fall ill and die as a result of the bad behavior of men.[1] This model of illness obviously resists Dixon's, in which women bear the responsibility for their own illnesses, but it reveals the weakness in domestic ideology itself. Domesticity not only separates the world into two spheres—the private and the public—and restricts women to just one but questions whether women can ever really prosper in that private sphere. In suggesting that women may have to wait for heaven to receive their reward, domesticity forces yet another division into "this world" and "the other world." While domesticity clearly privileges woman's moral power, and holds out infinite hope for spiritual reward, it offers women only a modest promise for reward in this world. As a form of spiritual salvation, domestic ideology was a strong force, but as a political strategy against restrictive definitions of womanhood, domesticity was too close to the medical and cultural definition of woman as "other" to offer coherent resistance.

In Jane Tompkins's formulation of sentimental power, foregoing reward in this world for the promise of the next presents no fundamental difficulty. It fits perfectly within a Christian value system that privileges spirituality over materiality and a social system that privileges the family over the individual. Her reading contradicts other critics, though, who see domesticity as having specifically material interests. Tompkins, of course, does argue that domesticity was potentially revolutionary in scope, but she sees the locus of that power as spiritual. In contrast, Nina Baym in *Woman's Fiction* sees in the novels an effort to expand matriarchal values in an attempt to center cultural power in the home, thereby making women rule supreme (27). Ann Douglas carries this argument even further in her highly critical study, *The Feminization of American Culture*, arguing that these writers placed too much emphasis on otherworldliness, leading to a cheap emotionalism that opened the door for twentieth-century mass-market consumerism. Douglas sees these novels in a context that is specifically material and political.

Even when critics are sympathetic to women's political goals, though, they tend to concentrate on only one sphere of influence. Barbara

Bardes and Suzanne Gossett's recent book, *Declarations of Indepen-dence,* is an excellent study of the close ties between women's fiction and serious national political questions of the times, but they direct little attention to the "sentimental power" Tompkins describes. The critic who considers the power to shape emotional and spiritual life does not take the power to effect political change much into account and vice versa. And while critics more often discuss how changes in the private sphere could have effected change in the public one, this anal-ysis often stops short of understanding how much domesticity was concerned directly with larger public issues.

Early critics of domestic fiction tended to write about it as if it were a monological, even simplistic, discourse, but the disagreements among them illustrate the falsity of that claim. Herbert Ross Brown, writing in the 1940s, and even the more sympathetic Helen Papashvily, writing in the 1950s, read the fiction as if there were a simple moral not only to any given novel but to all domestic novels by women, but their conclusions are quite different. Brown, for instance, addresses the issue of respon-sibility and reward this way in *The Sentimental Novel in America, 1789–1860*: "The gravest indictment of these novels is their essential falsity to life. Too often their pages inculcated a prudential morality baited with attractive promises of comfortable material rewards. The religious life was fully guaranteed to pay substantial dividends in this world, here and now. If these promised payments in earthly goods were unaccountably deferred, the heavenly compensations were made to sound no less solid and material; celestial mansions were fully equipped with all modern conveniences" (357). Papashvily, on the other hand, in *All the Happy Endings* describes the novels as "handbooks of . . . feminine revolt . . . [that] encouraged a pattern of feminine behavior so quietly ruthless, so subtly vicious that by comparison the ladies at Seneca appear angels of innocence" (xvii). Barbara Welter, who set the grounds for the analysis of domestic fiction in her early study of the "Cult of True Womanhood," reads it as a uniformly detrimental text that taught self-denial, self-sacrifice, and self-control. The common ground for these critics is a dismissive attitude toward the fiction, which they saw as simplistically ideological; whether the novels offered a false, utopian "cozy cloudland" (Brown, *The Sentimental Novel in America,* 359), a primer for revolution, or a system of self-oppression, the critic was sure they did not offer a complex system of thought.

Contemporary feminist critics have been more sympathetic, but, like the earlier critics, they tend to see a fairly straightforward "message" in the fiction. A more recent reading of domesticity, Gillian Brown's *Domestic Individualism*, begins to redress this problem in her reading of Stowe's *Uncle Tom's Cabin*. Brown argues that Stowe's recognition of the relation between domestic- and market-oriented values leads her to a critique that is as directed toward domesticity as toward the public sphere, that Stowe recognizes the value of both "domestic self-denial" and "feminist self-seeking" (18, 28), and that her abolitionism exists side by side with her racism (see Brown's second chapter, "Sentimental Possession").

Did domestic fiction encourage only self-sacrifice, or did it encourage rebellion and domination in the home? Was it a "pragmatic feminism" or a uniform "cult of true womanhood" that taught only self-denial? It is likely that it advocated all of these positions—independence as well as dependence, otherworldliness as well as a deep concern with day-to-day comforts and pleasures, self-interest as well as self-denial. Like the concurrent medical definitions of women, the models were hardly simple and noncontradictory. As we saw in chapter 1, such contradictions could have themselves encouraged a retreat into "illness," where all these virtues could appear to be resolved: the invalid is naturally dependent, so any act of self-determination, however small, seems an act of independence; her nearness to death by necessity makes her otherworldly and also concerned with enjoying the present; every act directed at healing her body is simultaneously self-interested and self-denying.

Because it resolves the conflict between self-denial and self-interest, illness became one of the only coherent models of behavior for women and certainly one of the most often used figures in women's fiction. Joseph Satterwhite, describing the fiction in *Godey's Lady's Book* (a magazine whose stories were written by both men and women but were aimed at a female audience) in "The Tremulous Formula," explains that one of the most often employed resolutions to the tale of a broken heart was the " 'Pining' or 'Decline' " pattern, in which a woman pines away for a man who has died or left for some reason. This tale is resolved "most frequently by a slow decline and painful death" or "occasionally by a slow, painful recovery from acute mental and physical anguish." Another variation, which he calls the "Abnegation" pattern, depicts a woman who gives up her lover and chance for happiness for his benefit (rarely for her own) and then most often either pines away or bears up stoically under her grief. For each of the other two patterns he describes, Satterwhite cites the "painful decline" or sudden death of the heroine (106–7) as the first option for resolution. The stories in *Godey's* are representative of many other stories and novels. Papashvily claims that "the 'pale polished cheeks,' the general fragility" of fictional heroines during the 1840s and 1850s were "unfortunately far too common among women of the period, [and] frequently betokened serious physical disorders" (127). The woman who had spent her adolescence and young adult life reading such fiction had a ready-made "pattern" of illness, decline, and death that told her what she could expect from life. Thus the woman gained the moral superiority befitting the domestic exemplar at the cost of her health and happiness. Unable, and perhaps unwilling, to win (or seek) political power, young women were able to gain a sentimental victory through a refined illness.

So the fiction based on an ideology of women's power (within their own sphere, if not elsewhere as well) ends up at odds with itself. Advocates of the new domestic economy believed in women's innate strength, their ability to overcome great odds, and, implicitly, their natural good health, but women's fiction does not always offer this same vision. The paradoxical figure—the domestic invalid—results in part, then, from the contradictions within domesticity, but she also appears from the conflict between domesticity and medical models. What if seeking too much power leads to wasting away? What if the woman really is responsible for her own illness? Does she deserve the rewards of a loving household? Domestic fiction does not offer an easy answer to these questions, a simple ideology of responsibility and reward. The figure of the invalid woman reveals how the lack of a coherent political rhetoric left domestic fiction unable to resolve the political problems that it details so well.

Invalid Mothers

If domestic fiction establishes a "pattern" of dealing with crisis by taking to bed, that pattern was nonetheless not entirely consistent. The invalid was, in some cases, a good woman who had been cruelly wronged and whose illness only revealed her piety; in other cases, she was a manipulative shrew who used her illness to exact special treatment. In *Uncle Tom's Cabin* (1852), Harriet Beecher Stowe presents her reader with both of these figures of the invalid. Marie St. Clare and her daughter Eva represent the two extremes of mid-century representations of the female invalid. On the one hand, the invalid is a selfish, hateful, and spoiled woman whose illnesses are feigned to enable her to avoid any kind of work; she lives in luxury and thinks only of herself and her imagined ills. Her servants wait on her hand and foot; her every need, real or imagined, is answered because no one wants to listen to her continual complaints. On the other hand, the virtuous female endures her illness without complaint, more concerned with those who will be left suffering after her death than with herself. It is significant that this virtuous female is a child who, despite her age, represents the ideal woman. Selfless, she thinks only of others, no matter how bad her health. In response, people around her love and serve her, realizing all the while that she cannot live because she is too good for this world.

Stowe's two female invalids are drawn clearly from both the medical discourse on women's illnesses and the domestic ideology of the importance of women's work; they represent the division between the otherworldly and the all-too-worldly, the self-sacrificing and the self-interested. Both are upper middle-class women; the working women in the novel, from the slaves to cousin Ophelia, all maintain admirable health. One apparent exception is Eva's Mammy, who suffers from frequent headaches, but, as the novel makes clear, this is only because she gets no sleep at all. Marie wakes Mammy a minimum of four times a night for the duration of the novel—and sometimes as often as twenty—and does not allow her to sleep during the day. Surely a less sturdy woman (that is, a woman of the middle class) would have died from less strain; Eva, in fact, does die from less. The apparent cause of her death is an illness brought on by getting overly excited during a cousin's visit and being "stimulated . . . to exertions beyond her strength" (397).

In "Bio-Political Resistance in Domestic Ideology and *Uncle Tom's Cabin*," Lora Romero argues that Stowe's novel critiques patriarchal power through the "parallels her novel articulates between 'nervous' white women and overworked black slaves." Romero reads Marie's illness as a result of the "lack of wholeness" that results from "the division of labor into mentalizers and manualizers" (722). Romero is certainly right about the etiology of Marie's disease, but she brings a distinctly twentieth-century understanding of the origin of that disease to her reading of the text. Stowe does not suggest that Marie is a victim of the same abuse of power that victimizes the overworked slaves—it is Marie, herself, who is overworking the slaves.

Marie's illness is explicitly described as a function of her jealousy, laziness, and luxurious life-style: "From her infancy, she had been surrounded with servants, who lived only to study her caprices; the idea that they had either feelings or rights had never dawned upon her" (242). When Augustine St. Clare names Eva after his adored mother and lavishes attention on the child, Marie reacts with illness:

> The thing had been remarked with petulant jealousy by his wife, and she regarded her husband's absorbing devotion to the child with suspicion and dislike; all that was given to her seemed so much taken from herself. From the time of the birth of this child, her health gradually sunk. A life of constant inaction, bodily and mental . . . in course of a few years changed the blooming young belle into a yellow, faded, sickly woman, whose time was divided among a variety of fanciful diseases, and who considered herself, in every sense, the most ill-used and suffering person in existence.
>
> There was no end of her various complaints; but her principal forte appeared to lie in sick-headache. (243)

Calling these headaches her "forte" suggests the extent to which Stowe understands Marie's illness to be a performance, a tool for grabbing attention away from her own child. The satire of Marie's complaints suggests that Stowe sees them as a result not of the patriarchal system but of Marie's own abuse of that system.

Marie's headaches, if not completely feigned, result from just the kind of luxurious life E. H. Dixon warned so strongly against in *Woman and Her Diseases*. Stowe calls attention repeatedly to her softly cushioned lounge, her ornate clothes, and her dependence on servants. Despite Stowe's own parody of the "scientific" understanding of blacks as a "degraded race," in the words of Marie (268), she nonetheless represents this invalid woman in a manner consistent with that same scientific discourse. Like Dixon, Stowe attributes responsibility for the wealthy woman's illness to natural weakness and to her own luxurious and selfish life-style. Stowe and her sister Catharine would write in 1869 in *The American Woman's Home*, "The distinctive feature of the family is self-sacrificing labor of the stronger and wiser members to raise the weaker and more ignorant to equal advantages" (18). In *Uncle*

Tom's Cabin, Stowe uses this rationale to condemn Marie not just for her lack of self-sacrifice but for her lack of concern for the "weaker and more ignorant" members of the household. Her desire is entirely for herself, for her own luxuries, and she neglects both her household and her health in pursuit of them.

Recent readings of *Uncle Tom's Cabin* (no doubt influenced by Tompkins's ground-breaking study) tend to focus almost entirely on one pole of Stowe's interest—the spiritual power represented by Eva and Tom, where self-sacrifice is all.[2] What is ignored, however, is the other pole, the material and physical, represented by characters who have power and use it wholly within this world—Eliza, George, Rachel Halliday, Mrs. Byrd, Ophelia, and, in a negative sense, Marie. These characters do not rely solely on self-sacrifice (although they do perform "self-sacrificing labor" for others) and a faith in the next world; they act—and receive their reward—in this one. Marie's power is represented as extremely negative and distasteful, but it *is* power. To claim that "the hysteric and the slave, as discursive entities, serve simultaneously as figures of utter disempowerment and transcendental resistance" (Romero, "Bio-Political Resistance in Domestic Ideology," 726) is to ignore the efficacy of Marie's power in her household—she reigns supreme. However reprehensible her behavior, there is no doubt that it results in living in luxury.

The figure of Marie's hypochondria is not entirely consistent with Stowe's own claim that women "suffer . . . the sins of the beloved in their own bodies." Marie is no Christ figure. Her "suffering" is entirely self-inflicted and represented as almost entirely false. She makes a mockery of those mothers and wives who really do suffer from the wrongs of others. In this, Marie represents the doubt that exists even within Stowe's articulation of the utopian promise that mothers could rid the country of slavery—women's potential invalidity.

It is Eva's death that embodies Stowe's claim of female Christ-like suffering. It is not simply her "exertions" or even "consumption" that kills her but the force of the corrupt system she lives in. Oddly enough, though, Stowe does not, as she did in her private writing, assign this function to a wife or mother but to a small child. Because Eva is a child, she is outside the economy of desire and exempt from the corrupting influences that cause her mother's illness.[3] It is Eva's exemption from desire that simultaneously makes her the representative of an ideal domestic economy, the ideal domestic woman, and an invalid—in direct

contrast to Marie, whose desire makes her both the anti-ideal of domesticity and an invalid. In her powerful reading of *Uncle Tom's Cabin* in
Domestic Individualism, Gillian Brown argues that "Stowe's domestic
economy interprets [Catharine Beecher's] tenet of self-denial as
women's independence from desire. . . . This feminine virtue forms the
foundation of a feminine economy that redefines the notion of possession" (31). It is this independence from desire that Nancy Armstrong
argues in *Desire and Domestic Fiction* came to characterize "domestic
woman," the woman whose self-control cancels out the notion of a
physical body: "The rhetoric of conduct books produced a subject who
in fact had no material body at all" (95). But to become this subject
exempt from desire, Eva must die. To rid herself of self-interest and
desire, to deny her material body and become ideal, she must become
an invalid. As much as Eva's death accords her "sentimental power"
over the readers, it makes no difference in her own material world.
Insofar as *Uncle Tom's Cabin* demonstrates (rather than encourages) a
theory of feminine power in this world, Eva is not its exemplar. The
medical discourse that defines women as "natural invalids" runs
throughout the novel and questions the real potential for and efficacy of
women's power.

The figure of the invalid that emerges from *Uncle Tom's Cabin* is at
once schematic and contradictory. The sickly female is represented in a
dichotomy almost as rigid as the Victorian stereotype of the woman as
either virgin or whore. She is either literally too good for this world, in
which case her illness is but an entry into the heavenly home where she
really belongs, or she is the example of everything wrong with the
world, in which case her illness is an extension of her corruption.

Despite this schematic split, however, both invalids wield a kind of
power in the household. Both Eva and Marie St. Clare rule the family
and servants absolutely. Eva does so because the servants love her and
Marie because they fear her, but both invalids receive attention and
ministration to a degree that would have been beyond the dreams of
most of Stowe's readers. Oddly enough, only Marie is able to enforce
her will. Eva's deathbed request that the slaves be set free, especially
Tom and Mammy, is never accomplished. Marie, on the other hand,
because she does not die of her illness, is able to do whatever she
pleases.

Stowe's narrative, despite its schematic representation of good and
evil invalids, offers readers a contradictory message about gaining

power. On the one hand, as Jane Tompkins argues in *Sensational Designs*, Eva, through a pious and saintly death, gains the spiritual power to shape the lives of those who remain behind on earth.[4] On the other hand, although Marie proves incapable of exerting a moral influence on anyone, she nonetheless is able to use her "illness" to enforce her will in the household. For the reader nourished in the Christian tradition of heroic deaths, Eva's illness and death offer a clear path to spiritual salvation and redemptive power, but for the reader imbued with the bourgeois value of luxury and the domestic value of ruling the household, Marie's "illness" offers a way to absolute domestic domination. The reader is offered contradictory messages again about how to gain power in her household, but in either case, illness is depicted as the means to some kind of cultural power for women.

Eva and Marie St. Clare, even though they are relatively minor characters in Stowe's novel, and even though they stand at two ends of a continuum, reveal the conflicting cultural positions into which the representation of the invalid is figured. When the invalid woman becomes the central figure, as she is in E. D. E. N. Southworth's novel *Retribution* (1849), those complex social structures become even more complicated; as central figures they carry the conventions of literary as well as medical and social discourses. *Retribution* was Southworth's first novel, and it established her among the foremost writers of her time. Although she was largely forgotten and is still largely unread today (only one of her more than twenty novels is in print), Southworth, who was once called "the American George Sand" (Nina Baym, *Novels, Readers, and Reviewers*, 208), was a best-selling author in her own time and was very well received by major critics.[5] In his review of *Retribution*, John Greenleaf Whittier claimed that few American novels could surpass it and compared it favorably with *Jane Eyre* (Helen Papashvily, *All the Happy Endings*, 61). Another critic called it "one of the most intensely absorbing stories we ever read" (Baym, *Novels, Readers, and Reviewers*, 55).[6] *Retribution* remains an entertaining and absorbing novel. Although Hawthorne's jealous assessment of writers like Southworth as a "damn'd mob of scribbling women" (J. T. Frederick, "Hawthorne's Scribbling Women," 232, and Ramona Hull, " 'Scribbling Females' and Serious Males") has for the last century kept them unread in academic circles, a careful reading of *Retribution* reveals how wrong claims that women's fiction was "formulaic" and "simple" are.

The novel tells the story of Hester Grey, a plain and lonely orphaned heiress of "delicate health." Hester eventually marries her guardian, Colonel Ernest Dent (a politician who has no money of his own), and brings her best friend, the beautiful and poor orphaned Italian, Juliette (Nozzalini) Summers, to live with them. It soon becomes clear that, despite her denials, Hester is dying of tuberculosis, but Ernest and Juliette (who are by now in love with each other) conspire to do nothing to save her, and she dies on her twenty-first birthday, after signing manumission papers for her slaves. Ernest later nullifies the freedom papers on a technicality and marries Juliette only three months after Hester's death. They move to Paris, where, although their marriage is marked by worldly success—social and political—they are suspicious of one another and, after seventeen years, come to hate each other.[7] Juliette's unbridled Italian passions more and more frequently turn into hysterical fits, and her demands for luxurious surroundings bring Ernest to financial ruin. When he tells her he is poor and in political disgrace, she leaves him to become the mistress of a powerful European leader. Soon she is involved in political intrigues and executed. After her death, a phrenological examination of her skull reveals it to be "the quintessence of demoniac subtlety and malignity" (247). Ernest returns to America a broken man to live with his and Hester's daughter, having finally learned to value Hester's honesty and integrity.[8]

Southworth's title derives from the moral that she sets out in both her opening and her closing lines: "Human and legal retribution we may elude by concealment; divine retribution we may avert by a timely repentance; but moral retribution we must suffer; and that not by the arbitrary sentence of a despot but by the natural action of an equitable law, old as eternity, immutable as God" (250). This "moral retribution" is "simply the evil principle itself, in its final stage of development," which follows the "crime" "as surely as the plant is produced from the seed" (5). Implicitly, this moral calls into question the efficacy of all male-dominated institutions for achieving justice. Legal, political, and even religious systems may be evaded, but the novel purports to illustrate a structure in which justice operates outside of the conventions of the bourgeois discourse of wealth and power: the family and domestic harmony. In consonance with the "promise and betrayal" described by Mary Kelley, *Retribution* reveals both the revolutionary possibilities of domestic ideology and its implicit fears. The vision the novel offers is of a world exempt from patriarchal systems of justice. Those systems,

Southworth suggests, do nothing for Hester; her husband can easily use the law to subvert the wish she expresses in her will, but he can do nothing to overcome the seeds of adversity his own misbehavior sows in his family. But Southworth's world is also one in which women "suffer . . . the sins of the beloved in their own bodies." The novel suggests a second, and conflicting, structure of retribution that it does not recognize and that does exist completely within the conventions of the dominant bourgeois discourse: the medical discourse in which women's illnesses are a natural result of their inferior physical construction and a punishment for stepping outside of "proper" womanly roles.

All of the major female figures in *Retribution* suffer from a debilitating illness at some point: Hester dies a slow and painful death from tuberculosis; her daughter is left alone and neglected and becomes seriously ill after Hester's death; Hester's maid, the slave-heiress Minny Dozier who is sold, separated from her husband and child, and reduced from heiress to lady's maid, suffers from bouts of hysterical seizures, paralysis, and general dulling of the senses; and Juliette, after her marriage, suffers from violent hysterical fits. While the novel illustrates the principle of moral retribution for violating the ideals of domestic virtue, it more powerfully illustrates the principle of physical retribution for being born female. Therefore two moral discourses are at work in *Retribution*. One, the discourse of domesticity, avowed by Southworth openly, values spiritual beauty and domestic harmony, questions all male-dominated institutional structures, and centers cultural power in the mother. The other, the medical discourse of the rising middle class, values the material world, upholds political and economic power, and punishes women with madness, disease, and death, even though, as we have seen, this discourse is itself contradictory. *Retribution* is the site of a struggle between two systems of social order: one domestic and morally centered, the other public and economically centered. As such, the novel illustrates the strains of maintaining the domestic discourse of the woman's power in the home amid the powerful bourgeois discourses about woman's innate weakness.

If, as Helen Papashvily, Ann Douglas, and Nina Baym have all maintained, women's fiction sought to further domestic virtues in order to place women, specifically mothers, at the center of cultural power, then *Retribution* takes its place among these novels. Hester Grey Dent, the pious, plain—she is literally homely—and maternal heroine, is unquestionably Southworth's exemplum of the virtuous wife and mother.[9]

Repeatedly, the narrator implicitly and explicitly expresses her preference for Hester: "Dear reader . . . I loved Hester" (168). Hester is the
ideal Christian wife and mother; she is devoted to husband and child,
concerned with the welfare of servants, and absolutely selfless. Marriage and motherhood are, with two exceptions (buying gifts for Juliette
and freeing her slaves), the sole passions of her life.

Hester is represented in the novel as the only truly happy character,
and her joy is her only reward (since she takes no real joy in her wealth).
Because of her perfect innocence of heart, she is unaware of the passion
between Juliette and Ernest; when a friend and former suitor tries to
tell her about it, she entirely misunderstands his meaning because such
betrayal is incomprehensible to her (126–28). When she is finally faced
with the reality of her coming death, she needs only an hour to prepare
herself and she admits that her only dread is that heaven could hardly
be as wonderful for her as earth (132–33). Despite continual repri-
mands from Ernest—for minor emotional displays, loving him too
much, trying too hard to please him, not caring enough about her
appearance—Hester adores her husband and is completely happy with
her marriage. She dies a beatific death, assured that her husband loves
her, that her child will be well cared for, and that her slaves will be
freed. That none of these beliefs is true intensifies the pathos of her
death for the reader.

Yet the narrator's overt preference for Hester's behavior does not
obviate the fact that Hester is a very ambivalent role model for feminine
domination or even feminine virtue; she is not self-interested enough
and her self-sacrifice is to no avail. Hester may be happy, she may be
assured of a place in heaven, but the readers of *Retribution* are sure to
realize that her happiness is only a matter of self-delusion. "So Hester
Dent, the loving, but unloved; the gentle, yet oppressed; the confiding,
though deceived, was dead at last. . . . The little hands, ever so busy in
the service of them—the treacherous, who neglected and deceived
her—were cold, still and useless. Hester was dead—and out of the way"
(143). If Hester is to serve as a model for "feminine revolt," "complete
domination," or self-sacrifice, it is only as a negative example of women
who neither revolt nor dominate and whose self-sacrifice makes no real
difference. As this passage suggests, Hester is clearly the sort of victim
who makes her own victimization easy. She chooses friends and husbands unwisely and then places too much trust in them. As a result, she
ends up not only sick and alone but duped even in death. Even Hester's

virtuous plan to free her slaves is thwarted by this weakness. Her death, unlike Eva's, does not even bring salvation or a vision of holiness to anyone; everyone is asleep when the final moment comes. The completely virtuous woman, then, is shown to be at fault. Had she been fully aware of all that was going on in her household—as her responsibility as wife and mother dictated—she might have lived. Lack of vigilance, lack of attention to her own health and welfare, and too much concern for and faith in her friends and family leave her with no power at all. The only woman in the novel to have "complete domination" of the household, in fact, is the overtly wicked and self-centered Juliette.

Southworth's narrator makes no secret of her personal dislike for Juliette; even more frequent than her praises of Hester are her diatribes against Juliette. She spells out the "allegory": "To Ernest Dent, Hester and Juliette—the first pure love, the last insane passion—represented the principles of good and evil. . . . The parallel is perfect, as you will find, if you pursue it" (220–21). In the midst of her warnings against Juliette's "evil," however, the narrator makes it clear that Juliette is not an altogether unattractive or unsympathetic character. "Bad as she was she was a woman, and loved; and what woman, the proudest and fiercest, can bear her hearth and home and heart made desolate, and by her own rash hand? She was a woman, and her woman's nature amply avenged itself" (213–14). Many passages describe Juliette's beauty, her luxurious clothes, her exquisite taste in furnishings. Even when Southworth emphasizes Juliette's dangerousness, it is not clear that it is a completely undesirable thing: "I am fevered and excited with this dark Juliette, with whom one cannot even deal without danger of receiving and communicating evil. She comes upon me like a fiend, or a fit of insanity; so I wish to hurry on to the end of her story, and be done with her" (223). Juliette is an evil that causes illness, but it is an exciting illness, one enhanced by beauty, power, and intensity.

The ambivalence about Juliette is revealed in the outcome of her "story," which reveals a "moral" as questionable as that of Hester's story. Juliette comes to a bad end but only after living for seventeen years in luxury, wealth, and, except for occasional hysterical fits, good health. This ending is complicated by the almost parenthetical mention of the phrenological analysis of her skull. According to phrenological theories—at that time, as well-regarded a science as any—if Juliette's skull revealed "the quintessence of demoniac subtlety and malignity," she was not responsible for her behavior. Two other explanations are offered for her behavior as well: she is an Italian and was subjected to great horrors as a child. At a time of increasing distrust and fear of immigrants, the narrator's insistence that Juliette's "foreign blood" was responsible for much of her misbehavior would have rung true for most readers; such xenophobic sentiments would have been shared by most. The second explanation, that her bad behavior was the result of having witnessed a massacre, having been shipwrecked as a child, and having been left in the care of an insane mother, shows an almost twentieth-century understanding of psychology, prefiguring writers like Henry James. The net effect of all these explanations is to absolve Juliette of responsibility for her "crimes."

Retribution, therefore, despite its title, its moralistic introduction and conclusion, and its narrator's claims to having illustrated the principle of moral retribution, does not maintain a simple and consistent position toward the evils it excoriates or the judgment it ostensibly renders. It offers, instead, a punitive system consistent with the same political, economic, and medical institutions that the narrator so distrusts. Hester, the representative of good, is not blameless; Juliette, the representative of evil, is not really to blame; and Ernest, probably the most to blame, is the least punished of the three. The moral system in *Retribution* is drawn to reassure oppressed women that, despite appearances, evil people are eventually punished and the good rewarded, but this system is questioned in its own elaboration.

Despite the fact that it is men who are by far the most to blame here—Ernest ignores Hester when she needs him, and Minny Dozier's slave-owning father rapes her mother—it is women who suffer these wrongs in their bodies. Hester is punished as well as rewarded; Juliette is rewarded as well as punished; Minny Dozier is repeatedly and cruelly punished before being restored to her original happiness; and Ernest is only mildly punished, a sign that whatever the moral system, true retribution is the lot of women, no matter their guilt or innocence. The moral center on which the novel is so consciously grounded is therefore absent or empty.

The foundation of the narrator's moral system is, as in most domestic fiction, the harmony of the home. Nevertheless, the only happy family in the novel is Minny Dozier's, after she, her devoted husband, and her daughter are reunited, and she is thereby cured of her hysteria. The center of this moral system is motherhood, but the one position in the novel that is most strikingly empty is the mother's position. Hester's and

Ernest's mothers are never mentioned, except to make clear that both died very young. Juliette's mother also dies young, after having gone mad. The mother of the slave-heiress Minny Dozier also goes insane and dies young. Hester herself dies when her child is only a toddler. Minny Dozier is the only mother to live through the novel, and she is separated from her child for a time and, in the reunion of her family, is the passive figure, sought out by a virtuous husband. All of the main characters in the novel are therefore raised as motherless orphans. Not only are all orphaned, but what familial relations do exist are doubled and confused. Ernest's father, only nineteen years older than his son, is described as his "brother-father." Ernest is Hester's guardian before he is her husband. Juliette is described as Hester's "sister-friend." And Minny Dozier's father is also her owner, since her mother was a slave. Southworth elaborates the dystopian vision to which feminine power is the answer: without mothers to keep relations straight, even the institution of the family is subject to corruption. Male domination of the family leads to confusion or worse.

There are also two possible suggestions of childhood sexual abuse in the novel, emblems of the peril when women do not control the family. In the first, Minny Dozier tells Hester that she was forced to sleep with her father, against her will, from the time of her mother's death until she was ten (56). In the second, Juliette, speaking to a young cavalier many years after her marriage, explains that she is haunted by the vision of the shipwreck that occurred in her infancy. She continues, "Such was my infancy; but girlhood—oh! cousin, my girlhood!—that early, horrible initiation into all—" (230), at which point she stops herself. To suggest sexual abuse from these two instances is, of course, to read into the narrative somewhat, but, since there is no hint about what kind of event in girlhood could have been worse than a shipwreck and a massacre, it is possible that Southworth might have been alluding to sexual abuse. Clearly, vagueness on this point may also be a rhetorical ploy to allow the reader to imagine the worst. In either case, the import of these suggestions is ultimately to allude to the terrible fate that can befall a young girl when she loses her mother.

Mothers are absent from the novel because of illnesses. Every mother mentioned in the novel is described as an invalid; with only one exception (Minny Dozier), each is ineffective as a mother and then dies. Minny's mother, who was not her owner's "willing mistress," died, "her wild rebellious heart throbbing itself to death at last" (54). Juliette's mother—who survived her husband and all of her children, except Juliette, after the massacre of Santo Domingo, only to be shipwrecked on her way to America—sunk into "melancholy madness," became so apathetic that she would not change her clothes, and died only a year after being rescued (11–12). Hester dies after a prolonged illness, during which she was bedridden, and Southworth devotes an entire chapter to a description of Hester's two-year-old daughter's despair and sorrow after Hester's death ("The Orphan Babe," especially 162–69).

The absence of the figure of a powerful mother can be read as the child's cry at discovering that the "phallic mother" is an illusion. Unable to accept the fact that the mother is not actually omnipotent and capable of preventing all harm, the "child" (or the author in this case) reacts to the mother's powerlessness by removing her from the scene completely.[10] Despite writing in a genre that explicitly upholds the power of the mother's position, Southworth would nevertheless have to lay the blame for her characters' problems at the feet of mothers who have proved too weak to protect their children from all harm, but by absenting mothers from the narrative, she is able to maintain the fiction of their power. The absence of mothers allows Southworth to suggest implicitly that had the mothers lived, things would have turned out differently.

The absence of effective mother figures—and the corresponding abundance of invalid mothers—can also be understood as a result of the conflict between the discourse of domestic fiction and the nineteenth-century medical discourse of woman's frailty. The domestic discourse that would set up an institution in which women and justice would reign is threatened by a discourse declaring women too weak to hold such power. The power of the medicopolitical ideology of the male middle class proves strong enough to render domestic ideology inconsistent. The novel therefore asserts that women like Hester could improve the world and that domestic harmony is a final arbiter, but it cannot move apart from a cultural background in which women are assumed to be too weak to dominate either the political or the domestic sphere.

The ideology of the dominant culture threatens the novel's consistency at other important points as well. Despite questioning all traditional institutions, the novel must make use of one—religion—in order to achieve justice for Hester. And despite the doubts she expresses about wealth and power, the narrator lingers over descriptions of Juliette's clothes and the social possibilities offered to her by Ernest

Dent's position in the government. At one significant moment, the narrator justifies these descriptions: "Lady reader, I shall make no excuse for again describing Juliette's costume, for we women always like to know how celebrated belles dress—don't we? And gentleman reader, you are at liberty to skip the next half page, or any other portion of this veritable history, that you being a mere man may perhaps consider tedious" (172–73).

The fantasy of wealth, beauty, and social esteem that Juliette offers to Southworth's readers is a seductive one and is perhaps even more dangerous than Southworth herself was willing to recognize, because in one sense Juliette, the poverty-stricken orphan who marries into wealth and social prestige, represents the ideal middle-class woman. Unlike Hester, who has to be continually reminded to think of her appearance, Juliette accepts and revels in the role of woman as ornament, woman as art object. Further, she embodies the bourgeois ideal of rags to riches. But she does so in a way that threatens the moral order, through her betrayal of her friend, and the social order, through her refusal to stand by her husband when he loses his position. Her immigrant status complicates this indictment by making her ingratitude both more blameworthy and to be expected. It is probably unforgivable for an immigrant to marry a wealthy and powerful man; it is certainly unforgivable that she should leave him when his wealth and power are gone. Juliette's hysteria and ultimate death appear to come not as punishment for her betrayal of Hester but as punishment for her betrayal of Ernest and the rules of bourgeois conduct.

In fact, the novel can be read as an allegory of what happens to women who do not maintain their appropriate position in society. Hester refuses to be the proper object of her husband's attentions by neglecting her appearance and therefore falls into a wasting death; she compounds this inappropriate behavior by acting without his permission to have manumission papers drawn up by her lawyer. Juliette's case is even clearer. As long as she maintains decorous behavior toward her husband, concerns herself with her health and her appearance, she is happy and healthy; but every time she tries to reprimand her husband, tries to speak out against some perceived fault, she falls into hysterics. She captures the Grand Duke's affections by sitting silently and letting him come to her but dies after involving herself in German politics.[11]

Possibly her greatest crime, though, is one of omission and is never explicitly mentioned in the text: Juliette never becomes pregnant despite a seventeen-year marriage full of passion. To betray her friend, marry above her station, and then prove barren (or, worse, practice birth control or abortion) is, in the cultural discourse of the time—whether domestic, bourgeois, or medical—truly a crime against nature.

The novel does, then, illustrate a kind of domestic retribution in which the virtuous are remembered kindly and the evil harshly, but running contrary to the moral of retributive justice that Southworth sets out to illustrate is the moral of retributive illness that was firmly embedded in the cultural ideology of the nineteenth century. Ultimately, the invalidism that medical men like E. H. Dixon promised proves strong enough to threaten Southworth's challenge to male-dominated institutions. She offers a vision of a moral, feminine world that nonetheless reveals her fear that the claims of women's weakness were true: that women might prove too weak to rule in any world.

The Feminist Invalid

In one of the earliest antifeminist novels, Sarah Josepha Hale's *The Lecturess* (1839), women do prove too weak to be women's rights lecturers. The central character, Marian Garland, is a lecturess who falls ill on a lecture tour. She takes it as a sign that her husband is right in his disapproval of her work and decides to stop lecturing. She cannot stay away from feminism, though, and returns to the podium after a few years. She loses both her husband and her health and finally dies, lonely and ill, having learned the lesson of submitting her will to her husband's. Given Joseph Satterwhite's findings about the "pattern" of illness in *Godey's Lady's Book*, it is not surprising that *Godey's* editor, Hale, would use illness as the final resolution to her own domestic novel. It is significant, however, that the conflict between domesticity and feminism is so clearly set out in the figure of the invalid. The domestic opposition to feminism is founded on the grounds of the medical attack on women's claims to equality—the female body is just not strong enough to handle the stresses outside the home. The domestic and medical formulations of separate spheres are, in Hale's novel, indistinguishable.

In an 1856 feminist revision of *The Lecturess*, Laura Curtis Bullard's *Christine: A Woman's Trials and Triumphs*, illness again figures in the conflict between domesticity and feminism, but Bullard seeks to establish an alliance between the two ideologies rather than to highlight their differences. This little-read[12] but fascinating novel follows the career of Christine Elliot, a feminist speaker who overcomes the betrayal of a faithless fiancé, outwits her family's plot to have her declared insane, establishes a home to assist young women in getting better jobs, and finally marries the same man who had betrayed her years earlier, after he has reformed and become a supporter of women's rights himself.

Bullard, a little-known feminist author,[13] uses the domestic genre for her novel and even concludes it with her heroine's happy marriage. Like many domestic novelists, Bullard figures illness as the result of male abuse, and like advocates of domestic ideology, she offers a vision of strong, able-bodied women who are capable of running large households and setting the moral example for their families. But unlike the domestic writers, she bases her critique of the wrongs done to women in a public political philosophy. The relationship between medicine, domesticity, and feminism and their different understandings of self-denial and self-interest, responsibility and reward, are dramatized in the novel's representations of ill women.

The relationship between domesticity and feminism was as complex in the mid-nineteenth century as it is now. Today feminists argue for equal rights in the workplace, but they also argue that housework should be recognized and respected and that the workplace should make more allowances for the family. Antebellum feminists also often argued simultaneously for more hospitable home environments as well as for suffrage, education, and property rights. Harriet Beecher Stowe, who is today considered an exemplar of domesticity, also supported women's suffrage in 1869 and wrote a series of articles in the *Atlantic Monthly* on the woman question;[14] Elizabeth Cady Stanton, whose name is synonymous with the rise of feminism in the United States, idealized a "matriarchate" in which mothers would "reign supreme," because she recognized that "the necessities of motherhood were the real source of all the earliest attempts at civilization" (quoted in Josephine Donovan, *Feminist Theory*, 38).[15] It is not always easy or even necessary to distinguish between domesticity and feminism; Gillian Brown refers to Stowe's ideology in *Uncle Tom's Cabin* as "domestic feminism."

Nevertheless, there are some distinctions that we can clearly delineate and that made for dramatic contrasts between the two systems of thought. Proponents of the women's movement took equal suffrage as their primary goal and turned their attention much more toward the public sphere than the private. Even when they were interested in aspects of private life—relations between husband and wife, divorce, custody of children—they tended to focus their energies on the public laws that governed private relations.[16] Perhaps the chief ideological distinction is apparent in this difference of approach: suffragists did not recognize the validity of separate spheres ideology. A division between public and private that corresponded with the division between male and female was anathema to the suffragist because she believed it disempowered women politically.

Given their rejection of the idea of separate spheres, one would expect to find a concerted critique of medical practices from mid-century suffragists since such practices were based on a conception of the absolute difference between the sexes, but such a critique did not come until fairly late in the century. At mid-century, there were only rumblings of the assault on medical practice that would begin in the 1880s, after a substantial number of women had become physicians, and reach its height in Charlotte Perkins Gilman's "The Yellow Wallpaper" (1891). (Since it was not until the latter half of the century that physicians' power was consolidated, this is not that surprising.) Antebellum feminists were, however, active in many of the same health reform movements that domestic writers embraced: reforming dress styles, encouraging exercise, and regulating household activities. Some, like health issues lecturer Mary Gove Nichols, combined their advocacy for women's rights with their calls for better health care. Even Nichols, though, who married a physician, did not offer a coherent critique of medical practices that was tied to feminist theory; her reforms were based more on a belief in the efficacy of hydropathy than on a theory of gender.[17]

Suffragists were nonetheless threatened by medical pronouncements that women were too weak to step into public life. Elizabeth Cady Stanton confronted this issue directly in her address to the 1848 Seneca Falls Convention:

> Let us now consider man's claim to physical superiority. Methinks I hear some say, surely, you will not contend for equality here. Yes, we must not give an inch, lest you take an ell. We cannot accord to man even this much, and he has no right to claim it until the fact has been

fully demonstrated. . . . We cannot say what the woman might be physically, if the girl were allowed all the freedom of the boy in romping, climbing, swimming, playing whoop and ball. . . . Physically, as well as intellectually, it is use that produces growth and development.

But there is a class of objectors who say they do not claim superiority, they merely assert a difference. But you will find by following them up closely, that they soon run this difference into the old groove of superiority. (Ellen Carol DuBois, *Elizabeth Cady Stanton, Susan B. Anthony: Correspondence, Writings, Speeches*, 30–31)

Her refusal to accept even difference, lest it should become superiority, and her insistence on the developmental value of use separate the suffragist from domestic and medical writers, but her rhetoric does not amount to an argument against medical theory or treatment per se. Whether because they did not perceive medicine as a threat or because they were still developing a positive expression of their opinions rather than an attack on oppressors, mid-nineteenth-century feminists did not articulate a coherent critique of medical practices. The argument they used—the sameness of the sexes—was therefore as opposed to domesticity as it was to medicine.

Laura Curtis Bullard's *Christine* nevertheless offers its readers an interesting blend of feminism and domesticity. The novel is clearly written to advocate women's rights in voting, education, and equal opportunity in the workplace, but it also supports the "natural" inclination of some women to domestic duties. Christine is completely inept at housekeeping and obviously meant to be a scholar and lecturer, but almost all of her close girlhood friends are devoted to home and husband. One of them even disagrees with her political position. Bullard clearly knows that her audience is probably not already committed to suffragism and is inclined toward domesticity. She works at not alienating those women who do not want to lecture or work outside the home, while urging them to be more sympathetic with those who do.

In *Christine*'s parallel subplots, we follow the lives of three of the lecturer's closest friends: Mrs. Warner, a loving wife and mother who is a feminist but has given up her ambitions to raise her family; Helen Harper, a sensible young woman who marries an artist for love and who is poor but happy (in an interesting twist, the husband is pro–women's rights, but the wife is not); and Annie Murray, a spoiled and petulant woman who marries for wealth but ends up desperately unhappy, sick, and alone and dies in poverty. Bullard clearly tries to appeal to her audience of nonsuffragist women through these domestic figures and to avoid the confrontation between domesticity and feminism. As do domestic writers, she concentrates a great deal on the problems of unhappy home lives and on the ways in which male dominance of the household—in particular, male violation of domestic harmony—causes the ills of women. She also uses the same convention of opposing good and bad invalids that we saw in Eva and Marie St. Clare and in Hester Grey Dent and Juliette Summers. Christine, even when she is locked in an insane asylum, remains our innocent, selfless, and virtuous exemplar, while the selfish Annie Murray serves as a warning against self-interest.

Bullard approaches issues of women's rights through the conventions of the domestic novel; the subtitle of the novel, *A Woman's Trials and Triumphs*, could easily be the subtitle of a host of mid-century women's novels. The novel offers us two different marriage plots (Christine is engaged, breaks her engagement when her fiancé proves faithless, and marries him in the end after he has repented; her adopted daughter, too, goes through a courtship and wedding) and traces the destruction of one woman's domestic life. The novel also follows domestic convention in its use of illness as a plot device: sickness is decisive in all of the major episodes in the novel, and in every case but one, it is a woman who is ill.

Bullard sets herself against the same male-dominated institutions that Southworth opposed in the opening to *Retribution*, but instead of expecting the punishment to follow evil deeds naturally, Bullard offers a specific political program for reforming those oppressive legal, religious, and social institutions—feminism. Bullard does not, however, offer a specific corrective to male-dominated medicine, even though the novel clearly illustrates the threat offered to women by that discourse.

Bullard's use of domestic conventions and her obvious desire to ally herself with the domestic position create some difficult ideological conflicts. The most important of these conflicts is between an ideology based on a belief in the idea of separate spheres and one directly opposed to it. Whereas the traditional domestic novel offered a private victory for women, Bullard's feminist novel collapses the separation between private and public, offering a possibility of public argument as well as a public victory. But the two ideologies also figure women's self-interest and self-denial differently. Christine takes responsibility for all women and offers her self-denial for the good of the public sphere; her reward is correspondingly achieved publicly as well. But she also practices this self-denial in the domestic sphere and reaps rewards there as well. The novel never alludes to a heavenly reward, never holds out promise of spiritual salvation. It remains pragmatically tied to public and political salvation.

One episode in particular reveals Bullard's difficulty in suturing domesticity and feminism. Christine's girlhood friend Annie, who is rich, spoiled, and raised to be nothing more than a decorative object, foolishly marries a man much older than she who expects her to be a competent housekeeper. Predictably, their marriage becomes a casebook study in psychological abuse, as he makes more and more demands to which she cannot (and does not want to) respond. Annie finally seeks advice from a lawyer about getting a divorce and gets a lesson on married women's property and divorce rights: the lawyer advises her to learn to love her husband. When she tells him that she loathes her husband, he responds, "My dear child, you are ill. . . . You had better go to your chamber and try to sleep" (275). (Later, he tells her husband, "Man, you drove her mad!" [277]).

Instead of seeing her unhappiness as illness, Annie takes her daughter and her jewels— the only property to which she has access—and leaves. She lives well for a little while but soon runs out of money. She works for a while as a seamstress until the foreman's sexual harassment becomes too pressing; when her daughter grows ill, she takes to begging. A young man who had known her when she was a belle sees her, befriends her, and eventually sets her up in a house as his mistress. When he abandons her later, she ends up on a downward spiral that leads to consumption. We last see her when she calls Christine to her, admits her guilt, entrusts Christine with her daughter's upbringing, and dies.

Annie's narrative is a real hybrid of the domestic and the feminist; she is a mother and all of her actions have been taken to shield her young daughter from the harsh fate of growing up in a household with no love or the even harsher fate of starvation. The domestic side of the novel clearly illustrates that the fault lies with men, in particular with her abusive husband, as in many domestic novels. But Bullard shifts the critique of Annie's family from the particular to the systemic in her feminist analysis of the legal and social systems that created this situation in the first place. Her feminist rhetoric makes possible a satire against a legal opinion that would describe unhappy marriages as the result of the wife's illness. She places the blame for Annie's failed marriage squarely on that legal system and on a social system that teaches men to desire the ornamental and to expect the domestic.

Even in the representation of Annie, though, the ill woman is not without responsibility for her own condition. Annie did become a man's mistress (they go through a ceremony, but she knew "that in the eye of the law our union would not be valid" [297]), and the novel suggests that she became a prostitute after he left her. She tells Christine, "I was maddened—I was reckless. Oh, Heavens! . . . I can say no more. From that time I was utterly lost. . . . I sunk deeper and deeper, lower and lower, till here I am, a wreck of what was once Annie Murray—a vile, vile wretch, but with one spark of virtue remaining, my love for my innocent Rosa" (300). Where a domestic novel would offer us the scene of Annie's repentance and assurances of her heavenly reward, *Christine* does no more than to say "her spirit passed on to its Maker" (301). Christine thinks that "Annie had been ruined by her education" (303), making society at least partly responsible, but Annie remains ruined. Is her consumption the result of her own bad behavior or of men's abuse of her? The text affirms both answers.

As we have seen with domestic fiction, assigning blame and responsibility to men is complicated by a medical ideology that holds women themselves to blame. But in *Christine*, the emergent feminism itself makes this assessment more problematic: if women are strong enough to support themselves, to be self-determining individuals, are they not responsible for their own well-being? The example of Christine stands as an indictment of Annie, questioning whether she had to turn to begging or prostitution to support herself. In figuring Christine as the heroic and strong individual, Bullard leaves the door open for a critique of any woman's failure as a deserved punishment for weakness. Whether judged on domestic terms for violating familial norms, on medical terms for seeking luxuries, or on feminist terms for depending on men, Annie is responsible for her condition and to some extent "deserves" the punishment of illness.

Annie's self-interest is in the end outweighed by her self-denial for her daughter, but self-interest is her defining feature throughout the novel. Even the early chapters about their childhood represent Annie as naturally selfish and egocentric when she lets Christine suffer the punishment for something she herself did. The critique of institutions that Bullard mounts in Annie's case is undercut by the domestic conventions which necessitate that a woman who would come to such an end must have "deserved" it somehow. The morality of the domestic genre and the politics of the feminist discourse are at odds over Annie's actions. The only way to resolve such a contradiction is, as we have seen, the woman's illness and death.

Bullard's commitment to feminism emerges over her rhetorical use of the domestic genre in *Christine*. The villain of the novel is a woman, a member of Christine's own family, and the novel's spokeswoman for the domestic position. The beautiful Julia Frothingham, despite being a self-made entrepreneur of sorts (she runs her own exclusive finishing school for girls), is an avidly antifeminist advocate of preserving the woman's sphere. Like the present spokeswoman for "traditional family values," Phyllis Schlafly, she is an aggressively outspoken believer in woman's passivity.

It is Julia who traps Christine in the insane asylum and who convinces Mr. Elliot, Christine's father, to take part in it. Bullard dissociates herself from a particular kind of conservative domesticity and resists any idealization of familial—or even womanly—bonds. But Bullard's treatment of Christine's imprisonment in the asylum is as interesting for the critique it does not make as for the one it does. For while there is a strong indictment of familial abuses and of conservative domestic values, there is no direct resistance to medical practice.

Instead, the criticism is of Christine's family, in particular her aunt and her father. When disinheritance is not enough to stop Christine's lecturing, the family refuses to relinquish its control over her. Her aunt, who objects to the principles of women's rights, convinces her father, who objects to a woman's public speaking, to pretend that he is insane, and they use Christine's sense of guilt for betraying her father's wishes to lure her to the asylum. While she is inspecting the room "for her father," she is locked in and left. Julia visits Christine and explains the conditions on which she will be released: "You must promise, first, never again, by voice or pen, to defend the foolish doctrines of that ridiculous cause which you have espoused." Christine refuses the condition, warning Julia, "You will drive me mad!" (242). Eventually, Christine does escape and exposes her aunt's deceit in front of witnesses, guaranteeing her freedom.

The novel never leaves us in any doubt of Christine's sanity. Even though she reacts to being locked up with the "wildest excitement," it is clear that her response is not out of proportion to her circumstances; she quickly controls herself, realizing that "her violence had been so much against her" (229). But after almost a year of solitary confinement, Christine begins to doubt herself, fearing that she is sinking into "the most hopeless of any kind of insanity, that of a gentle, but settled melancholy." Under these conditions, her health begins to decline; "She was growing weaker every day, and she rejoiced in this gradual decay which she felt stealing over her" (245). Even so, she has enough presence of mind to seize her first chance for escape and to work out a plan that will guarantee not only her release but her safety from any future plots by her family. Her release is not the only reward—or revenge—Christine achieves. Her lecturing and writing prove profitable, and she becomes moderately wealthy; her father, on the other hand, almost loses his farm and is saved from bankruptcy only when Christine pays off a loan for him. She wins both material and moral victories in the end.

Bullard never explicitly criticizes medicine and medical practices. Since Christine's family commits her under a false name without telling her what it is, her assertion of her real identity becomes a sign of her insanity to the physician and something of a vindication of his role in her imprisonment. He comments at one point, "There, too, is a mono-maniac, who imagines herself to be Christine Elliot; sane in all other respects, apparently—quite gentle, yet almost a hopeless case" (230). Her letters to friends, which are confiscated, of course only reinforce this false diagnosis. At one point, the man who eventually helps Christine escape acknowledges that the doctor has no interest in helping her ("He's paid for keepin' on ye here and 'taint likely he's over-anxious to get rid on ye" [255]), but that is as close as the novel ever comes to a critique of a medical practice that would lock up a woman solely on her family's word.

The critique in this novel remains domestic: it is an aunt and a father who are guilty. Bullard's condemnation on this point remains private, not public. Oddly enough, the family is not represented as emblematic of society at large, nor is the asylum described in terms that make it representative of a larger system. In contrast to a later story like "The Yellow Wallpaper," there is no nameless narrator in an "ancestral estate." Christine remains throughout the novel such an individualized character that her fate never seems symbolic. There is none of the direct address so common in other novels of the period, forcing the reader to recognize this situation as representative—no expression directed to a "Dear Reader" that would force us to see Christine as a representative figure.[18]

Perhaps 1856 was too early to mount a concerted campaign against medical practices. Although allopathy was becoming a dominant cultural force, it was not the power—or the threat—it would be by 1891 when Gilman wrote "The Yellow Wallpaper." Christine's dilemma was not, however, a purely fictitious or idiosyncratic situation. In the first volume of the *History of Woman Suffrage* (1881), Elizabeth Cady Stanton reminisces about an event during the winter of 1861:

> While [we were being ridiculed] publicly, we had an equally trying experience progressing day by day behind the scenes. Miss [Susan B.] Anthony had been instrumental in helping a fugitive mother with her child, escape from a husband who had immured her in an insane asylum. . . . Though she was incarcerated in an insane asylum for eighteen months, yet members of her own family again and again testified that she was not insane. . . . The result proved the wisdom of Miss Anthony's decision, as all with whom Mrs. P. came in contact for years afterward, expressed the opinion that she was perfectly sane and always had been. *Could the dark secrets of these insane asylums be brought to light*, we should be shocked to know the countless numbers of rebellious wives, sisters, and daughters that are thus annually sacrificed to false customs and conventionalisms, and barbarous laws made by men for women. (469, emphasis added)

By 1881, when Cady Stanton's account was published, women had begun to resist in an organized way medical definitions of women and to develop a rhetoric for that resistance. It was therefore not difficult for Cady Stanton to generalize from the case of Mrs. P. to "the dark secrets of these insane asylums." Certainly Laura Curtis Bullard's critique runs aground on her own individualistic idealization of Christine, but her failure to generalize Christine's experience also follows from the lack of any real discourse of resistance on which to base such a critique.

In contrast to Hester Grey Dent, who must trust in a natural retribution for any justice, Christine Elliot finally "gets it all": a successful career, her health, and a loving—and feminist—husband.[19] While this nascent feminist position does not offer a coherent argument against medical definitions of women as "natural invalids," it is stronger in resisting that medical ideology than the domestic tradition. The domestic position, in its agreement with the medical insistence on absolute difference, falls prey to the fear Cady Stanton expressed in Seneca Falls: that difference would be run "into the old groove of superiority." Later feminist writers, like Charlotte Perkins Gilman, would have to reassess the relation between domesticity and feminism after medical theory adopted the rest cure, an exaggerated, cartoon version of domesticity. But Bullard's *Christine* offers a variation of "domestic feminism" that, although conflicted and contradictory on many points and limited by the lack of both a coherent discourse and a fully workable genre, could still imagine a woman's recovery and triumph.

Domesticity and feminism, however, were neither the only nor the most influential discourses resisting mid-century medical theory. Before we return to the engagement between feminism, domesticity, and medicine in Gilman's and Edith Wharton's work at the turn of the century (in chapter 4), we will examine the relation between medicine and American romanticism in the texts of male writers in the 1840s and 1850s. Like their female counterparts, Washington Irving, Edgar Allan Poe, and Nathaniel Hawthorne both resisted and were intrigued by the increasingly powerful medical formulation of the figure of the invalid woman.

Chapter **3**

(Super)

"Natural"

Invalidism:

Male Writers

and the

Mind/Body

Problem

Now, never losing sight of
the object of supremeness, or
perfection, at all points, I asked
myself—"Of all melancholy
topics, what, according to the
universal understanding of
mankind, is the most melan-
choly?" . . . The death . . .
of a beautiful woman is,
unquestionably, the most poetical
topic in the world.
  —Edgar Allan Poe,
    "The Philosophy of
    Composition" (1846)
But Nature's got rules and
Nature's got laws
  —Laurie Anderson,
    "Monkey's Paw" (1990)

Few texts so relentlessly celebrate the feminine invalid as
Washington Irving's *Biography and Poetical Remains of the Late Mar-*
garet Miller Davidson (1841). Margaret, a tubercular child poet, died
just a few months short of her sixteenth birthday, a victim of the same
disease that had, fourteen years earlier, claimed her older sister Lucretia (who was, herself, a famous poet). The biography is usually ignored in the Irving corpus. When it is noticed, the criticism is usually
derisive. Stanley T. Williams, Irving's 1935 biographer, one of the few

critics to even mention the *Biography*, calls it a "sweet confection" that is "the ultimate of the sentimental tendency in him and probably his worst piece of writing" (*The Life of Washington Irving*, 108). Expressing his incredulity over a passage of the biography, Williams considers whether "such idiocies [are] a devastating proof that Irving had gone quite to seed" but concludes that "Irving was not a mawkish donkey; it is rather that he understood certain emotional criteria of the age" (110). But Irving's contemporaries reacted to it quite positively: Edgar Allan Poe, reviewing it in *Graham's Magazine*, heaped great praise on the biography (despite his doubts about Margaret's poetical abilities), writing, "Few books have interested us more profoundly" (93).

The biography may be too sentimental for the cynical tastes of late twentieth-century readers, but it was extremely popular in its time; it went through eleven editions between 1841 and 1857. The biography is actually a collaborative text, written by Irving who borrowed heavily from the notes given him by Margaret's mother, herself an invalid (Irving describes his meeting with her: "She was feeble and emaciated, and supported by pillows in an easy chair, but there were the lingerings of grace and beauty in her form and features" [10]). It represents an interesting blend of the sentimental and the romantic. Margaret's mother describes her as what we would recognize as a Little Eva figure, sent as a Christian exemplar to the world, and Irving describes her as a type of the doomed artist. In the intersection between these two voices we can read the struggle between these two discourses.

The Domestic and the Romantic (Super)Natural

The struggle between discourses is staged in the question of what Margaret's life had meant; that is, whether the world was better off for her poetry or would have been a better place had she lived—for, within the medical model of closed energy, her health and her writing are considered completely inimical. On his first meeting with Margaret, Irving had cautioned her mother "against fostering her poetic vein" after he had seen that she was "prone to the same feverish excitement of the mind" as her sister had been (10). The next time he sees Margaret, three years later, he notices that the interval had "rapidly developed the powers of her mind, and heightened the loveliness of her person, but [his] apprehensions had been verified. The soul was wearing out the body" (11). The whole biography is dedicated to tracing the battles between Margaret's mind and her body, documenting the alterations in her health and her intellect. When she is writing poetry, she is happy but her body wastes away; when she agrees to stop her diligent studies (she teaches herself the classical languages and French and reads world history as well as world literature voraciously) and her writing, her health improves but she becomes despondent.

Irving turns the narration of Margaret's death entirely over to her mother, Mrs. Davidson, quoting at great length a letter she wrote to Catharine M. Sedgwick when Margaret had died. (Sedgwick had befriended the family years earlier when she wrote Lucretia's biography.) In the course of this letter, the sentimental vision becomes the clearest. Mrs. Davidson sets the scene and outlines the powerful lesson to be learned from Margaret's example:

> Oh, my dear madam, the whole course of her decline was so unlike any other deathbed scene I ever witnessed; there was nothing of the gloom of a sick chamber; a charm was in and around her; a holy light seemed to pervade every thing belonging to her. There was a sacredness, if I may so express it, which seemed to tell the presence of the Divinity. . . . My dear Miss Sedgwick, how I have felt my own littleness, my total unworthiness, when compared with this pure, this high-souled, intellectual, yet timid, humble child; bending at the altar of her God, and pleading for pardon and acceptance in his sight, and grace to assist her in preparing for eternity. (144)

At the end of the letter, Mrs. Davidson refers to Margaret as her "angel child" and describes a packet of papers she had found, sewn together (like Emily Dickinson's "fascicles" would be), which contained Margaret's religious self-examinations. Although they are "of too sacred a nature to meet the public eye," we are told that they are evidence of "a heart chastened and subdued by the power of divine grace" (151).

Mrs. Davidson's narrative concentrates on Margaret's holiness, her bravery, and her dedication to making her family happy. When she mentions Margaret's poetry, it is always a kind of domestic poetry that she celebrates—a poem dedicated to Mrs. Davidson herself about the powers of motherhood, or a poem that contrasts worldly fame (as a poet) and heavenly happiness, finding the former greatly lacking. For Mrs. Davidson, Margaret's poetry makes her different, but it is her piety, her kindness, and her bravery that make her exceptional and notable. Her implicit argument is that Margaret's death is linked to her holiness, a visible sign of it and a means to its propagation in the world.

Irving's interest in Margaret is poetical. He is by no means antithetical to Mrs. Davidson's position, but when the narrative shifts to the domestic or the sentimental, he leaves the text in her words.[1] But when he turns to Margaret's work or her poetry, he resumes control of the narration. When Irving narrates, his attention is focused on her reading, her relationship to nature, and her writing. He dwells on her precocious storytelling, her quickness to learn, the diversity of her reading. Throughout, however, he evinces the worry that such efforts were making her more interesting and attractive at the same time that they were killing her: "Her highest pleasures were intellectual," he writes, but he notes that "it was necessary to keep her in check, lest a too intense pursuit of knowledge should impair her delicate constitution" (20–21).

For Irving, Margaret represents the romantic, tubercular artist, a kind of female John Keats whose intellectual and poetical brilliance literally *consumes* her body.[2] While Mrs. Davidson concentrates on Margaret's possession by the Holy Spirit, Irving concentrates on her possession by a poetic spirit. He writes of the "almost unearthly lustre of her eye" (11) and her "premature blossomings of poetic fancy" (18).

Periodically, Margaret is told to halt her studies and her writing (she is "especially warned" about the "exciting exercise of the pen" [65]), and she does, to the apparent benefit of her physical condition, but she finally cannot restrain her need to write and in every case ends up back at work. And in every case, this return to work is accompanied by a worsening of her physical condition: "A few weeks of this intellectual excitement was followed by another rupture of a blood-vessel in the lungs, and a long interval of extreme debility" (69). What is striking about Irving's contribution to the *Biography* is his absolute wonder at the intimate connection between mind and body. He completely accepts the medical model of closed energy and the need to maintain balance but without the medical sense of the girl's guilt for exciting "bad natural tendencies." He seems to accept Margaret's death as her tragic destiny as a poet and even sees it as evidence that she *was* a poet.

Irving's attitude toward the female child-poet offers us a way into an exploration of Poe's and Hawthorne's representations of invalid women and is suggestive of a mid-nineteenth-century belief system in which questions of mind and body, agency and subjectivity, gender roles and "separate spheres," come into complex interaction. The doubled discourse of the *Biography*—with its narration by both Mrs. Davidson and Washington Irving—is more obviously contradictory than that we will see in Poe's and Hawthorne's work but is indicative of a doubleness we will encounter in all of their writings about female invalids.

Despite the rigid distinction that has been made in American literary criticism between "domestic" or "sentimental" and "romantic" writers, American authors during the mid-nineteenth century were all responding to the same cultural situation, and often in very similar ways, as the example of Washington Irving's and Mrs. Davidson's collaboration demonstrates. But while chapter 2 focused on women writers, this chapter takes up the male response to the changing discourses on medicine and women. The women in Edgar Allan Poe's and Nathaniel Hawthorne's fiction are a particularly sickly lot. These male writers adopted the cultural and medical figure of the invalid woman and, as Poe reveals in "The Philosophy of Composition," elevated her death to the status of the "most poetical" subject. Nowhere does she appear more often than in Poe's stories, and nowhere is she as consistently placed in the context of science and art than in Nathaniel Hawthorne's tales. Scrutinizing the shape of her figure in several short texts—"Ligeia" and "The Oval Portrait" (Poe), "The Birthmark" and "Rappaccini's Daughter" (Hawthorne)—and in a longer work by Hawthorne—*The Blithedale Romance*—will illuminate why the invalid woman became so firmly established in the fiction of male writers at mid-century.[3]

I have separated Stowe, Southworth, and Bullard from male writers here not because I have chosen to privilege either set of writers or because I agree with the critical segregation that has occurred in the past but because the male and female authors in the mid-nineteenth century had different ideological agendas. While women writers were trying to set out a place in the culture where their worth could be established and their value(s) upheld, male writers found themselves with the need to reassess their own roles in the culture and their relationships to women, to women's work, and to their own work. The fundamental reorganization of culture suggested by both domesticity and feminism made the question of what men were to do problematic.

For example, as Jane Tompkins argues in *Sensational Designs*, Stowe's *Uncle Tom's Cabin* leaves "groom[ing] themselves contentedly in a corner" as the only viable male role in human history (146). For male writers who wanted to do more than groom, then, domesticity, not to mention feminism, could have been perceived as being as much of a threat to men as was medical discourse to women. Their writing would have had to reject certain tenets of domesticity and feminism; the medical model of invalid women would certainly have been an appealing alternative for men who questioned the ideology of the female-dominated discourses.

In a culture as dramatically segregated by gender as was mid-nineteenth-century American society, it is to be expected that male and female concerns were separate and, at times, antithetical. G. J. Barker-Benfield argues in *The Horrors of the Half-Known Life* that men experienced a very different kind of pressure than did women. These pressures—which he describes as the need to suppress emotion, to develop themselves as individuals without reference to a family or the larger community, and to prove themselves capable within the harsh public sphere of competition—amounted to a continual need for strict self-control that was often translated into a need to control women and to resist their civilizing influence.[4] The need to interpret and understand gender roles, for men and women, was strong.

Both male and female writers, therefore, were writing literature that was, as Kenneth Burke in *The Philosophy of Literary Form* argues literature always is, "equipment for living . . . [that] would *protect*" them against some threat (61). But male and female writers sensed different threats: women were responding to the threat that they perceived medical science offered (as I explain in chapter 2), while men were responding to the possible threat of women's growing social power as well as to the increasingly straitened roles prescribed for men, including medical restrictions on male roles. Despite these distinctions, it is important to keep in mind that "women's fiction" (written by and for women) and "men's fiction" (written by and for men) appeared side by side in the same popular magazines and periodicals. The easy differentiation of the "quality" of these stories by such earlier critics as J. T. Frederick, who writes in "Hawthorne's Scribbling Women" that the female editors of these periodicals "took in each other's wash, so to speak" (236), cannot bear up under close scrutiny. The difference between them is more a matter of the questions they seek to resolve than of quality.

That ideological difference gives shape to the figure of the invalid woman in Poe's and Hawthorne's tales, an ideology that questions the claims made by women for feminine moral power and for the importance of women's role in the household at the same time that it seems to resist the medical discourse on which "separate spheres" ideology rests. In "The Oval Portrait," "Ligeia," "The Birthmark," "Rappaccini's Daughter," and *The Blithedale Romance*, Poe and Hawthorne directly address the problematic relation between mind and body as it appears in medical discourse. Whereas the medical man asserted that the body could be exercised only at the expense of the mind, and vice versa, Poe and Hawthorne search for a new union of mind and body in which the two do not compete for primacy. Eventually they cannot resist the power of the medical definition, though; however desirable the union appears, the stories make it finally impossible, unless through unnatural or supernatural means. The woman's death, then, besides being an aesthetic moment, allows for the transcendence of certain natural laws (as understood by nineteenth-century science). The dead woman's "supernatural" power is not, as it is in women writers' texts, a result of her legacy of faith and good works but a result of some diabolical, unnatural force, tinged with gothic horror. That horror in turn questions the aestheticism of her death and reinscribes it with a different kind of power.

Running alongside their questions about nature are also questions of responsibility. At moments, Poe and Hawthorne seem to follow E. H. Dixon's lead and blame the woman for her own death, or they blame at least a specifically female nature, but at others, they seem to follow Stowe and blame their male protagonists for insensitivity and outright cruelty. In every case, the question of responsibility for a woman's invalidism and death becomes a central question of the text and one that both authors refuse to settle. Like Washington Irving, then, they leave the question of the meaning of the woman's life and her death open.

The remainder of this chapter will trace this interaction of the natural, the unnatural, and the supernatural aspects of women's illnesses in Poe's and Hawthorne's fiction against the background of the same discourses on women's health that were examined in chapters 1 and 2—definitions of women as invalids, as civilizing forces, as the equals of men. Here my focus will be on the particular problem for the nineteenth-century male writer of defining the relationship between man and woman as the relationship between mind and body.

The Mind/Body Problem

Poe and Hawthorne were influenced by European romantic thought, as were most American writers in the mid-nineteenth century. But, as Americans steeped in the Puritan and expansionist traditions of the new country, they could not import European theories of mind and art without some conflict and confusion. The romantic faith in the primacy and natural goodness of the individual mind, confidence in the wonderful and supernatural, rejection of empirical scientific thought, and belief in the power of the artist came to America through a filter of ethical and religious thought that stressed seriousness, held to a doctrine of natural sinfulness, and expressed faith in the "divine light" of individual spiritual direction. The romantic celebration of the primitive and the natural was complicated in America by expansionist and bourgeois faith in the goodness of progress, the value of wealth, and the importance of material possessions.

For the European romanticist, the power of an individual man's mind was exactly that—a male power. In the romanticism of such writers as Jean-Jacques Rousseau, William Wordsworth, and even Mary Wollstonecraft, it was the male who was associated with the mind and culture; woman was associated with the body and nature.[5] This association was never without its discontents in European thought, but in a country that in its early days granted enormous freedom to women and that had a history of strong and independent females in its religious and prairie life (if not elsewhere), such an association would have been especially uncomfortable. Nevertheless, woman as nature is a frequent trope in American writing,[6] as is the dissociation of woman and mind. This dissociation stands behind Poe's images of women who are terrifying to the degree that they are intellectual (especially Morella and Ligeia) and behind Hawthorne's problematic representations of women writers and artists (his comments on the "damn'd mob of scribbling women" and his portrayal of a female intellectual in *The Blithedale Romance* and of women artists in *The Marble Faun* can easily be read as condemnations of female artistic and intellectual work).[7]

This envisioning of intellectual women as anomalous is common, according to anthropologist Michelle Zimbalist Rosaldo in "Women, Culture, and Society," whenever women "defy the ideals of male order" (32). She argues that "whatever violates a society's sense of order will be seen as threatening, nasty, disorderly or wrong" (31) or, we might add, sick. But at the same time that romanticism equated woman with nature and the principles of nonrationality, its emphasis on self-determination and individuality established an intellectual atmosphere in which the debate on women's rights could be opened.[8] As Sherry Ortner explains in "Is Female to Male as Nature Is to Culture?," "Woman cannot be consigned fully to the category of nature, for it is perfectly obvious that she is a full-fledged human being endowed with human consciousness just as a man is" (75–76). The result of this contradiction is that women are "seen to occupy an intermediate position between culture and nature" (84).[9]

This intermediacy, this existing in both nature and culture, results in the confusingly doubled representation of women in so many cultural texts: "We can begin to understand then how a single system of cultural thought can often assign to women completely polarized and apparently contradictory meanings, since extremes, as we say, meet. That she often represents both life and death is only the simplest example one could mention" (Ortner, 85). Woman can be represented as not only both life and death but, as we shall see in Beatrice Rappaccini and Zenobia, both abundant health and tragic illness.

This contradictory representation of women is borne out in other ways in Poe's and Hawthorne's fiction. Alongside the ambivalent relation between women and nature is the equally ambivalent relation between women and culture. The tales ask: what if women were removed from their roles as arbiters of culture? They reveal the fear that "if you [change] woman's position by removing her from her moral superiority, her pedestal, by blurring the lines between the spheres, she would threaten order" (G. J. Barker-Benfield, *The Horrors of the Half-Known Life*, 48). But there is also a recognition in the fiction that the real threats to order "were men, craving autonomy, tempted to repudiate political authority as well as the ties of heterosexual obligations. Men were projecting onto women what they feared from themselves" (ibid.). The contradictions in the fiction result from the confrontation between these two views. In these texts, men attempt, but cannot fully succeed, to make women entirely body. Women try to assert their powers of mind but cannot, finally, assert their own intellectual strength.[10]

This contradiction returns us to a central problem in the medical discourse on women—the relation of mind and body to the establishment of separate spheres. For while the female discourses of domesticity and feminism were threatened by the medical discourse (as we saw in the previous chapter), it is equally true that the whole medical understanding of the body was threatened by those female discourses. If woman could develop her mind without ruining her body, then not only were the medical men wrong about women, but the whole basis for maintaining separate gender spheres was wrong, too. If body and mind could coexist without draining each other, then their relation to each other would become troubled.[11] And while this new relation would seem to offer remarkable potential, it also offers an enormous threat to a worldview that had been developing for centuries, a threat to the very fabric of society.

Women's role would not be the only role in this society that would change with a new understanding of the mind/body relation. The correlative, that man could likewise develop his body without risk to his mind, was equally threatening in that it would require a complete rethinking of male roles.[12] The dissolving of the comfortable divisions among men, into laborers and thinkers, for example, would be as problematic as would that of divisions between the sexes. But, again, the potential must have been tantalizing to men for whom the status quo meant a devotion to either thought or body but not both. Men faced different medical strictures than did women, but they were strictures nonetheless.

In short, the conflicts between medical, domestic, feminist, and romantic discourses are played out in the shifting relations between sets of paired terms—mind/body, culture/nature, health/sickness, man/woman. Those conflicts appear in texts by Poe and Hawthorne as contradictions, as impossibilities within the tales, and as doubts about male roles as well as female, about male as well as female illness.

The figure of the invalid woman in Poe's and Hawthorne's fiction is shaped by these contradictions in the cultural representations of woman. On the one hand, she is nature, to be worshipped and admired in her native state, as well as an object to be possessed, exploited, and developed.[13] So the invalid woman also represents an imperfect and even threatening nature. On the other hand, she is an individual, with human powers of mind and responsibility for her own self-determination. In fictions concerned with the individual and the difficulties and necessities of maintaining a sense of individuality, the figure of woman as nature represents several dilemmas. How can woman be both representative of nature and a self-determining individual? How can she be both mind and body? Can she?

One "solution" to the problem of woman's representation was to figure her into the one place accepted and expected by the culture: that of the invalid. As invalid, woman takes her place on the side of the body and nature—since these are "naturally" the defining features of the invalid. In this figuration, woman specifically symbolizes a nature that is in keeping with expansionist belief; that is, she needs man's intervention. Representing women as "natural invalids" creates its own problems, however. As nature, woman becomes inhuman. As the *object* of man's (medical) intervention, she loses her standing as *subject* to a large degree. Treated as natural invalid, woman stands as a challenge to the faith in the validity and self-determination of the individual and, in being defined almost exclusively as body, as a threat to the hope for a unity of mind and body. If she is understood as only a representative of nature, as something other than a being with the power to direct her own fate, then she must either be discounted as human or stand as a threat to the notions of individuality and freedom.

Further, the cultural climate at mid-century would not easily allow such an equation. Women like Margaret Fuller and Elizabeth Cady Stanton were speaking out openly against such definitions; an entire feminist movement was beginning to assert female equality. The domestic writers who published in the same periodicals as Poe and Hawthorne were redefining the culture/nature distinction in such a way that women's moral guidance in the home came to represent the civilizing force of culture, while the male world of competition came to represent a kind of reversion to nature.[14] It would not be possible (or, perhaps, even desirable) to represent woman as equal to nature. But what would be entailed in an acceptance of women as intellectual equals? There were almost daily claims to both the feminine power of mind *and* the civilizing power of women in the home. Such claims complicated the representation and understanding not just of women's roles but also of men's roles.

The power of this conflict for male writers becomes apparent when we include in it the issue of reproduction. Sherry Ortner in "Is Female to Male as Nature Is to Culture?" explains, using Simone de Beauvoir's *Second Sex*, that one basis for the association of men with culture and women with nature is woman's ability to bear children. Men, to assert their creativity, must reproduce " 'artificially' through the medium of technology and symbols . . . [creating] relatively lasting, eternal, transcendent objects, while the woman creates only perishables—human beings" (75). In other words, men reproduce intellectually, while women are restricted to physical reproduction. For men to accept women's abilities to reproduce culture as well as nature would be, therefore, tantamount to admitting their own inferiority in being able to reproduce only culture, only mind, while women have access to both means. What we will see in "The Oval Portrait," "Ligeia," "The Birthmark," "Rappaccini's Daughter," and *The Blithedale Romance* is the desperate questioning of the mind/body relation. The texts take several tacks on the problem: they represent masculine attempts to redefine women as natural invalids (to deny women's association with culture), to imagine a male ability to reproduce nature, and to deny outright the power of the female mind and body. Poe and Hawthorne illustrate that such strategies for dealing with the contradictory, intermediate position of women are only partially successful, at best.

While other male writers avoid this contradiction by largely ignoring women—Ralph Waldo Emerson, Henry David Thoreau, and Herman Melville are the most obvious examples—Hawthorne and Poe "resolve" it with the woman's death. But this death itself "solves" the problem of female figuration in contradictory ways. In death, the woman becomes no longer human, so she can be nature as well as something more than human; she becomes perfect or supernatural. Granting the woman this measure of power and transcendence compensates her for the power and individuality that she is denied. At the same time, the fiction of self-determination is preserved by making the woman responsible for her own sickness; her death then becomes a punishment for her inability to overcome nature's inadequacy. In agreement with the contradictory position held by E. H. Dixon and other medical authorities, here woman is condemned to suffering, illness, and death both by nature and by her own willful misbehavior. But this male discourse is disrupted in Poe's and Hawthorne's fiction by the domestic and feminist claim that women are really made to suffer by the misbehavior of men. There is ample evidence in all five texts that women are the victims of male abuse. Their deaths end the question of responsibility in the texts but not for the reader (nor, perhaps, for the writers). The "resolutions," then, offer no solution to the dilemma. The figure of the invalid woman in Poe's and

Hawthorne's fiction compounds the contradictions already found in the culture, especially in medicine and popular fiction. Woman is the principle of nonrationality—nature—and is therefore good, but she also needs improvement; further, she both is and is not personally responsible for her "inadequacies." The male characters fare no better—their own troubled and doubled relation to mind and body, to culture and nature, often leaves them sick, or alone, or both.

Making Natural Art of Women

Two tales reveal much about the contradictions of woman's representation. In Edgar Allan Poe's "The Oval Portrait" (1842) the narrator, who is wounded and ill, sees a fascinating portrait of a beautiful young woman and reads a brief story of its painting: she had obediently acquiesced to her husband's desire to paint her portrait and had fallen ill while sitting for it; he did not notice her rapid fading and, at the moment of his completing the portrait, she died. Hawthorne's "The Birthmark" (1846) is the model for the old doctor joke, "The operation was a brilliant success, but, unfortunately, the patient died." In that tale, a talented scientist becomes obsessed by a birthmark on his beautiful wife's cheek and, in the process of removing it, kills her.

The similarities between these tales are remarkable; it seems likely that Poe's tale was an inspiration for Hawthorne's.[15] Both husbands are devoted to their professions and find that the only way to maintain passion for their wives is to combine it with passion for their professions. Both wives are strikingly beautiful. Both husbands are explicitly trying to equal the feats of nature in order to "reproduce" nature: Poe's artist cries, "This is indeed *Life* itself!," at the moment he finishes his portrait (and his wife's life); Hawthorne's scientist openly pits himself against the power of nature in trying to "perfect" Georgiana. Finally, both tales center on the question of whether the wife was merely the price that had to be paid for the husband's exceptional accomplishment or whether the husband is guilty of monomania and murder.

Hawthorne's tale has often been interpreted as being about the dilemmas facing the artist. These readings focus on Aylmer as "tragic hero," to use Robert Heilman's phrase, rather than as villain. Aylmer's fault lies not with his treatment of his wife but with his failure to recognize soon enough that perfection is not attainable in this world.

This view is endorsed by the entry in Hawthorne's notebook that was the origin of the story: "A person to be the death of his beloved in trying to raise her to more than mortal perfection; yet this should be a comfort to him for having aimed so highly and holily" (*The American Notebooks of Nathaniel Hawthorne*, 624). Poe's story, too, can be read as an artist's tragedy, losing a "beloved" in trying to achieve a high and holy art.[16] Such readings make woman the symbol either of the price nature exacts for such knowledge and achievement or of nature itself, receding always into unreachable distances as the heroic artist nears her.

In contrast, Judith Fetterley in *The Resisting Reader* describes "The Birthmark" as a story not of failure but of success. Her description of it as "the demonstration of how to murder your wife and get away with it" (22) seems as appropriate to Poe's tale as to Hawthorne's. Fetterley argues that the criticism of the tale as a story of misguided idealism misleads readers. Instead of a story about "the unhappy consequences of man's nevertheless worthy passion for perfecting and transcending nature," it is actually "a brilliant analysis of the sexual politics of idealization and a brilliant exposure of the mechanisms whereby hatred can be disguised as love, neurosis can be disguised as science, murder can be disguised as idealization, and success can be disguised as failure" (22–23). She argues that it is really a story about "the sickness of men" and their diseased relation to feminine sexuality and woman's power to reproduce (27–28). Furthermore, it destroys the image of science as an objective and rational endeavor that exists outside of morality, values, and emotions (30). Leland Person, in his reading of the story in *Aesthetic Headaches*, agrees with Fetterley, but he credits Hawthorne with anticipating her critique: "Hawthorne explicitly criticizes his protagonist and indicts his sadistic treatment of his wife" (109).

These two tales are about both the tragedy of the noble artist and wife abuse. In the same way that Aylmer and the painter in Poe's story cannot maintain passion for their wives without recourse to art and a challenge to nature, Poe and Hawthorne cannot work out their complicated relationship to art and nature without recourse to woman. At the heart of both stories is the conflict that I outlined earlier: woman both is and is not a symbol of nature, is and is not a self-determining individual. Her death "resolves" this contradiction.

Both tales are stories of exploitation and a kind of failure. The husband is not able to have his wife and make art of her, too. In each story, as Fetterley notes of "The Birthmark," the husband displays much hostility toward his wife, but it is clear that he nonetheless recognizes the woman's value as possession, since he wishes, in one case, to duplicate it and, in the other, to increase it. The tragedy of the stories, then, becomes the failure to recognize the woman's "true worth," which is, as the "value" of women has been for centuries, her ability to reproduce, to act for her husband in creating "life itself." Luce Irigaray explains in "Women on the Market" that in the patriarchal system in which men exchange women and in which, therefore, women are treated as objects, women have one of two kinds of value. They can have commodity value as objects that can be traded or, once traded, utility value as objects with the ability to produce heirs. Women in this system never have value in and of themselves, then, but only in relation to male needs. "When women are exchanged, woman's body must be treated as an abstraction. . . . The exchange operation cannot take place in terms of some intrinsic, immanent value of the commodity. . . . They are exchanged . . . as women reduced to some common feature. . . . *Woman has value on the market by virtue of one single quality: that of being a product of man's labor*" (175, emphasis in original).

Poe and Hawthorne represent the man's failure as a failure to recognize his own value as the creator/reproducer of culture and his wife's value as the reproducer of nature. In both stories, the man is armed with the necessary technology and art to create "relatively lasting, eternal, transcendental objects" but wastes his energies trying to "merely" reproduce nature. The husband fails to see his wife's utilitarian value as a producer of babies because he is overwhelmed by her commodity value as a beautiful object, and thereby he loses the opportunity to produce heirs through her.

In both tales, therefore, the husband is ultimately a loser. He not only loses his original "capital" (his wife), he also misses out on the reward of his labor, his creation of culture—the painter's lifelike work is hidden away in a dark recess in a tiny room of an abandoned chateau, and Aylmer can hardly exhibit a dead Georgiana's cheek to the scientific community. These failures of art and science mirror Poe's and Hawthorne's contradictory representations of woman and nature. The authors share the European romanticist's view that nature cannot be bettered, that man is subject to nature, but they also share the capitalist, expansionist, patriarchal notion of nature as that which is to be subjected to man's control. Women, who here represent the "natural" ability to (re)produce "life itself," must die in these tales because of the ultimately impossible resolution of these two forces.

The wives' deaths here also apparently resolve another ideological problem: that raised by women's insistence on their own power in the home. Here, neither wife can assert her power, first, because the husband in each story has relegated her to the status of material for his work and, finally, because he kills her. In so doing, he unequivocally returns her to a state of nature, for she has ceased being human—ashes to ashes, dust to dust. But just as the women in Stowe's and Southworth's novels gain moral power at their deaths, so, too, do these women. Just as the woman's death fails to resolve her intermediate position between nature and culture, so, too, does it fail to resolve her ambiguous relation to power. Poe's narrator leads us to believe that the woman in "The Oval Portrait" endows the painting with her life, achieving a gothically supernatural effect over viewers, and even though Georgiana tells Aylmer not to repent, hers is the moral voice at the end of the story explaining to him that he had "rejected the best the earth could offer" (*The Complete Novels and Selected Tales of Nathaniel Hawthorne*, 1032). These women do not leave the legacy of faith and good works that female characters in women's fiction so often do, but they do leave behind men who are finally defeated by woman's ultimate supernatural power.

The tales illustrate the impossibility of maintaining a consistent symbolic equivalence between woman and nature in a narrative system that emphasizes individuality and autonomy. The invalid is both innocent victim and, because she willingly acquiesces to her husband's will, conspirator in her own demise. She is both beautiful and in need of perfecting. She represents nature as well as culture. Finally, she accedes to the role we have seen established by nineteenth-century society and medicine: she is both subject to nature's whim and guilty of aggravating bad natural tendencies.

The scene in "The Oval Portrait" could well represent a more personal dilemma for Poe. The artist in the narrative enacts what Poe himself might have felt he was doing: making art out of the deaths of women. As Marie Bonapart argues in her early ground-breaking *The Life and Works of Edgar Allan Poe: A Psychoanalytic Interpretation*, Poe's tales about women have their origins in his mother or wife, both of whom died from tuberculosis.[17] Given Poe's unrelenting motif of sickly women, Bonapart's biographical reading is persuasive. Still, writers do not produce texts exclusively out of their own private experiences. The particular economic, intellectual, and political milieu in which a writer works also shapes the text. Poe, as an active editor of a number of magazines and journals, was intimately involved with contemporary culture. That culture is as much a part of his fiction as are his own psychological idiosyncracies. Cultural constructions of gender and illness played as important a part in his portraiture of women's illness as did his personal experience.

Edgar Allan Poe's female characters stand out in American fiction as the most unrelentingly sickly. They are, almost to a woman, beautiful, mysterious, and fated to die. Poe's narrators, usually mad or ill themselves, frequently concede that the women's deaths are a result of their having been too good for this world. Like Stowe's Eva and Southworth's Hester Grey, they are too perfect for its corruption. Like the title character in "Eleonora," they are often "made perfect in loveliness only to die" (*The Complete Tales and Poems of Edgar Allan Poe*, 651). And like the women in domestic fiction, their deaths do not necessarily end their stories. Poe's women, sickly and weak in life, gain power at their deaths—power over the narrator or their near relations—through supernatural means. Whether it is Madeline Usher breaking free of her tomb, Berenice being found alive after burial,[18] Eleonora speaking in the wind, or Morella taking over her daughter's body, Poe's female characters show even more energy and power in death than in life. Poe's stories thus share much common ground with the women's fiction of the decade and, like those stories and novels, invite a reading in the context of the discourses on medicine and woman's power in the home.

One story in particular encapsulates Poe's problematic figure of the powerful female invalid—"Ligeia" (1839), the tale that Poe himself in 1846 called "undoubtedly the best story I have written" (quoted in Joan Dayan, *Fables of Mind*, 172). This story hinges on an understanding of the mind/body relation as well as the man/woman relation. It sets out the difficulties of understanding what man's relation to the "new woman" could be and uses the conventions of gothic horror to explore the woman's new power. This story also dramatically reveals the troublesome doubleness we encounter in the representation of the invalid, leaving the question of exactly what happens in the story finally unanswered.

Poe sets out the question of a kind of mind/body relation in the epigraph to the story, from Joseph Glanvill, which states that "the will therein lieth, which dieth not. Who knoweth the mysteries of the will with its vigor? . . . Man doth not yield himself to the angels, nor unto death utterly, save only through the weakness of his feeble will" (654). The tale is, indeed, a question of will, of whether a woman can will herself to resist death, of whether a man can will himself to see her return to life. The opening of the story, too, dwells on questions of mind and body. The narrator describes himself only in terms of mind; the opening lines are about his memory: "I cannot, for my soul, remember. . . . My memory is feeble" (654). But Ligeia, despite "her rare learning," which was "immense," is described almost entirely in terms of body, the one thing our feeble-memoried narrator has not forgotten: "There is one dear topic, however, on which my memory fails me not. It is the *person* of Ligeia" (654, emphasis in original). He dwells for two pages on the wonders of her body, looking for classical analogies and finding her to exceed even these.

When he finally gets to her mind and intellectual abilities, he does it through Glanvill again and notes that she had "an *intensity* in thought, action or speech . . . [and a] gigantic volition" (657, emphasis in original). In fact, all of his descriptions of Ligeia's mind, character, and emotions cast her in the mold of "too muchness"; he uses adjectives of size ("immense," "gigantic") and quantity (the "overflowing of her heart" is "more than passionate"; her devotion to the narrator is "more than womanly" [657–58]). But it is her body that takes precedence, her body that he remembers, despite his sense that it was her will, her powers of mind, that made her exceptional. As we will see with Zenobia in *The Blithedale Romance*, it is this too-muchness of mind, this superabundance, that kills Ligeia. As did Margaret Miller Davidson's, Ligeia's "soul was wearing out the body" (Washington Irving, *Biography and Poetical Remains of the Late Margaret Miller Davidson*, 11); "Ligeia grew ill. The wild eyes blazed with a too—too glorious effulgence; the pale fingers became of the transparent waxen hue of the grave; and the blue veins upon the lofty forehead swelled and sank impetuously with the tides of the most gentle emotion" (657–58). Ligeia's illness, in other words, intensifies her too-muchness. But where Margaret's supernatural powers were holy, Ligeia's become horrific when, after her death and her husband's remarriage to the Lady Rowena, she possesses the dead body of Rowena.

As are the deathbed scenes in domestic fictions, Ligeia's death is full of pathos, but it is a very different kind of pathos. Rather than accepting her death as a transition to a holier plane, Ligeia struggles against it and resists. Our narrator confesses his surprise at this: "There had been much in her stern nature to impress me with the belief that, to her, death would have come without its terrors; but not so. Words are impotent to convey any just idea of the fierceness of resistance with which she wrestled with the Shadow. I groaned in anguish at the pitiable spectacle" (658). This struggle outlines the problem with Ligeia. Against the backdrop of sentimental heroines who accept their deaths, her resistance to death must seem a fear of the afterlife, a fear of some kind of retribution. Is Ligeia guilty of some crime? Our narrator cannot discount this possibility, since he confesses to the fact that he never even knew her patronymic. Has she some guilty past? We can, of course, only speculate, but it would have been precisely the kind of speculation a nineteenth-century reader, accustomed to the conventions of representing guilty women, would have engaged in. Like Juliette Summers, Ligeia's abundance makes her questionable; her "wild desire for life—for life—*but* for life" (658, emphasis in original) makes her suspicious. If there is a contrast drawn between women in this tale, it is not really between Rowena (who likewise fears death) and Ligeia, but between Ligeia and the female figures in domestic fiction.

The division in this story is not really between the two women; despite the fact that one is "dark" and the other "light," one intellectual and strong (even as she fights death), the other a feeble and weak-willed invalid, they are, finally, interchangeable. Both sicken and die, and Rowena's body, on its bier, becomes Ligeia's body, too. The real division in this story is between the genders: the narrator is all mind (if weak minded) and the women are all body (despite Ligeia's great will and mind). In fact, the use to which Ligeia puts her mind (if we are to believe the narrator's story that she wills herself to kill Rowena and then assume her body, a question to which I will return) is to become, again, a body. And as Cynthia Jordan has pointed out in *Second Stories*, despite the fact that the narrator repeatedly mentions the "almost magical melody, modulation, distinctness, and placidity of her very low voice" (657), he never actually records anything she says.[19] She remains, in his version of the story, at least, always all body.[20]

Whether we are to trust this version of the story, though, remains an open question. Over and over Poe casts doubt on his narrator; the narrator tells us about his opium habit, claiming to have married Rowena during a "mental alienation" caused by that habit.[21] He admits the uncertainty of his vision when he describes the moment that he believes Ligeia has poisoned Rowena ("I saw, or may have dreamed that I saw" [663]) and when he describes his "visions of Ligeia" while watching the "hideous drama of revivification" going on in Rowena's body. If our narrator is all-mind to Ligeia's all-body, he remains a pitiful excuse for mind. Poe leaves us with an insoluble dilemma: either Ligeia returns from the dead to inhabit the dead body of her successor, or an opium addict believes that he has seen his dead second wife return to life as his dead first wife.[22]

Early in the story, our narrator admits his inferiority to Ligeia: "I was sufficiently aware of her infinite supremacy to resign myself, with a child-like confidence, to her guidance through the chaotic world of metaphysical investigation" (657). We are left to decide whether it is because he is without her continued guidance that he turns to opium, or whether it is because of the guidance he *had* received from her. A tale that so prominently features questions of will leaves open the central question of the man's power of will. Does Ligeia's power drive him to drugs? Are all men to become "child-like" in the presence of powerful women and profligate when that influence is gone? Poe leaves open the question of whether we are to read the story as one about the horrors of a woman with a will of her own or as a tale of the horrors of the divisions between mind and body, men and women.

The Natural *Pharmakon* in the Garden

Woman's complicity in her own illness and death and her relation to science become the central questions in "Rappaccini's Daughter." This tale would seem, at first glance, to remove the question of the woman's blame for her own illness. Beatrice, like many of the other invalid women we have seen so far (and will yet see), is the victim of abuse: without her consent, or apparent foreknowledge, her father has tainted her with his poisons. She is, symbolically, a victim of sexual abuse; it is a liquid produced by her father that "taints" her and makes her an unsuitable love object for a young man.[23] Nonetheless, her father lures a young man, Giovanni Guasconti, to his garden and, to provide a mate for Beatrice, imbues him with poisons, too. As soon as Beatrice realizes her part in the tainting of Giovanni, she proclaims her despair at the turn of events, claims her innocence, and takes her own life by drinking an "antidote" to the poisons that permeate her system, an antidote that has been given to Giovanni by Rappaccini's rival, Baglioni.[24]

The clarity of Beatrice's innocence, though, is clouded. Returning to the entries in Hawthorne's *American Notebooks* that provided the basis for the tale, one finds that Hawthorne's model for Beatrice was a legend of a woman fed on poisons who was sent to Alexander's court to murder him (623).[25] Hawthorne's attitude toward the symbol of physical disease is ambiguous in that he writes that he would like to "symbolize moral or spiritual disease by disease of the body" (625).[26] Closer to the tale, however, is the most damning indictment of Beatrice: Hawthorne's playful preface to the story. Attributing the story to M. de l'Aubepine (French for "hawthorn") and professing to discuss de l'Aubepine's works, Hawthorne discusses instead his own tales, offering French titles that are literal translations of his English titles, with one glaring exception. "Rappaccini's Daughter" becomes "Beatrice; ou la Belle Empoisonneuse," that is, "Beatrice, or the Beautiful Poisoner." The change in this title is significant because it gives Beatrice her own name rather than introducing her by her father's. In so doing, it emphasizes her autonomy and, by describing her as a "Beautiful Poisoner," suggests that her role is an active one—she is not the poisoned but the poisoner.[27] Furthermore, it is a specifically feminine role (*empoisonneuse* rather than *empoisonneur*), one which allows her to use her beauty to accomplish the poisoning.[28]

The suggestions of Beatrice's guilt leave open the crucial question of the story: is she the innocent victim or the guilty one caught in her own trap? Hawthorne manages to have it both ways. Like women in the medical and cultural discourses of the time, like Georgiana, Ligeia, and the woman in Poe's "Oval Portrait," she is both innocent and guilty, beautiful and horrible. Like Ligeia, she is made attractive by that which also makes her horrible. Beatrice is nature that has been "improved" by science—she is the most beautiful woman in Padua (a city where many have died of love)—but she is also nature that has been made unnatural. The poison in her system makes her alluring and more attractive, but it also makes her unapproachable. She is pure but tainted at the center of her being. Her representation is polarized in the same way that Sherry Ortner describes cultural representations of women generally: she is pure, but polluted ("Is Female to Male as Nature Is to Culture?," 72).

Reading "Rappaccini's Daughter" as "Beatrice, or the Beautiful Poisoner" emphasizes her role as not the innocent victim of male abuse but the active, if misled, temptress and destroyer of men, a fallen Eve. The poison in her system, though instilled in her by her father, is the essence of what she is and of what gives her enormous power to tempt men and to lead them astray. Although Beatrice represents an altered nature that is evil, perverted, and cruel—her breath kills animals and wilts flowers—she also embodies the innate danger of a femininity that is corrupt and tainted. Her father's evil is represented outwardly by his "sickly and sallow" appearance (1052) and by an "infirm voice" that signals that he is "affected with inward disease" (1046), but hers is hidden by a mask of beauty and "a bloom so deep and vivid that one shade more would have been too much. She looked redundant with life, health and energy" (1046). Beatrice represents extremes: she is "redundant" with health, but she is also diseased. Beatrice's surface beauty hides the underlying menace of femininity from men. In this respect, Beatrice resembles two other figures of feminine illness from the 1840s. In a New England schoolbook, children were introduced to two women, Dissipation and Housewifery; Dissipation, like Beatrice, has a pretty mask and a pleasing appearance that hide "a countenance wan and ghastly with sickness" (quoted in Barbara Epstein, *The Politics of Domesticity*, 75). An illustration from 1840 represents syphilis as existing under the guise of beauty; the drawing features a fashionably dressed woman holding a mask of beauty over a skeletal face of corrupt flesh (Sander Gilman, *Difference and Pathology*, 106). As in these representations of feminine illness, Beatrice's "abundant health" is but a mask for her true invalidism.

As Aylmer does Georgiana, Giovanni and Baglioni diagnose Beatrice, deciding that she is ill and in need of Baglioni's medicine. Her disease is even worse than Georgiana's because hers is contagious. Giovanni, like the lover Socrates describes in Plato's *Phaedrus*, is infected by a disease that is transmitted through the eyes: "He is in love. . . . He does not understand his own condition and cannot explain it; like one who has caught a disease of the eyes from another, he can give no reason for it; he sees himself in his lover as in a mirror, but is not conscious of the fact" (255d). After watching Beatrice from the window of his room, he no longer can concentrate on work; "She had at least instilled a fierce and subtle poison into his system" (1051). She transforms his previous "remarkable beauty of person" (1044) to the point that when he meets Baglioni in the street, the professor comments on the change in his appearance (1052). Beatrice leaves her lover corrupted and cut off from normal human relations. Read in this way, Beatrice's death is less a tragedy than was her perverted life. The end of the story represents the proper end of all evil things, however beautiful and tempting.

We should note that one of the things that makes Beatrice so frightening is her supposed unnatural development of mind. Baglioni, despite his ignorance of Beatrice's real nature, suggests this possibility to Giovanni: "I know little of the Signora Beatrice save that Rappaccini is said to have instructed her deeply in his science, and that, young and beautiful as fame reports her, she is already qualified to fill a professor's chair" (1049). Beatrice denies that she has this knowledge, but the suggestion of it lingers. Like Ligeia's immense learning, Beatrice's supposed combination of great powers of mind with great youth and beauty leave her questionable; her unnaturalness tinges her with the gothic supernatural.

Persuasive as this interpretation is, Hawthorne did not entitle the story "Beatrice." Instead, his title calls attention to familial relations, to Beatrice's subjection to a tyrannical and abusive father, and to her passive position in the social system. Beatrice becomes the innocent victim of male abuse and misuse of power.[29] She retains the power of allure and temptation, but these are unwitting and, to the extent that they corrupt Giovanni and herself, unwanted gifts. She is just another of her father's possessions—imprisoned and tainted by him, kept from normal society and from normal pursuits. Like her "sister"—the large violet flower she resembles, embraces, and wears as an ornament—she is the innocent but perverted creation of a man who would use science to tamper with nature.

Read as "Rappaccini's Daughter," the story becomes not one of a misguided, star-crossed love affair between a young man and a beautiful but tainted young woman; it becomes instead a story about the struggle between two older men for control over a beautiful and intelligent young man, a story of homosocial desire.[30] Professor Rappaccini uses Beatrice's altered nature to lure Giovanni away from Baglioni, a rival professor. Baglioni, in turn, questions Beatrice's purity in hopes of defeating Rappaccini's hold over Giovanni. At one significant point, Baglioni thinks to himself, "It is too insufferable an impertinence of Rappaccini, thus to snatch the lad out of my own hands" (1053). In this arrangement, Beatrice becomes merely the object of exchange that establishes a relation between men. She is forced into a position that, according to feminist theorists Gayle Rubin and Luce Irigaray, negates woman's existence as a subject:

> The circulation of women among men establishes the operations of society, at least of patriarchal society. Whose presuppositions include the following: the appropriation of nature by man; the transformation of nature according to "human" criteria, defined by men alone; the submission of nature to labor and technology; the reduction of its material, corporeal, perceptible qualities to man's practical concrete activity; the equality of women among themselves, but in terms of laws of equivalence that remain external to them; the constitution of women as "objects" that emblematize the materialization of relations among men, and so on. (Irigaray, "Women on the Market," 184–85)

Thus, the end of the story takes on a feminist cast; Beatrice recognizes her function in the contest between her father and Baglioni and, refusing to be an object of exchange, disqualifies herself for that role. In a symbolically significant move, she drinks the "antidote" that will remove the flowers' poisons from her system; that is, she "de-flowers" herself.[31] A deflowered woman, of course, has no value as an object of exchange. "Once deflowered, woman is relegated to the status of use value, to her entrapment in private property; she is removed from the exchange among men" (ibid., 186). Beatrice's final act is explicitly that of a subject; she moves to cure herself of the poison in their (patriarchal) system. Her taking of her own life is meant to teach Giovanni and Rappaccini a lesson. Her last words are, "Oh, was there not, from the first, more poison in thy nature than in mine?" (1065). But this one act as an independent subject leads to her death, that is, to the end of her subjectivity, as she becomes an object whose only power is to edify men.

Neither reading of the tale, as "Beatrice, or the Beautiful Poisoner" or as "Rappaccini's Daughter," entirely accounts for every aspect of the figure of the invalid woman as Hawthorne draws it. As Nina Baym notes of this story, it "may be too rich, in the sense that it is susceptible to a number of partial explanations, but seems to evade any single wholly satisfactory reading" (*The Shape of Hawthorne's Career*, 107).[32] Beatrice is the unnatural, artificial, and dangerous creation of a perverted science as well as the innocent natural child untouched by civilization, the "noble savage" that Rousseau envisioned. In Beatrice, the conflicted attitude of the male writer toward woman and nature is dramatized; man's "improvements" on nature make it, in fact, more attractive and alluring, but they also contaminate it. There is, however, no way to approach nature without altering it. In this system, woman is made both more alluring and more unapproachable by man's intervention. The figure of the invalid drawn here is not simply natural or unnatural, good or bad, innocent or guilty. Nor is it altogether clear who in the story is sick or well. Baglioni and Giovanni decide that Beatrice is ill and therefore needs to be "cured" by the antidote. But throughout the story, it has been Rappaccini and Giovanni who have been described as ill. Beatrice, even as she accepts the antidote, questions whether she is more ill than the men around her. Like the Greek word for poison, *pharmakon*, which means both remedy and poison, Beatrice is both the cause of and the cure to Giovanni's illness. As Jacques Derrida explains in "Plato's Pharmacy," *pharmakon* is a sign that represents mutually exclusive properties: it is both poison and remedy; both natural, since it comes from herbs and plants, and unnatural, since it is distilled and blended; and it is that which, even though "exterior" to the subject, nevertheless enacts a profound change within the "interior" of the subject. Like the *pharmakon*, Beatrice represents mutually exclusive properties. In Rappaccini's inside-out garden, antidotes are poisons, improvements are corruptions, evil is innocence. Beatrice's "illness" makes her, as her father explains, invulnerable to the ordinary "condition of a weak woman" (1064), but it makes her vulnerable to the charms of the first man she meets. Beatrice is the *pharmakon* in Hawthorne's garden.

"Rappaccini's Daughter" is ultimately a tale centered on the question of who has the power to define illness, to define what is natural and unnatural. Beatrice asserts her right to decide her own fate, but this assumption of power kills her and leaves all three men still alive. The tale may question the propriety of masculine definitions of femininity, but one cannot take it outside the context of nineteenth-century aesthetics, in which woman's weakness is "poetic" and "beautiful." Any "lessons" from such stories are therefore subsumed into aesthetic evaluation. Questions of the woman's power to shape culture are elided in the definition of women as "unnatural nature" and "supernatural invalids."

A Return to the Garden: The Healthy Invalid

Beatrice Rappaccini is not Hawthorne's only superabundantly healthy heroine who ends up dead; Zenobia, in *The Blithedale Romance*

(1852), fits this pattern as well. Coverdale, the narrator, describes her in terms that make her a type of "able-bodied womanhood" (to use Martha Verbrugge's phrase):

> It did one good to see a fine intellect (as hers really was, although its natural tendency lay in another direction than towards literature) so fitly cased. She was, indeed, an admirable figure of a woman, just on the hither verge of her richest maturity, with a combination of features which it is safe to call remarkably beautiful, even if some fastidious persons might pronounce them a little deficient in softness and delicacy. But we find enough of those attributes everywhere. Preferable—by way of variety, at least—was Zenobia's bloom, health, and vigor, which she possessed in such overflow that a man might well have fallen in love with her for their sake only. (447)

It is all the more striking that this model of healthy womanhood ends up drowning herself and becoming, by novel's end, *just* body, and a horrible one at that. It is tempting to argue that Hawthorne resolved the doubleness of Beatrice Rappaccini's characterization by splitting the female figure in this work into two women, Zenobia and Priscilla—the famous dark and light ladies of his later romances.[33] But what we see in *The Blithedale Romance* is that Zenobia refigures the same doubleness, that she even reenacts Beatrice's own suicidal "resolution," and that Hawthorne still manages to have it both ways by disclaiming the narrative (through his troublesome narrator).

I do not want to offer a full-fledged reading of *The Blithedale Romance* here; I intend to examine the repetition in that text of the earlier figures from "Rappaccini's Daughter" and to place them within the mid-century debate over women, medicine, and gender roles. What we see in the romance are specific repetitions of the scene from the earlier tale: a marked identification between women and flowers; a setting that is specifically pastoral, gardenlike, and isolated; strong homosocial desire between men;[34] the interaction between an innocent-in-love and a beloved who is ambiguously represented as both ideal and tainted (Priscilla and Zenobia);[35] and a narrative that establishes its own "plausible deniability." The significant change from Beatrice to Zenobia is that while Beatrice's intellectual abilities are suggested in the tale but denied by her, there is never any doubt that Zenobia represents the absolute union of mind and body. As we saw above, Coverdale describes her as a "fine intellect . . . fitly cased."[36] Even in his praise of her,

Coverdale notes that "fastidious persons" would find her body too much but states that he finds her "preferable." Of course, by novel's end, in his "confession," he admits that he has come around to the "fastidious" point of view, preferring the "softness and delicacy" of Priscilla. Much has been made in the criticism of the threat Zenobia offers to Coverdale, but the real threat Zenobia poses is to the whole foundation of medical and social thought: she is a fully sexual woman with a fully active mind, suffering from no obvious medical ill effects of this superabundance. This is the threat that has to be contained within the novel.

Leland Person argues in *Aesthetic Headaches* that "Zenobia resists containment by type or by language; her presence always implies more than Coverdale or Hawthorne can denote" (148), but what we see in Zenobia's suicide is precisely the containment of the threat she offers to the sociomedical definition of the female. This is not to deny the power of Zenobia's voice within the text or the potential disruptive force she represents. Several recent critics have recognized the dialogism of *The Blithedale Romance*.[37] Leland Person contends that "like Beatrice Rappaccini, Zenobia effectively demands that Coverdale encounter a woman in her fully human nature; she subverts his inclination to idealize." He goes on to suggest that, in incorporating Zenobia's pronouncements on the oppression of women, Hawthorne allows the revolutionary potential of her voice into his text (152). Dale Bauer, in *Feminist Dialogics*, argues that Zenobia's language "cannot be fully appropriated and, therefore, is a constant threat" (48) but that she is finally violently silenced to maintain the social order.

The threat that Zenobia offers to the system represented by the de facto patriarch of Blithedale, Hollingsworth, and Coverdale is precisely the same threat that the Blithedale experiment offers to American culture at large, as is the promise that she offers—the utopian ideal of the perfect union of mind and body, intellect and sexuality. From the first, the Blithedalers anticipate the rewards of developing both their minds and bodies, but the reality casts doubt on the possibility. Coverdale describes both the hope and the reality they confront:

The peril of our new way of life was not lest we should fail in becoming practical agriculturists, but that we should probably cease to be anything else. While our enterprise lay all in theory, we had pleased ourselves with delectable visions of the spiritualization of labor. It was to be our form of prayer, and ceremonial of worship. Each stroke of the hoe was to uncover some aromatic root of wisdom, heretofore hidden from the sun. . . . Our thoughts, on the contrary, were fast becoming cloddish. Our labor symbolized nothing, and left us mentally sluggish in the evening. *Intellectual activity is incompatible with any large amount of bodily exercise.* The yeoman and the scholar . . . are two distinct individuals and can never be melted or welded into one substance. (477, emphasis added)

The ideal of becoming farmer-poets, of uniting intense intellectual work with hard physical labor, is never realized at Blithedale. Zenobia teases Coverdale with being no Robert Burns and tells him that her vision of him in the future is modeled on Silas Foster, with the *Farmer's Almanac* for his literature and nothing on his mind but the farm. Hollingsworth defends Coverdale's abandonment of poetry because it is unfitting to his new physique: "Coverdale has given up making verses now. . . . Just think of him penning a sonnet, with a fist like that!" (478).

In "The Birthmark" and "Rappaccini's Daughter," Hawthorne had represented intellectual men as not at all physical. Both Aylmer and Rappaccini are pale, sallow, and sickly looking men, defined by their great intellectual powers to the same extent that the women in the texts are defined by their physicality. When a man is physical—as with Aylmer's assistant, Aminadab, or Silas Foster—he is correspondingly nonintellectual. Such division is, as we have seen, in harmony with nineteenth-century models of health and gender roles. What the Blithedalers propose to do violates not just *social* restrictions but the restrictions of *nature*, as they were defined in the nineteenth century. As the character who is most clearly defined as both intellectual and physical from the outset, Zenobia *embodies* this violation of natural laws.[38]

As with Beatrice Rappaccini, it is this very unnaturalness that makes Zenobia so attractive. A man "might well have fallen in love with her" for the sake of her "overflow" of health and intellect. Throughout the romance, until his "confession" of his love for Priscilla (and perhaps even afterward), we suspect Coverdale of having done just that. Her attraction, though, is the same attraction that Blithedale holds—a violation of the rules of nature and society. There are a lot of reasons why the utopian experiment fails, as Coverdale indicates, but the central reason is that its attempt to unite mind and body, to combine the production of culture with the natural production of agriculture, to question the differences between men and women, dooms it to failure not just by violating social norms but by violating the laws of nature.[39] Just as Blithedale must cease to exist to maintain the social order, Zenobia must cease to exist to maintain the natural order on which society is based.

That maintaining of order is not accomplished by the murder of Zenobia, as some critics tend to suggest, but by illness.[40] For during the mid-nineteenth century, suicide was explicitly understood as a disease. In his study of American suicide, *Self-Destruction in the Promised Land*, Howard Kushner traces the changes in attitude toward suicide from Puritan times to the present and writes, "By the 1830s melancholy and suicide, no longer religious or legal issues, had become almost exclusively the concern of medical men. And if melancholy were a disease, a melancholic individual was no more responsible for committing suicide than for contracting smallpox. This transformation of consciousness signalled the medicalization of suicide that had emerged unchallenged by the 1840s" (34). The association between suicide and illness was so strong that witnesses and juries at suicide inquests in Victorian England "sometimes seem to have been puzzled when they could remember" no examples of past instances of insanity, nerves, or depression, "and yet death did indeed seem to be self-inflicted" (Olive Anderson, *Suicide in Victorian and Edwardian England*, 227).[41]

It is neither Hollingsworth nor Coverdale nor guilt over her treatment of Priscilla that does Zenobia in but the very condition that had at first appeared to Coverdale as an "overflow" of "bloom, health, and vigor." The cost of such overdevelopment of mind and body, intellect and sexuality, medical convention held, would have to be a complete physical or mental collapse, just as the social experiment of Blithedale would necessarily have had to collapse. What we see in Zenobia's final scene is her final mental breakdown.

The last time we see Zenobia alive is in chapter 26, "Coverdale and Zenobia." There, we finally witness her collapse, the impossibility of "bloom, health, and vigor" to "fitly case" such an intellect. After Hollingsworth's judgment of her and his choice of Priscilla, Zenobia "began slowly to sink down" (569). The chapter describes her "woman's affliction" in terms that are clear indications of a suicidal melancholy, or that would have been to the reader in 1852. When Zenobia's sobs finally abate, Coverdale describes her appearance: "[She] stared about her with a bewildered aspect, as if not distinctly recollecting the scene through which she had passed, nor cognizant of the situation in which it left her. Her face and brow were almost purple with the rush of blood. They whitened, however, by-and-by, and, for some time, retained this deathlike hue. She put her hand to her forehead, with a gesture that made me forcibly conscious of an intense and living pain there" (570). Such a description could almost be (and would have been recognized as) testimony at an inquest; the "intense and living pain" in Zenobia's head would have been a clear indication of the "incipient brain illness" or "derangement of mind" that Anderson and Kushner describe as typical of testimony at such hearings. Later in the chapter, Coverdale remarks on the "strange way in which her mind seemed to vibrate from the deepest earnest to mere levity" (572), and Zenobia herself claims to be "sick to death" (573). Certainly, Hollingsworth's judgment of her triggers this descent, but Zenobia's own assertion, that "the whole universe, [the female] sex and yours, and Providence, or Destiny, to boot, make common cause against the woman who swerves one hair's breadth out of the beaten track" (571), finally holds. The "whole universe . . . and Providence, or Destiny" cannot allow the divergence from the "beaten track" that Zenobia's intellectual physicality represents. It is nature's law that decrees that she must collapse, not Hollingsworth's.[42]

Her final appearance in the novel, as a horribly misshapen "spectacle," completes Zenobia's transformation to all body. As with Georgiana, she becomes a thing to be looked at, an almost-art *object*: "She [is] the marble image of a death agony" (578). Despite his recognition that he should not describe the scene ("Were I to describe the perfect horror of the spectacle, the reader might justly reckon it to me for a sin and a shame" [578]), Coverdale dwells on the scene at length, not just on its horror but on the display of Zenobia's body ("Her knees . . . her arms . . . her hands . . . her lips . . . the poor thing's breast"). He is convinced that, had she known how she would look, Zenobia would never have committed this act: "Being the woman that she was, could Zenobia have foreseen all these ugly circumstances of death . . . she would no more have committed the dreadful act than have exhibited herself to a public assembly in a badly fitting garment" (579). The body that Coverdale had once believed a "fit" casing for her great intellect is now no more than body and is, to that degree, horrible.

We can read in this final scene some of the same doubleness of Georgiana's and Beatrice's deaths: it is a death of the woman's own choosing, yes, but it is also not her fault but the fault of nature. Hers is a death caused by the cruelty of men, by their insensitivity and refusal to recognize her as a sentient being in her own right, but, again, it is not really their fault either. Zenobia even reenacts the "de-flowering" of self that we saw in Beatrice's death, when she removed the flower that had been her symbol throughout the romance. Like Beatrice, Zenobia signals that she is no longer "on the market" and available to men. But are we to finally understand the unfairness of that market, or is this a symbolic suggestion that Zenobia's cover (her mask of innocence) has finally been blown?

At mid-century, a woman's death by drowning carried with it cultural connotations that defy a simple reading of Zenobia's death. Coverdale, trying to understand why a woman of Zenobia's great beauty would have chosen a mode of death he finds "the ugliest," reasons, "She had seen pictures, I suppose, of drowned persons in lithe and graceful attitudes" (578–79). Such pictures and sculptures were abundant in the nineteenth century. Joy Kasson discusses the impact of Edward A. Brackett's very popular sculpture, *Shipwrecked Mother and Child* (1850), in *Marble Queens and Captives* and traces its origins to a 1788 engraving of Jacques-Henri Bernardin de Saint-Pierre's *Paul et Virginie* (by T. Johannot and E. Isabey), depicting the graceful dead body of a drowned woman. Olive Anderson shows that in London in the 1840s the stereotype of female suicide was deeply romantic and usually featured "a distraught girl flinging herself from a high bridge, or a beautiful woman's damply draped body 'Found Drowned' and lying by moonlight." She cites example after example in popular novels, paintings, prints, ballads, songs, and melodramas. (*Found Drowned* is, in fact, a painting by G. F. Watts, based on Thomas Hood's poem, "The Bridge of Sighs," which Anderson reproduces [202].)

But while the victim of shipwreck was undeniably a victim, the female suicide, Anderson argues, was more ambiguous: "For the middle class, the female suicide was essentially a sinner; for the working class, she was a victim. For the former, suicide was the inevitable final retribution for fornication or adultery. . . . By contrast, the unchanging message conveyed by the songs and melodramas which working-class people favoured was that 'the woman always pays' and 'the poor get all the kicks'" (199). But by the 1840s, she shows, even middle-class people were beginning to see female suicides as "the result of cruel wrongs"

(202). The children of criminals and drunkards, in particular, were depicted as victimized, and we learn in the course of the novel that Zenobia's father had been a criminal.

How, then, do we read Zenobia's suicide? As a result of disease brought on by the unnatural exercise of both mind and body? As a sign of "fornication or adultery," the possibility of which tantalizes Coverdale throughout the romance? As a sign of her victimization at the hands of men throughout the text (her father, Westervelt, Hollingsworth, Coverdale)? The medical explanation of her death is certainly persuasive, but it does not overrule the other explanations or even exclude them all. And the fact that we have only Coverdale's version of the events, which is surely of only dubious reliability, means that again, as with the doubled titles of "Rappaccini's Daughter," Hawthorne refuses to give an answer. Is it a feminist romance? A medical parable? He finally has it both ways.

The "Feverish Poet"

During the illness that initiates him into Blithedale society, Coverdale whispers to Hollingsworth that Zenobia is a witch, that she would vanish if he were to take her secret talisman, her exotic flower. When Hollingsworth reports Coverdale's accusations to Zenobia, she responds, "It is an idea worthy of a feverish poet" (465). One aspect of "The Oval Portrait," "Ligeia," "The Birthmark," "Rappaccini's Daughter," and *The Blithedale Romance* that I have left, as yet, unexplored is the sickness of the men. Poe's narrators are almost always sick: the narrator of "The Oval Portrait" is in a "desperately wounded condition"; the narrator of "Berenice" is "ill of health, and buried in gloom"; the narrator of "Eleonora" admits, "Men have called me mad." Both of Hawthorne's scientists, too, are of questionable health: Aylmer and Rappaccini are both pale and look unhealthy, even though nothing is ever noted explicitly to define them as ill. *The Blithedale Romance* makes the illnesses of men a little clearer: Coverdale confides, "It is my private opinion, that, at this period of his life, Hollingsworth was fast going mad" (471), and Coverdale is the only one in the romance to define himself as "an invalid" (which he does twice in the chapter describing his recovery from the flu [468, 469]).

Leland Person argues that these sickly men signify Poe's and Hawthorne's understanding of the unhealthy separation of character traits by gender:

> In projecting women into art objects in order to contain their creative energy, male characters repress those aspects of their own minds— especially their own creative power—with which women are identi- fied; they thus run the risk of committing themselves to a creative process that is not only destructive of women but self-destructive as well. Most important, these male writers seem aware of the problem. The objectification of women which feminist critics have decried, in other words, should be understood as an extreme that male authors themselves recognized to be destructive both to the male self and to a masculine poetics. (*Aesthetic Headaches*, 6)

Such an explanation works beautifully within the framework of Lain- gian psychology that Person uses, but it is not very persuasive within the historical frame of a nineteenth-century understanding of mind and body. Poe's and Hawthorne's men are certainly understood to be self- destructive to the extent that they indulge in their monomanias[43] and to the extent that they develop their minds at great cost to their bodies, but such self-destruction would not have been understood as part of the oppression of women.

If we follow the argument made by G. J. Barker-Benfield in *The Horrors of the Half-Known Life*, it would have been the pressure ex- erted on the nineteenth-century man to succeed —to develop his mind and earning potential at the expense of his body and feelings—that would have *caused* the representations of women as objects and con- tributed to the oppression of women. Barker-Benfield argues that nineteenth-century theories held that male insanity was caused by both the harsh "realities of the world" of business and the greater sexual appetite of men. Since the business world and male sexuality were considered part of the "restless, insatiable, vicissitudinous, and essen- tial nature of male society . . . the male tendency to insanity was [there- fore regarded as] ineluctable." He contends that this had a deleterious effect on men's attitudes toward women:

> The effect of this was first to register the enormous pressure on men, intensified by their feeling that it was a given of their society (the instability of which was accordingly and necessarily a given too), and of their sexual role within it. The characteristic disorder of boom and

slump was, as Tocqueville put it, an "endemic disease" of the demo-
cratic "temperament." The corollary of accepting such conclusions
about men was to direct social/medical/psychological expertise at
that area of society that was not a given, that was not held by men to
be so inalienable as the nature of their own existences, and conse-
quently was more controllable, that is, to direct it at women. (57)

To make claims that Poe or Hawthorne were mid-nineteenth-century
feminists who saw the dangers of the objectification of women even
more clearly than did women authors of the time is, probably, to engage
in too much wishful thinking. It does seem likely, however, that in the
same way that female authors like Stowe, Southworth, and Bullard
chafed against the medical definitions and restrictions on women, Poe
and Hawthorne chafed against medical definitions of men that promised them insanity if they tried to combine "too much" exercise of the
intellect with "too much" exercise of their bodies and their sexuality.
That such medical pronouncements were uncomfortable seems clear.
That they could develop a twentieth-century understanding of the role
of these definitions in oppressing women and restricting men seems
unlikely.

Ultimately, whether one believes that Poe and Hawthorne joined their
male artist/scientist figures in the objectification and destruction of
female figures or that they represent those artist/scientist figures as
horrors who oppress women and bring on their own destruction depends on one's reading of their attitudes toward those sickly male
narrators and characters. Is *their* illness the illness that Hawthorne in
his notebooks meant to use to "symbolize moral or spiritual disease by
disease of the body"? Or does that illness remain the province of
women? Finally, it is both—a critique of the patriarchal medical language that would define woman as always (an) invalid by projecting the
"sickness of men" onto her and an embodiment of that patriarchal
language. At best, the texts enact the invalidization of women they
criticize. Like the female-authored texts we saw earlier, however much
these tales resist the power of the medical discourse, they are finally
incorporated by or into it.

Later in the century, as medical theory became increasingly powerful,
much of this kind of uncertainty would disappear in novels like Oliver
Wendell Holmes's *Elsie Venner* (1861). In this physician-authored novel
about a young doctor's encounter with a snake-woman, there are ques-

tions of whether the woman is evil or just misguided, whether she is natural or supernatural, but there is no question of the need for a physician's intervention and no question of any male guilt. The towns-people in the story are divided not by religious differences but by their physician preference (the town has two), but everyone defers to the medical men. Questions about medicine, like those raised by Laura Curtis Bullard, Poe, and Hawthorne, would have to take on new forms to combat an increasingly solidified medical profession at the end of the nineteenth century.

In the first half of the nineteenth century, the invalid woman was established permanently as a literary figure in the conventions of American fiction. Aspects of the figure determined by the social conditions of the mid-nineteenth century have remained part of her representation long after those conditions changed. The contradictory shape of the figure—simultaneously representing power and weakness, innocence and guilt, blamelessness and fault, subservience and independence—carries on into later works. The invalid woman not only shapes literary conventions of how illness is represented but also helps determine how our culture defines illness, femininity, and normality.

Chapter 4

The Writing Cure: Women Writers and the Art of Illness

By the 1870s, the invalid had become such a popular object for both writers and artists that she was one of the most familiar cultural figures. Abba Goold Woolson devoted a whole chapter in *Woman in American Society* (1873) to "Invalidism as a Pursuit," in which she complained that "the familiar heroines of our books, particularly if described by masculine pens, are petite and fragile, with lily fingers and taper waists. . . . A sweet-tempered dyspeptic, a little too spiritual for this world and a little too material for the next, and who, therefore, seems always hovering between the two, is the accepted type of female loveliness" (136). In *Idols of Perversity*, a recent study of turn-of-the-century painting, Bram Dijkstra notes that the same was true of women in art: "Throughout the second half of the nineteenth century, parents, sisters, daughters, and loving friends were kept busy on canvases everywhere, anxiously nursing wan, hollow-eyed beauties who were on the verge of death" (25). Joy Kasson has identified a fascination with the "romantic invalid" in nineteenth-century American sculpture. Wherever women turned—in literature, art, medical or religious tracts, or even their own parlors—they were confronted with the figure of the invalid woman. Sickly women and, to a lesser extent, sickly men were thought more aesthetically pleasing and interesting than healthy people.[1] As Susan Sontag explains in *Illness as Metaphor*, the "tubercular" look was fashionable and was considered romantic. Abba Goold Woolson claimed that "with us, to be ladylike is to be lifeless, inane and dawdling. . . . Instead . . . of being properly ashamed of physical infirmities, our fine ladies aspire to be called *invalides*" (*Woman in American Society*, 192–93). Women courted ill health in an attempt to be "beautiful," eating arsenic to achieve pale skin, wearing corsets, avoiding exercise. Whether these habits were destructive to women's health (as nineteenth-century feminists claimed), positive expressions of independence and sexuality (as David Kunzle argues in *Fashion and Fetishism*), or simple signs of continuing human interest in appearance and eroticism (as Valerie Steele contends in *Fashion and Eroticism*) ultimately may be impossible to tell. What we can know for sure is that in the mid- to late nineteenth century, illness became not only the subject of art but itself a kind of cosmetic art.

The invalid was not the only model of womanhood offered in the late nineteenth century, however. By the late 1880s and through the turn of the century, thousands of women were rejecting the cultural stereotype of woman as weak and sickly. Through both feminist and domestic social housekeeping movements women were becoming activists. They were entering both the professional world and the world of social work, thereby forming increasingly important political forces. Educated and intelligent women had more options than ever; as a result, though, it was incredibly difficult to define a proper womanly role. In *Imaging American Women*, Martha Banta claims that "the images by which ideas about the American female were being offered to the public between 1876 and 1918 were . . . varied to the point of potential self-contradiction" (32).

Feminists were more organized than they had been in the middle of the century to respond to claims that female physiology stood in the way of women's political progress, but they were still worried by doctors' claims and uncertain about their own assertions of strength. M. Carey Thomas, who headed Bryn Mawr College, looking back to the 1870s, wrote in 1908, "We did not know when we began whether women's health could stand the strain of education" (quoted in Mary Walsh, "Doctors Wanted: No Women Need Apply," 124). The medical discourse had grown so powerful in the late nineteenth century that even feminists had begun to doubt their own claims.

One influential physician who was sure that women could not stand the strain of equality was Dr. Edward H. Clarke, who published *Sex in Education; or, A Fair Chance for the Girls* in 1873. He argued that menstruation necessitated regular rest periods that would make it impossible for girls to receive an equal education with boys. Perhaps no other work so solidified the feminist resistance to male medical pronouncements; an almost instant best-seller, *Sex in Education* nonetheless elicited a deluge of counterattacks. Julia Ward Howe edited a volume of replies to Dr. Clarke in 1874, and at least three other collections of feminist responses were published that year.[2] More importantly, Clarke's claims led to the first scientific study of women, menstruation, and education: Mary Putnam Jacobi's *The Question of Rest for Women During Menstruation* (1877), which concluded that normal work was more beneficial to menstruating women than was bed rest. Feminists finally found the means to make their resistance to medical definitions of woman as invalid coherent. Clarke's monograph ultimately had the effect of strengthening the feminist opposition to medical practice.

Given the climate of activism, change, and conflict at the turn of the century, one would expect to find that fictions written by active and productive women who had, themselves, overcome invalidism would represent equally active and productive women who defy the stereotype of the invalid woman. Instead, in fictions like Charlotte Perkins Gilman's "The Yellow Wallpaper" (1891) and Edith Wharton's *The House of Mirth* (1905), we find the same passive and defeated invalid that had figured in the fictions of Southworth, Hawthorne, and Poe fifty years earlier. Despite the fact that Gilman and Wharton themselves worked hard to avoid invalidism, they nonetheless continued to create female figures in their fiction that appear strikingly similar to the earlier ones. The woman in "The Yellow Wallpaper," like Poe's women, goes mad and, apparently, takes her husband with her. Even though, as Annette Kolodny argues in "A Map for Rereading," her story is a "willful

and purposeful misprision" of "The Pit and the Pendulum" that emphasizes that Gilman's narrator cannot be "released to both sanity and
freedom" as can Poe's (456), it nonetheless leaves the figure of the
invalid woman as drawn by Poe intact—driven insane by her intellectual needs. In the same way, Lily Bart in *The House of Mirth*, like
Georgiana in "The Birthmark," Beatrice in "Rappaccini's Daughter,"
and Zenobia in *The Blithedale Romance*, dies at the end of the story, her
body serving as an edifying object for the male gaze.[3]

The apparently stable figure of the invalid woman in turn-of-the-
century women's fictions is related specifically to issues of women's
power through and over illness. Much recent feminist criticism of "The
Yellow Wallpaper" and *The House of Mirth* has evaded the questions
about individual power these texts specifically raise, celebrating the
power of the author even though the texts work to challenge the possibilities for individual action. While much medical treatment at the turn
of the century was still "somatic," that is, treating all ailments (even
mental ones) with physical cures, theories stressing the power of mind
over body came into prominence during the 1890s and 1900s. Physicians and laypeople alike were fascinated with "mental illnesses"—
both insanity and psychosomatic illnesses—and with new cures that
sought to directly treat the mind. "Mind cures" ("New Thought" as well
as neurology and psychology) developed the idea that the individual has
the ability to control his or her mind and therefore his or her body,
regardless of environmental factors or social inequities. These medical
and social theories emphasized the power of the individual rather than
the normative power of society, so that illness became a mark of individual, not social, failure—of individual, not societal, "dis-ease."

Many of these new mind cures were religious in origin, like Mary
Baker Eddy's Christian Science, and sought cure through belief. Others
were secular or only vaguely religious, celebrating a "life force" or an
"All-Supply" of energy. For the purposes of this discussion, I will refer to
both the religious and the secular mind cures as "New Thought," as they
were called at the time. Perhaps the simplest definition of New Thought
was set out in the purpose statement of an early New Thought group, the
Metaphysical Club of Boston, in 1895: "To promote interest in and the
practice of a true philosophy of life and happiness; to show that through
right thinking one's loftiest ideals may be brought into present realization; and to advance intelligent and systematic treatment of disease by
spiritual and mental methods" (quoted in Charles Braden, *Spirits in*

Rebellion, 5). New Thought eventually became the medical equivalent of the economic individualism urged in the "success" literature at the turn of the century. Elizabeth Towne, who published her own religious New Thought poetry with the New Thought Publishing Company, started a publishing house and printed Bruce MacLelland's *Prosperity through Thought and Force* (1907), a treatise that explained how to use New Thought to achieve wealth as well as health. Just as one could rise on the corporate ladder with hard work and willpower, so, too, could one achieve perfect health. The discourse of self-help, mind over matter, and *willed* health may have provided Gilman and Wharton with the chance to effect for themselves a "writing cure," a personal version of Freud's "talking cure," that was related to New Thought.

Nonetheless, in "The Yellow Wallpaper" and *The House of Mirth*, Gilman and Wharton resist this representation of the individual's capacity for health. Instead, they portray seriously "sick" societies in which social and sexual oppression makes women ill. But these writers' own experiences of "willed" health, as well as their immersion in contemporary culture, make it impossible for them to maintain a consistent stance: the New Thought that had saved the writers indicts their heroines. Illness in these texts becomes, then, a matter of both subversion and collusion. Illness becomes a way to resist the sexist norms of nineteenth-century society, a specifically feminine form of revolt against male control, and a sign of *real* health in a *sick* world. At the same time that Gilman and Wharton celebrate this kind of resistance—almost to the point of glorifying victimage—they also condemn the women who allow their own victimization. Illness also becomes, then, a sign of acceptance of patriarchal power. As Deirdre David argues of George Eliot in *Intellectual Women and Victorian Patriarchy*, Gilman and Wharton were "collaborateurs" and "saboteurs" whose heroines' ends help reconcile the writers' ambiguous attitudes to past and present, to the male and female traditions in fiction, and to the ideology of "self-advancement" through "disciplined work" (209, 215).

Mental Healing at the Turn of the Century

By the turn of the century "New Women" and suffragists had begun to challenge Victorian stereotypes of femininity. Of course, most women were not "New Women." Even at the height of the first women's movement, only a very small percentage of women (around 4–5 percent) actually went to college (although by 1910, 40 percent of all college students were women [Glenda Riley, *Inventing the American Woman*, 47]) and only about half of female college graduates went on to actively pursue professional careers (ibid. and Carroll Smith-Rosenberg, *Disorderly Conduct*). Still, 17 percent of all women were in the work force in 1900—four times as many as there had been in 1870 (Riley, 55). Another of the major changes in the lives of late nineteenth-century women was their involvement in various reform movements. After the Civil War, many were involved in actively feminist causes, but even greater numbers of women led, organized, and staffed social housekeeping campaigns like the temperance movement, care for orphans and veterans, urban planning, aid for the poor, and educational and health reform. Some women undertook these causes as active feminists. Most, however, saw their activism as consistent with the ideology of domesticity: they were expanding their role as moral guides from the nursery and kitchen to the world outside the home.

One of the most active of these reform movements was aimed at health; these activists read the dire assessments of women's failing health and, guided both by feminism and by domesticity, determined to do something about it. Following in the footsteps of Mary Gove Nichols, health reformers like Dorothea Dix, Marie Zakrzewska, Elizabeth Blackwell, Jane Addams, Margaret Sanger, and Mary Putnam Jacobi, to mention but a few of the most famous, were instrumental in reforms of health and medicine (see Regina Morantz-Sanchez, *Sympathy and Science*, and Judith Leavitt, *Women and Health in America*). They founded hospitals; advocated dress reform, diet reform, health education, better hygiene, and birth control; and fought for reforms in regular medical practice that became standard policy by the mid-twentieth century. Women's movements of various kinds caused great changes in nineteenth-century culture, but a side effect of those reforms was increased contradiction among differing definitions of "woman's proper sphere." More than ever, women declared themselves fit to hold responsible positions outside the home; more than ever, medical authorities decried the public health dangers created when women devoted themselves to activities other than mothering.

Turn-of-the-century medical authorities by no means presented a unified front, however. The profession was still fragmented by differing theories of disease and treatment. Until the discovery of bacteria and specific etiology for disease at the end of the nineteenth century, allopathy was only one among many competing techniques.[4] "Irregular" practices, like homeopathy, hydropathy, Grahamism, mind cure, and eclecticism, seemed pretty much equal at the time.[5] Self-doctoring, accomplished with the help of the growing patent medicine business, was much in vogue.[6] The medical profession was further fragmented by the entry of a fair number of women into active competition. By 1900, 6 percent of the practicing physicians in the United States were women; in some cities, like Boston and Minneapolis, women accounted for 20 percent of the physicians (Morantz-Sanchez, "So Honoured, So Loved?"). These women served as living proof against the accepted "regular" medical position that women were not strong enough to be professionals or to step outside limited roles in the family.

A decades-old (if not centuries-old) belief does not die easily. Despite growing evidence that women could leave the home and not face life-long suffering and despite new theories of disease based on a medical model of specific etiology rather than closed energy, male physicians continued to caution against women taking on roles outside the home. Many of these medical authorities turned their attention from specific physical ailments to interest in "nervous diseases." Late nineteenth-century physicians were fascinated by mental disorders. In Europe, this fascination would lead to Freud's development of psychoanalysis; in the United States, it led to S. Weir Mitchell's development of the "rest cure" and William James's *Psychology*, as well as the proliferation of mind cures.

The second half of the nineteenth century saw an unprecedented increase in the diagnosis of "nervous" illnesses. Medical and cultural observers everywhere noted the staggering and ever-increasing numbers of people (male and female) who suffered from ailments grouped under the general label "nervousness." Edward Wakefield, a physician writing in *McClure's Magazine* in 1893, called nervousness the "national disease of America." Despite studies showing no rise in the actual incidence of insanity between 1885 and 1910, neurologists like George M. Beard and S. Weir Mitchell, among many others, believed that nervousness posed an imminent threat to modern civilization.[7] Not surprisingly, the diagnosis of "nervousness" often represented cultural attitudes toward both disease and its sufferers; similar symptoms in men and women, the rich and the poor, those of American stock and those who had recently immigrated, were attributed to different causes.

Therefore, while recent immigrants and the poor went insane, members of the upper middle class most often became "nervous." One study reveals that in 1911 the foreign-born were almost twice as likely as the native-born to be committed to insane asylums in New York State (Nathan Hale, *Freud and the Americans*, 80). Middle-class men, no matter the severity of their symptoms, were most often described as having "neurasthenia," a disease newly discovered (or at least named) by Beard in 1869; middle-class women, too, were often diagnosed as neurasthenic, but if the symptoms were more severe, especially if they included "paroxysms" or "fits," women were described as "hysteric" and the blame for the disease was placed on their sexual organs (as the etymology of the word *hysteria*—from the Greek *hyster*, meaning "womb"—suggests).[8]

Neurasthenia was the disease of the upper middle classes; almost any symptom could be a sign of it (the same was true of hysteria for middle-class and upper middle-class women). Robin and John Haller describe it in *The Physician and Sexuality in Victorian America* as the late nineteenth-century "pathological dumping ground for moralists within and outside the medical world" (8). Almost anything, from tenderness of the scalp, forgetfulness, and ticklishness to dyspepsia, insomnia, and abnormal secretions, could be a sign of neurasthenia; in a few cases, impotence, headaches, yawning, and depression were also symptoms. Nineteenth-century physicians, influenced by Herbert Spencer's Social Darwinism, believed that neurasthenia in a man was the result of a too-speedy evolution from physical to mental work; his illness, though certainly not pleasant, was nonetheless a sign of his "higher" evolution and, therefore, at least tolerable. Many neurologists and psychologists, including Weir Mitchell and William James, were themselves sufferers of neurasthenia.[9]

Nervousness in women, on the other hand, did not have such a specific etiology. Neurasthenia and hysteria, as one encounters them in medical writings of the time, seem to differ only in the severity of symptoms, but that, too, varies from doctor to doctor and among patients.[10] (I will use "nervousness" to refer to mental ailments unless the context calls for a specific designation of either neurasthenia or hysteria.) Nervousness was sometimes understood in the same light as male neurasthenia: troubling but a sign of good breeding and intellectual achievement. More often, though, nervousness was interpreted as female inadequacy to deal with any intellectual endeavor at all and a tendency toward the more severe disease, hysteria. Nineteenth-century physicians believed male neurasthenia was the result of man's ever more demanding role in society, while female neurasthenia was the result of her inadequate brain capacity for dealing with complex thought and roles outside of the home (Haller and Haller, *The Physician and Sexuality in Victorian America*, 42).

Nor was cause the only gender differentiation in neurasthenia. Treatment for male nervousness was increased activity, a return to physical exertion that was seen to counteract too much mental exertion. This treatment signaled the beginnings of a changed attitude about the relation between mind and body. Unlike the mid-nineteenth-century belief in the necessity of shepherding energy, new theories advocated balancing energies and even building energies in the treatment of men. But physicians most often suggested an intensified domesticity as the "cure" to female nervousness, assuming that domestic life was more peaceful than the world outside the home. If the disease were caused by over-exertion, rest could be its only cure and a quiet life the only way to prevent it. One could describe the rest cure, which kept women not just at home but in bed in their rooms, as an almost parodic exaggeration of domesticity. Even some women physicians advocated a return to the domestic sphere for nervous women (see Morantz-Sanchez, "So Honoured, So Loved?," and Haller and Haller, *The Physician and Sexuality in Victorian America*, 35). As Tom Lutz observes in *American Nervousness, 1903*, "Both cures [for women and for men] were represented in terms of a return to traditional values of passive femininity and masculine activity" (34). Domesticity, which had begun as a woman-led movement to establish feminine power within the home, became by the turn of the century the means for doctors to confine women there. The suturing of difference between medical and domestic ideologies that we saw at work in Southworth's *Retribution* had, by an intensification of their similarities and a dismissal of their differences, become a tool for doctors to use to extend their own cultural and professional influence. (This occurred despite the extension of one kind of domesticity out of the home into "social housekeeping" reforms.)

Some physicians, however, suggested that female neurasthenia might be the result of boredom and idleness; one such physician, Herbert Hall, argued in 1905 that neurasthenia most often happened to creative women who were generally more clever and artistic than other people (Haller and Haller, *The Physician and Sexuality in Victorian America*,

40). Even those who held this theory of the disease, however, usually suggested not professional or artistic work but charity work. Whatever their theory, though, theorists of nervousness agreed that it was somehow a culturally induced disease. "Their descriptions of the commonest nervous disorders of women and men emphasized conflicts within individuals who could not fulfill social norms, yet, because they had internalized them, could not consciously reject them" (Hale, *Freud and the Americans*, 59).

Regular, allopathic, treatments for neurasthenia between about 1880 and 1910 were usually physically oriented. Nathan Hale, in *Freud and the Americans*, has characterized medical treatment during this period as the "somatic style" because it sought to treat mental ailments by exclusively physical means. Weir Mitchell, a pioneer in the field of neurological treatment, argued against what we would today identify as mental treatment. While he recognized that the causes of patients' ailments "are often to be sought in the remote past" and that patients will tell their physician "more than he may care to hear," Mitchell did not advocate eliciting such "confessions" (Mitchell, *Doctor and Patient*, 10). It will surprise modern skeptics to learn that the somatic style did achieve notable results; rest, diet, exercise, electrical stimulation, hydropathy, and drugs often worked wonders. These means did not, though, work as well as the claims made for them; many patients tried doctor after doctor, treatment after treatment, and still found no real relief. This dissatisfaction led to widespread experimentation with "irregular" treatments, many of which were genuinely mentally oriented; hypnosis and New Thought were extremely popular during this period. According to Hale, "medical and popular interest in hypnosis, suggestion, mental healing and multiple personality peaked in the early 1890s, declined slightly after 1895, then waxed rapidly after 1900" (*Freud and the Americans*, 229–30).

These new kinds of cures share some characteristics with the earlier somatic cures, especially with Mitchell's "rest cure." This is not particularly surprising since many curists started out as neurologists or as the patients of neurologists. The most significant aspect of all the cures—whether rest cure, hypnosis, hydropathy, dietetic treatment, or New Thought—was a confidence that nervous illness was a matter of an *intent* to be ill, that if the patient decided to be well, she could be. Weir Mitchell rejected almost all of the new psychotherapeutics, but his treatment reveals an attitude toward nervous disease that suggests, at root, an understanding of illness as intentional and of cure, therefore, as a matter of will. His cure's aim was to instill the self-discipline to fight against the "moral failures" of "selfish invalidism" (quoted in ibid., 61). New Thought, while holding that cure could be achieved by "floating in harmony" with the deity, nevertheless encouraged its practitioners to "hit hard and win" against illness (Gail Parker, *Mind Cure in New England*, 10). Freud, at least in his earlier works, shared this attitude and even extended it. In the "Dora" case, he discusses "motives of illness," noting that some diseases are "the result of intention" and even weapons "as a rule leveled at a particular person." He further notes: "The crudest and most commonplace views upon the character of hysterical disorders—such as are to be heard from uneducated relatives or nurses—are in a certain sense right. It is true that the paralysed and bed-ridden woman would spring to her feet if a fire were to break out in her room and that the spoiled wife would forget all her sufferings if her child were to fall dangerously ill or if some catastrophe were to threaten the family circumstances" (*Complete Psychological Works*, 7:45). Arguing that the "intention to be ill" is an unconscious rather than conscious process, Freud nevertheless asserts that in many hysterical diseases, a prerequisite to cure is "an attempt . . . to convince the patient herself of the existence in her of an intention to be ill" (ibid.).

The attitude that illness was the result of the will to be ill developed from the rethinking of the relation between mind and body that occurred at the turn of the century. Many late nineteenth- and early twentieth-century physicians and psychologists agreed with the idea described in an early article by William James called "We Are Automata" (1879): "Feeling is a mere collateral product of our nervous processes, unable to react upon them any more than a shadow reacts on the steps of the traveler whom it accompanies. . . . It is allowed to remain on board, but not to touch the helm or handle the rigging" (quoted in Hale, *Freud and the Americans*, 54). But a larger number, including James himself in later works, were fascinated by the possibilities that the mind and body were not as profoundly split as philosophers had suggested since Descartes. The effect of questioning the mind/body split was the burgeoning of a whole new attitude toward the power of the mind to make the body ill and, in turn, to cure it.

In the United States, this attitude reflected a refinement and scientific verification of transcendentalism adapted to an age of pragmatism. Practitioners of New Thought saw Emanuel Swedenborg and Ralph

Waldo Emerson as their immediate precursors and would find an ally of sorts in William James. Like transcendentalism, New Thought explicitly rejected the Calvinist religion of sin and death and substituted instead a faith in an "All-Supply" of light and hope. New Thought taught that disease was a man-made entity, because God would never have created something so bad. In complete agreement with the position Emerson propounded in "The Transcendentalist," New Thought maintained that changing one's thinking would change one's reality. Unlike transcendentalism, though, New Thought was both pragmatic and active; practitioners and patients believed in it because they saw its results, and they saw themselves not as passive recipients of the deity (the "transparent eyeball") but as active workers, trying to achieve the deity's will in the world.[11]

The activism of New Thought, its insistence that one must work hard for health, reveals its ties with the reform and self-help movements of the day, reflecting the strong American faith in the individual's ability to determine his or her own fate. One of the most popular mind cure authors, Orison Swett Marden, published the self-help journal *Success* (a publication, incidentally, for which Charlotte Perkins Gilman wrote frequently). Marden's work altered the focus of success literature from instructions in how to achieve professional success to "a call for methodical character-building" (Parker, *Mind Cure in New England*, 31). One of the most important proponents of a kind of New Thought, Mary Baker Eddy, extended the reformism and woman-centeredness of domesticity. She used women's social reforms as patterns for self-reform, their control of the household as a model for self-control. She developed the domestic notion that woman could best direct the moral life of the nation into a belief that women were the chosen of God (see Gail Parker, "Mary Baker Eddy and Sentimental Womanhood"). Mind cure, in most of its forms, united several turn-of-the-century reformist and materialistic movements; it combined women's rights, health, and social reforms with a determination to "succeed" worthy of a Horatio Alger novel.[12]

The popularity of mind cure and various other psychotherapies was supported and extended by the new style of sensational mass journalism. Journalists, many of whom had themselves been "saved" by the revolutionary mental therapies, extolled the virtues of the treatments. This journalistic fervor for mental cures was the strongest in women's magazines (Hale, *Freud and the Americans*, 232). In fact, women were quite involved with the New Thought movement, finding in its teachings an outlet for their ambitions and beliefs. Many feminists discovered that it could prove to be a philosophical basis for their demand to be treated as equals as well as a relief from the prevailing sexism of medical treatment. Elizabeth Cady Stanton was an early proponent of mind cure, urging that a woman should become her "own physician of body and soul" (quoted in Parker, *Mind Cure in New England*, 11).

New Thought helped provide the discourse for a coherent and articulate critique of the medical profession that had been lacking in earlier decades (as we saw in chapter 2 with Laura Curtis Bullard's *Christine*). "Mind cure became one outlet for an articulate feminism that demanded equal access to positions of spiritual leadership, freedom from the pretensions of a male medical elite, and the right to use sexual intercourse (as experienced by women) to depict the relationship between mortals and the All-Supply [the deity]" (Parker, *Mind Cure in New England*, 14–15). In New Thought, women found a way to take their cure into their own hands, a way to try to avoid the patriarchal dicta of the medical men. Many other women embraced it merely because it offered a cure for their ailments, but once they had been cured, they often joined the crusade for mental healing. Mary Baker Eddy is perhaps the most famous of these women, but she is far from alone; the health reformer Annie Payson Call, the popular poet Ella Wheeler Wilcox, and popular mind cure authors Elizabeth Towne and Mary Ferriter were but a few of the other women who took mind cure as their personal crusade.

Other women, many of them "regular" physicians and feminists, also argued that women should take charge of their own lives, direct their own health, and resist the cultural tendency to seek femininity through illness. Abba Goold Woolson spoke for many when she argued for health education and a reform in the attitudes toward sickness and health: "When women shall learn to desire good health as essential to both beauty and efficiency, and shall look upon their present pernicious indulgences as not only inexpedient but as morally wrong, we may hope to see our people taking a vast stride in all departments of progress" (*Woman in American Society*, 195). As early as the 1840s, Mary Gove Nichols had urged the same; by the turn of the century, women's health reformers following in Nichols's footsteps continually exhorted women to take charge of their lives and health.

The Writing Cure

One of the most famous women who took up this call for better health through self-discipline was Charlotte Perkins Gilman. In her auto-biography, she claims to have cured herself by working and writing, despite her doctor's orders to stop both activities (*The Living of Charlotte Perkins Gilman*, 106). She claimed that it was writing, especially, that had returned her to health and that had helped other women to follow her example. Gilman had been a victim of "nervousness" throughout her childhood and continued to suffer periodic bouts throughout the rest of her life. But shortly after the birth of her first (and only) child, her symptoms worsened and she feared a complete break-down. As is well known by now from the numerous studies of "The Yellow Wallpaper" and Weir Mitchell's rest cure,[13] Gilman rejected Mitchell's advice to "never touch pen, brush, or pencil" and to "live as domestic a life as possible" (*The Living of Charlotte Perkins Gilman*, 96) in favor of a life of writing, public speaking, and feminist crusading. Gilman later claimed that "The Yellow Wallpaper" had even convinced Mitchell to change his rest cure to include, for some patients, the chance to write.

One of the beneficiaries of this change was Edith Wharton. Wharton, like Gilman, was a sufferer of "nervousness"; she had suffered a serious breakdown in 1894–95, and when she felt another coming on in early 1898, she went to Weir Mitchell's clinic in Philadelphia for treatment (she was, however, an outpatient and was treated by one of his col-leagues, not by Mitchell himself [R. W. B. Lewis, *Edith Wharton: A Biography*, 76]). While there, like most rest cure patients, she was isolated, forced to rest and eat abundantly, given massages, and, unlike Gilman, encouraged to write. R. W. B. Lewis rebuts the "legend" that Wharton began writing during the rest cure as a mode of therapy (a claim mentioned and accorded respect by Suzanne Poirier in "The Weir Mitchell Rest Cure" [31]), pointing out that she had published enough for a small volume before her first breakdown (76), but he admits that 1898 marks the beginning of her sustained career as a writer (82).[14] Wharton may not have *learned* to write from her cure, but she did learn that writing could be encompassed in a cure and did not have to be, as Lewis suggests it had been, illness inducing.

Gilman and Wharton found that writing could be curative, whether they had consciously undertaken it as therapy or not. It became for them their own independent form of mind cure because it allowed them to "remake their circumstances," to change their "thoughts and motives" in order to transform their "conditions and economies." It also seemed to work; Gilman was never entirely free of her nervousness, but after becoming an active writer and speaker, she never suffered from it to the same degree as she had earlier. Wharton became healthier in direct relation to her success as an author. But in the texts that mark each woman's emergence as an important writer, the fictions generally accepted as their first "masterpieces," the female characters are not granted the authors' newly won health. The woman in "The Yellow Wallpaper" descends dramatically into a complete breakdown just as Gilman ascends from the threat of a breakdown; in *The House of Mirth*, Lily Bart's physical health deteriorates as a result of her increasing depression. She falls into a cycle of insomnia and drug abuse and finally succumbs to an overdose that may or may not be accidental.[15] The defeat of these female characters may well have been the price of Gilman's and Wharton's own victories over illness and invalidism. In *writing* the story of the invalid, they were able to avoid *living* it.

In *The Madwoman in the Attic*, Sandra Gilbert and Susan Gubar argue that the activity of writing, or producing art, was fraught with anxiety for most nineteenth-century women. They argue that the lively or imaginative girl growing up in the nineteenth century was "likely to experience her education in docility, submissiveness, self-lessness as in some sense sickening. To be trained in renunciation is almost necessarily to be trained to ill health, since the human animal's first and strongest urge is to his/her own survival, pleasure, assertion. . . . Learning to become a beautiful object, the girl learns anxiety about—perhaps even loathing of—her own flesh" (54). This is the reason, they contend, that so many women in the nineteenth century were ill. Gubar, in " 'The Blank Page' and the Issues of Female Creativity," argues that "many women experience their own bodies as the only available medium for art" (248); she associates this art of the body with blood and pain.[16] She argues that women who have not been allowed the education or opportunity to write, paint, or sculpt have learned to make art of their bodies through clothing, makeup, and their shapes: "The woman who cannot become an artist can nevertheless turn herself into an artistic object" (249). For Gilbert and Gubar, making art of the body is itself illness inducing.

In contrast to this view, David Kunzle and Valerie Steele argue that learning to turn herself into an art object was, for the Victorian woman, a way of taking control over her own body. Kunzle goes much further on this point than Steele; he argues that Victorian men were, if anything, against the corsets, cosmetics, and elaborate dresses worn by Victorian women. He sees such body shaping as forms of sexual expression and self-assertion, even of independence from male norms. In his view, it was the corseted lady, not the feminist, who was the real sexual radical in the nineteenth century. Steele's view is more moderate than Kunzle's—in part because her research leads her to believe that reports of corset wearing and tight lacing have been much exaggerated—but she contends that the art of fashion has always been a healthy way to express self and sexuality and accepts the idea that nineteenth-century fashions were, at least in part, a way for women to express self-control rather than male control.

If we allow that illness could be a kind of "cosmetic" for women, as Abba Goold Woolson claimed it was, and if the cosmetic arts were a way to rebel against male control, then illness itself could become both an art and a form of rebellion against patriarchy. The woman who grew up with nineteenth-century standards of moral and social conduct would then have found illness a congenial role in several ways. First, if she, like the women Gilbert and Gubar describe, came to loathe her own flesh, she could punish that flesh with illness. But if she also discovered that the illness with which she punished her body was aesthetically pleasing, then she could turn her self-punishment into art. In this way, the woman who had grown up with fiction and visual arts that exalted the holy and beautiful illnesses of female characters could come to experience suffering and making her body ill as artistic activities. For the woman caught between medical discourses that defined her as ill, aesthetic discourses which asserted that she was better that way, and New Thought arguments that she could take control of her own life and urged her to do so, the self-discipline of willed and artistic illness could offer the simplest resolution to these competing forces.

Making an art of illness, then, represents one extreme kind of self-control. If illness can be understood as a kind of artistic self-discipline, a way of taking control of one's own body, of "working" it to artistic ends, then illness can be *both* a matter of art and of self-punishment, a way of enjoying and loathing the flesh. In *Discipline and Punish*, Michel Foucault argues that punishment, as a part of discipline, "has the function of reducing gaps. It must therefore be essentially *corrective.* . . . Disciplinary systems favour punishments that are exercise—intensified, multiplied forms of training" (179). If illness comes to be a *discipline*, then, it can be both punishment and art. It can be either an art intensified into punishment or a punishment meant to "correct" imperfections of the body. It can therefore be both collusion with moral and social standards that oppress women and a subversion of those standards at the same time. The woman who makes an *art* of her illness accedes to her "place" in a patriarchal system, but *she* controls that place.

Alice James may serve as an illuminating case in point. She writes repeatedly in her *Diary* of "achieving" illness and of "getting herself dead" as a feat equal to or surpassing Henry's and William's writing (211). Jean Strouse, Alice James's biographer, argues that Alice maintained a kind of "negative superiority" about her illness. "All her life Alice had been in conflict over just who she could be. . . . The intelligence and energy Alice might have used in some productive way went into the intricate work of being sick. . . . Her miserable health *was* her career" (*Alice James: A Biography*, 291). And Ruth Bernard Yeazell writes, "Alice retired permanently to her bed and took up the profession of an invalid" (*The Death and Letters of Alice James*, 4). At one point, quoting "un ange philosophe," she explicitly describes suffering as a way to make one's life a work of art:[17] "Sous cette inspiration [souffrance] les existences les plus humbles peuvent devenir des oeuvres d'art bien supérieures aux plus belles symphonies et aux plus beaux poèmes. Est-ce que les oeuvres d'art qu'on réalise en soi-même ne sont pas meilleures? Les autres, qu'on jette en dehors sur la toile ou le papier, ne sont rien que des images, des ombres. L'oeuvre de la vie est un réalité" (55–56). Alice's "work" was directed destructively at her own body, not exactly as punishment but as self-discipline, as making a work of art of her life. It was this destructive, punishing work that allowed her to construct a sense of self and self-control. The self she defined was ill; the one piece of writing she published in her lifetime, a letter to the editor of *The Nation* (4 July 1890), was signed "Invalid." Alice's writing of her diary was an extension of this work, not a revision of it, because she attempted to write *herself*, as invalid, into it.

Writing could then be an extension of illness-as-art. Gilbert and Gubar claim that it was the stress of making art that caused women writers' illnesses in the nineteenth century, that moving from the "feminine" art of the body to the "masculine" art of the pen was illness inducing.[18] But it seems more likely that illness and writing exist not as opposing options for women but as different points along a continuum of artistic self-discipline. Therefore, as a woman began to make other kinds of art, she no longer needed to experience her sense of art through making herself ill. Ironically, then, the best way to overcome the sense that one's body and illness are the only media for art would be to make art in other ways. Illness would, then, resume its original character as punishment, not self-discipline, not art. Gilman and Wharton both came to believe that writing made them feel better—Wharton had, in fact, used "making up" stories as a kind of a therapy since she had been a child (see Cynthia Wolff, *A Feast of Words*). This was true of other women writers, too. Kate Chopin consciously took up writing as therapy for the depression she experienced after her husband's and mother's deaths, and even Alice James believed that writing her *Diary* helped to relieve her illness.[19]

Writing and making art also were part of the prescription offered by female mind curists to women. Harriott K. Hunt, one of the first female physicians in this country (although she never attended a medical school because none would admit her), was one of Mary Baker Eddy's early proponents and wrote in her autobiography, *Glances and Glimpses*, that her treatment of women consisted of "telling [them] to throw away their medicines, begin a diary, and think of their mothers" (quoted in Ann Douglas Wood, " 'The Fashionable Diseases,' " 46–47). Mary Ferriter, a popular mind cure author, wrote in 1923: "Tell the girl that every twenty-eight days she will have a call from nature and that then she will have the sex urge, or the creature instinct, strong upon her; that then is the time for her to express in art, music, poetry" (from *Truth of Life—Love—Liberty*, quoted in Gail Parker, *Mind Cure in New England*, 98). Gilman and Wharton, who were both extensively exposed to New Thought philosophy, undoubtedly internalized some of this thinking, especially when they found it so successful.[20]

This "writing cure" would, of course, have been coincident with Freud's development of the "talking cure," through which patients were able to speak their anxiety and stop directing it internally. It also parallels much current feminist psychoanalytic theory about the role of language in effecting cures. Psychoanalysts like Luce Irigaray and Michèle Montrelay argue that women growing up in a world dominated by masculine signifying systems often lack the necessary representational structures to articulate sexuality and anxiety: "Women do not manage to articulate their madness: they suffer it directly in their body" (Irigaray, quoted in Diana Adlam and Couze Venn, "Women's Exile," 74). Language, the "pure cathexis in the word as such," they argue, allows the woman to turn painful experiences into a discourse in which "words are *other*" than herself (Montrelay, "Of Femininity," 96). Freud wrote that "hysterics suffer mainly from reminiscences" (*Complete Psychological Works*, 2:7). Irigaray and Montrelay argue that by articulating those reminiscences, women no longer have to live them.[21]

For women writing at the turn of the century, this "writing cure" went further than just articulating painful reminiscences, though. It also fundamentally changed the woman's role. As Jonathan Culler puts it, women have historically been the subject *of* literature, or the inspiration *for* literature, but not the subject who writes literature (*On Deconstruction*, 167). But in becoming a writer, a woman comes to inhabit an altogether different position in society and history. Writing about illness, then, allows the woman writer to separate the experience of it from herself; becoming a writer who creates narratives of illness allows her to control it, to avoid experiencing the sickness herself. Unlike Alice James, who merely wrote her self into her text as invalid, Gilman and Wharton wrote the *illness* into their texts, leaving themselves apart from it, as *authors*, not invalid women.

By writing, Gilman and Wharton produced irrefutable evidence of their changed position from invalid women to writers: a visible, material creation that attests to their activity. In *Discipline and Punish*, Foucault maintains that "disciplinary power . . . is exercised through its invisibility; at the same time it imposes on those whom it subjects a principle of compulsory visibility" (187). This visibility, he argues, allows them to be controlled. In "The Yellow Wallpaper" and *The House of Mirth*, Gilman and Wharton try to make the disciplinary power of patriarchy visible, to reveal the painful effects of women's compulsory visibility (both female characters are "watched"), and to redefine that visibility in the process, in favor of something that can stand for the woman writer herself—the writing.

The "writing cure" is a remedy that provides a way for the woman writer to present her illness so that it is "written and simultaneously erased, metaphorized; designating itself while indicating intraworldly relations; it [is] *represented*" (Jacques Derrida, "Freud and the Scene of Writing," 229). The writing she produces will *take her place* in two ways, then: first, it can be Other, it can represent the illness she no longer has to embody, and second, it can represent her in her absence.[22] But like the *pharmakon*, writing is a cure that is also a poison because to cure the woman writer, it must kill the invalid woman.

The Art of Illness

Both "The Yellow Wallpaper" and *The House of Mirth* center on female characters who are in some sense frustrated artists, trapped in an ugly and uncomfortable world that does not allow them viable alternatives to the traditional world of wifehood and motherhood. These two women, the narrator of "The Yellow Wallpaper" and Lily Bart, therefore turn their artistic urges destructively on themselves. Both Gilman and Wharton refuse the ideal of feminine domesticity in these narratives and, with it, the traditional happy endings of women's fiction. Both narratives reject domestic ideology—marriage and the home do not provide a happy alternative to the heroine's problems—and domestic narrative structure—the heroine does not save herself from an exterior threat but succumbs to an interior one. The emphasis both texts place on art and the rejection of dominant ideology is important to the notion of a "writing cure" and to the place of these narratives in feminist literary history.

"The Yellow Wallpaper" is written in first-person narrative, in the form of the journal of a nameless woman who has been taken to an "ancestral hall," "a hereditary estate," to spend the summer on a modified rest cure while recuperating from some "nervous" condition. Since the narrator remains nameless—she neither mentions her own name nor records anyone calling her by name—she seems not to experience herself as a subject but as a wife, her child's mother, a "sick" woman, or as "a woman" in the "hereditary estate" of all women, which, under patriarchy, makes women sick.

While the woman maintains that she is sick, her husband, a physician, maintains that she is not. This contradiction of her experience leaves her confused; as she puts it, "If a physician of high standing, and one's own husband, assures friends and relatives that there is really nothing the matter with one but temporary nervous depression—a slight hysterical tendency—what is one to do?" (3). She is "absolutely forbidden to 'work' until [she is] well again" (4), even though she is told she is not sick and even though she disagrees with the prescription:

"Personally, I believe that congenial work, with excitement and change, would do me good. But what is one to do?" (3–4).

Throughout the story, her doctor-husband contradicts her representations of reality and imposes his representations on her. She tells him she feels something strange and ghostly in the house, and he says it is a draught and closes the window (4). Confessing that her "nervous troubles are dreadfully depressing," she states, "John does not know how much I really suffer. He knows there is no *reason* to suffer, and that satisfies him. . . . Nobody would believe what an effort it is to do what little I am able" (6). She does, however, keep trying to tell John how she feels. In every case, he tells her she is wrong, that he knows better than she what is true for her. Still, she tries to maintain her role as speaking and desiring subject, even though John continues to treat her as a child—as *infans*, the one who does not speak, the one who is to be taken care of. She tries to tell him that she "is not gaining" and that she wants to leave the old house; John's response is, as we might expect, "Of course, if you were in any danger, I could and would, but you really are better, dear, whether you can *see* it or not. I am a doctor, dear, and *I know*" (11–12, emphasis added).

Despite these repeated instances reinforcing her idea that "nobody would believe" her, she continues trying to tell someone. Her writing of the journal we read is one indication of this attempt to continue representing, even though it is the very work she has been told not to do. She is, at least initially, trying to somehow maintain her subjectivity despite male interdiction. She rebels against John's attempts to control her by instituting her own system of self-discipline: writing. Such a rebellion on her part, however, has marked consequences. She says, "I did write for a while in spite of them; but it *does* exhaust me a good deal—having to be so sly about it, or else meet with heavy opposition. I sometimes fancy that in my condition if I had less opposition and more society and stimulus—but John says the very worst thing I can do is to think about my condition, and I confess it always makes me feel bad" (4). When she writes at one point, "I would not say it to a living soul, of course, but this is dead paper and a great relief to my mind" (3), the effects of the continual denial of her representations of reality start to become apparent. In writing only for "dead paper"—writing only *to* death—her language use becomes less governed by existence in the world outside her. She ceases to function as a "speaking-subject" in the world. Continually denied recognition as a subject, treated as a nonspeaker, as one whose representations are invalid (because they are the representations of an invalid?), she comes to reject the effort of maintaining this "invalid" subjectivity: "I don't know why I should write this. I don't want to. I don't feel able. And I know John would think it absurd. But I *must* say what I feel and think in some way—it is such a relief! But the effort is getting to be greater than the relief" (10).

The narrator's attempts to produce her reality, to realize her "representations," are failures and are eventually more frustrating than helpful. Gilman presents not just an image of a woman's "education in docility" but also the defeat of a woman writer, as Annette Kolodny and Paula Treichler have both pointed out. Kolodny describes the story as a woman's giving up writing in favor of reading "the symbolization of her own untenable and unacceptable reality" in the wallpaper ("A Map for Rereading," 459). Treichler argues that the diagnosis imposed by the physician-husband is not merely a representation of reality that contradicts the narrator's but a mechanism for controlling her ("Escaping the Sentence," 71). For Treichler, the wallpaper becomes a symbol of the escape from this control: women's writing "becomes possible only after women obtain the right to speak" (64), but women's language remains merely "metaphorical and evocative" (74).

But if we understand that writing here is a form of "control," too, then we see that although her system of self-discipline is radically at odds with that which her physician-husband would impose on her, eventually the distinction between the two becomes unclear. Studying the wallpaper, becoming one with its unknowable artistic principles, is another attempt at self-control but one that eventually becomes indistinguishable from the control of her husband: the wallpaper, like John, watches her.

"The Yellow Wallpaper" is a story about the loss of distinctions—between writing and reading, doctor and patient, medical and self-discipline, art and the body. Early in the story the narrator begins to reexperience her childhood sense that the furnishings of her room have a life of their own. Later, the wallpaper develops "absurd, unblinking eyes" (7), and she eventually sees another woman in the wallpaper. In other words, the furnishings in her room seem to take on a threatening subjectivity of their own; they watch her, attempt to frighten her, and eventually cooperate with her. Throughout, she continues to assert her identity as a speaking subject, but that sense is continually denied by John, who does not listen to her or contradicts her when he does, and becomes more and more difficult to maintain. Coupled with her treatment as an object—something to be watched (by John and the wallpaper) but not listened to—we see that the distinction between subject and object becomes meaningless for her. She does not come to an awareness or rejection of her own "untenable and unacceptable reality"; rather, she becomes part of the world of objects. Her existence as a subject breaks down. Frustrated in her attempt to produce a readable text, she becomes one. Her body—through illness—becomes the outlet for her creativity. Denied the opportunity to make external representations, to write, she is forced to turn these creative impulses on herself. Gilman here illustrates how similar the two activities are.

Walter Benn Michaels, in his introduction to *The Gold Standard and the Logic of Naturalism*, argues that "The Yellow Wallpaper" is not about "a woman being driven crazy by Weir Mitchell's refusal to allow her to produce, [but] is about a woman driven crazy . . . by a commitment to production so complete that it requires her to begin by producing herself" (5). He is right to claim that Gilman accepts the notion that the self must be produced, but he reads past the indications that "The Yellow Wallpaper" is the scene of a battle over who has the *right* to that production. The conflict in this story is between culturally accepted and culturally forbidden modes of self-production. The point of the woman's desire to write is not, as Michaels argues, to "produce evidence that [she is] still the same person" (7); it is, instead, to produce evidence that she is *different*. Gilman does not write "herself *into* her body" (5, emphasis added), as Alice James had done. She writes her way *out* of it. While all other distinctions in the story break down, one remains: the distinction between Gilman and her narrator, a distinction Michaels collapses. For even though it is an autobiographical story, Gilman maintains a sharp difference between herself, as writer-producer, and the woman in the story whose writing fails.

The problem in "The Yellow Wallpaper" is not production itself but who has control over production. The story becomes a rewriting of the Poe and Hawthorne stories examined in chapter 3 at the point when the woman resists the male attempt to produce her as the perfect woman (in this case, the quiet and domestic wife). Unlike the cooperative Georgiana or the painter's wife in "The Oval Portrait," the narrator of "The Yellow Wallpaper" does not submit entirely to her husband's productive efforts. But the woman's resistance is not much more successful than the earlier women's cooperation had been; she does not end up dead, but she does end up mad.

The difficulty of "The Yellow Wallpaper" springs from uncertainty about the woman's writing and its relation to her illness. In the second half of the story, it is not clear who is writing or when. As the woman's position as a subject becomes more tenuous, it becomes impossible to sort out who—or what—is writing. Tenses shift back and forth between present and past ("I am securely fastened now" and "Now he's crying" to "said I" and "I kept on creeping" [18–19]), the persona shifts from the woman in the room to the woman in the wallpaper, and the final scene—the tethered woman crawling around the edges of the room, creeping over her unconscious husband—leaves open the question of whether we are reading a madwoman's text, a sane woman's post facto description of madness, or an entirely impossible text, one that could never have been written. As a feminist critic I would like to read this story as that of a woman who has achieved "transcendent sanity" (Treichler, "Escaping the Sentence," 67) because she has been able to imagine "mirages of health and freedom" (Gilbert and Gubar, *The Madwoman in the Attic*, 91), but I must eventually recognize that it is a tale of defeat. As Treichler herself has pointed out, the woman is tied up in the nursery and will undoubtedly be "sent to Weir Mitchell" when John regains consciousness.

A happy ending is not compatible with the tone or context of this story. In fact, "The Yellow Wallpaper" may go out of its way to avoid a happy ending, to emphasize its complete rejection of domesticity and the ideology of domestic fiction. Far from upholding motherhood as a means to power and self-expression, Gilman here represents motherhood and domesticity as the paths to confinement and madness, the death of self-expression. The narrative instability at the end of the story, then, is not the "communal voice" that Treichler finds but the voice of no one, the voice of one with no self. It is the voice of domesticity as Gilman imagines it: confined and mad. Denied the opportunity to make art, or the audience to appreciate it, the woman turns her artistic impulses to her own body, becoming thereby just another of the indecipherable furnishings of the "hereditary estate."

In *The House of Mirth*, the relationship between illness and art is central to an understanding of the character of Lily Bart and to Wharton's writing. Throughout the novel Lily is depicted and admired as an artistic object. Lily's beauty is central to her existence and is represented by Wharton as the result of painstaking production. Our first view of Lily is through Selden's eyes and shares his "confused sense that she must have cost a great deal to make" (5). Lily's value is directly related to her beauty, to her status as a beautiful object. She has no money, no real family connections, and not much of a desirable character; she is a shallow gambler with no interest in high art, literature, or anything practical. Lily's one talent is as an artist of the body; as Dale Bauer argues in *Feminist Dialogics*, she "creates herself as a work of art" (97).[23] She is merely a beautiful commodity on the marriage market; she is in many ways the exemplar of Thorstein Veblen's women who are valuable to a future husband only to the extent of their ability to represent his wealth.[24] As we saw in the previous chapter (with Beatrice Rappaccini), Lily's value in the marriage market is doubly dependent on her beauty and her remaining virginal. The novel is, in one sense, a tale about the difficulties of "keeping up appearances"—both Lily's physical appearance and the appearance of innocence. Lily's life is devoted to the "art" of appearances. When that art fails—when she can no longer make art of her body by traditional methods (for example, clothes and makeup), Lily gradually becomes ill, losing sleep and abusing drugs. Her death, which leaves her body artistically arranged on her bed, is a culmination of her art of the body and her illness.

Wharton goes out of her way to emphasize that Lily is an artistic object, turning her at one point into "living art": at the Brys' *tableaux vivants*, Lily appears, unadorned, as a painting. She does not need decoration; she is decoration. It is significant that this moment—when she is merely a silent painting—is Lily's one moment of unmitigated triumph and the moment when it is *she* who becomes the producer. But, as Bauer points out, she only gains recognition "by inserting [herself] as the representation of another woman in a male-created text" (*Feminist Dialogics*, 97).

Susan Gubar argues that Lily's overdose is a logical extension of her objectification into art; once she had become an artistic object, there was little else to do but "kill herself into art" (" 'The Blank Page' and the Issues of Female Creativity," 250). Gubar points to the fact that before taking the overdose, Lily examines her beautiful dresses and thinks about the *tableaux vivants* and then "thinks that there is 'some word she had found' to tell Selden. . . . This word is Lily's dead body; for she is now converted completely into a script for his edification, a text not unlike the letters and checks she has left behind to vindicate her life" (ibid., 251). Gubar argues further that this equation of body and word "illustrates the terrors not of the word made flesh but of the flesh made word." Like Alice James, Lily had to "get herself dead" in order to speak to Selden. But in contrast to Georgiana in "The Birthmark" and Beatrice Rappaccini, Lily is not made into an object by a man but turns herself into one. (Gubar's use of the passive disguises this.) She therefore takes control and refuses to let society define her; she does not merely leave her body as a text but also leaves those same checks that Gubar mentions and then looks past. She pays off Gus Trenor, making herself completely independent from his demands. Unfortunately, neither her checks nor her body are easily readable. Like the woman in the wall-paper, she finds that women's "language" remains, at least in part, incomprehensible. Lily's death exemplifies how "artistic discipline" can intensify into punishment, how the subversion of society's norms can be interpreted as collusion with them.

Lily fails at every artistic attempt that is not directed at her own body. Even when she is employed at the millinery shop in the "art . . . of [creating] ever varied settings for the face of fortunate womanhood" (282), she is a complete failure, unable to make straight or even stitches. Lily's every attempt at communication is a failure, too. Finally, she even fails at her artistic specialty, herself: her looks begin to fail and she loses her reputation. Lily's only artistic success, the only effort that achieves the effect she desires—the compassion and love of Selden—is her death. She (as Wharton does in creating Lily's character) makes an art of death.

Gubar does not examine the artistry involved in Lily's death scene. Lily does not merely become "a word"; she also becomes, as she had done in the *tableaux vivants*, a painting. In *Idols of Perversity*, Bram Dijkstra shows that one of the most popular genres of turn-of-the-century painting was the "death" or "sleep" painting; Shakespeare's Ophelia and Tennyson's Lady of Shalott and Elaine were among the most popular subjects for the visual arts, as were anonymous dead women. These paintings were an extension of the drowned women paintings and sculptures described by Joy Kasson and Olive Anderson and, as Dijkstra maintains, exhibited "the erotic ambiguity of the Victorian ideal of passive womanhood—the dead woman—indicating how easily a painterly homage to feminine self-sacrifice could shift toward a

Lucy Hartmann, Albine *(ca. 1899). (From* Idols of Perversity: Fantasies of Feminine Evil in Fin-de-Siècle Culture, *by Bram Dijkstra [New York: Oxford University Press, 1986], 59)*

necrophiliac preoccupation with the erotic potential of woman when in a state of virtually guaranteed passivity" (58).

Many of these paintings, especially those depicting Albine (the heroine who dies at the end of Emile Zola's *The Sin of Father Mouret* [1875]), surround the dead woman with flowers; the dead woman is "nature's flower" who will "die like a flower among the flowers" (Dijkstra, *Idols of Perversity*, 58).[25] Lily, as her name indicates, is also a flower, and like the women in Romaine Brooks's *Le Trajet* or *Dead Woman* (ca. 1911), Hermann Moest's *The Fate of Beauty* (1898), Paul-Albert Besnard's *The Dead Woman* (1880s), John Collier's *The Death of Albine* (ca. 1895), Lucy Hartmann's *Albine* (ca. 1899), Frances MacDonald's *The Sleeping Princess* (1897), Madeline Lemaire's *Sleep* (1890), and Sarah Bernhardt's self-portrait, *Sarah in Her Coffin* (ca. 1870s), Lily, too, becomes a dead but aesthetic object for a male viewer. It is only at her death, when she has literally embodied one of these paintings—her body aesthetically arranged on the bed, in stark contrast with her dingy surroundings—that Selden, like the Victorian male Dijkstra describes, is able to love her.

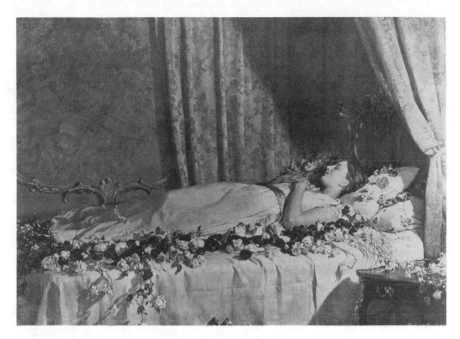

John Collier, The Death of Albine *(ca. 1895).*
(Courtesy of the Royal Academy of Arts)

It seems remarkable that many of these paintings, like *The House of Mirth,* were created by women artists. Even on the stage, the undisputed queen of the theater, Sarah Bernhardt, specialized in death and madness scenes; her *La Dame aux camélias* set the worldwide standard for beauty and grace. Dijkstra argues that these women artists participated in and refined a male-defined genre. But if we examine their works in the context of the stresses involved in being a woman artist, these works appear not so much to conform to the male-defined genre as to turn that genre to their own psychic needs. If these women produced artistic objects to satisfy the demands of patriarchal disciplinary power, then those productions could take their places in that power structure; the women would therefore not have to turn themselves into artistic objects. "Killing the invalid," then, could become an activity quite similar to the one described by Virginia Woolf as "killing the angel in the house": an act of violence necessary to free the female artist from a dangerous and debilitating system of power ("Professions for Women," in *Collected Essays,* 285–86). That dead invalid would then shield the woman artist from having to embody cultural norms.

Romaine Brooks, Le Trajet *(or* Dead Woman*) (ca. 1911).*
(Courtesy of the Smithsonian Institution, National Museum
of American Art)

Elaine Showalter argues in "The Death of the Lady (Novelist)" that this kind of exorcism of the "Perfect Lady" in *The House of Mirth* allowed Edith Wharton to become a novelist:

> In choosing to have Lily die, Wharton was judging and rejecting the infantile aspects of her own self, the part that lacked confidence as a working writer, that longed for the escapism of the lady's world and feared the sexual consequences of creating rather than becoming art. . . . If Lily Bart, unable to change, gives way to the presence of a new generation of women, Edith Wharton survives the crisis of maturation at the turn of the century and becomes one of our American precursors of a literary history of female mastery and growth. (146–47)

Lily's death thus serves two purposes: it shows the horror of the body's objectification, the dangers for women of the self-discipline of body-art, and it also provides Wharton with the same kind of surrogate ill woman that Gilman found in "The Yellow Wallpaper." For in creating ill flesh in words, Wharton was able to will herself not to create illness in herself.

Like Wharton, Charlotte Perkins Gilman managed to cure herself through her representation, her "story" of a breakdown. Just as *The*

Sarah Bernhardt, Sarah in Her Coffin, *self-portrait (ca. 1870s). (From Mem-ories of My Life, by Sarah Bernhardt [New York: Benjamin Blom, 1968])*

House of Mirth is a narrative of the world Edith Wharton had experienced when she was younger, so, too, is "The Yellow Wallpaper" a representation of much of what Gilman herself experienced. But while the woman in her story does not benefit from her writing, Gilman's writing proved to be restorative. In writing out an alternative narrative, in writing a breakdown rather than continuing to have one, Gilman not only made the patriarchal disciplinary system and woman's place in it visible, but she found that the writing could *take her place*. In creating a narrative of her hysterical condition, she no longer had to embody illness directly but could represent it in her text. Her story and her subsequent writings were published and allowed her a revision of her metaphorical place. She became a social worker, feminist crusader, and *writer*—a visible subject in the outer world, with new concrete possibilities open to her.

The "writing cure" as it can be seen in Gilman's and Wharton's work is not identical to turn-of-the-century mind cure or New Thought. Neither woman could "let go" and "surrender" her individual will to the "All-Supply," as most curists advocated.[26] But in another sense, their writing does conform to the strain of New Thought and mind cure that developed in tandem with economic individualism. Success authors like Orison Swett Marden linked health, wealth, and character; health and wealth were signs of moral strength, sickness and poverty of moral failure (see Gail Parker, *Mind Cure in New England*, 25). Writing became for Gilman and Wharton a self-reliant, active, and determined attempt to defeat the will to illness; they regarded illness as weakness and a moral failure (as Wharton's attitude toward her husband's illness reveals and as we will explore at length in chapter 5), to which neither writer would succumb.

Happy Endings

While *The House of Mirth* and "The Yellow Wallpaper" may have proven curative for their writers, they have nonetheless left an interesting dilemma for the feminist critic. These two fictions surely must be among the unhappiest of the fictions of feminine defeat in American literature. In both, the women's repeated mistakes and bad judgments, or at least their acquiescence in others' bad judgments, becomes, to the modern feminist reader, almost embarrassing. In both, the lack of viable alternatives is frustrating.

As a result of our desire to read past this defeat, contemporary feminist critics often attempt to "recover" a happy version of these unhappy endings. We either rewrite the endings—Lily's suicide becomes a release into freedom from social strictures, or the narrator's madness at the end of "The Yellow Wallpaper" becomes a burst into female creativity—or we turn, as I have done, to biography to deal with these two works. Rewriting the endings, it seems to me, is to argue that women's only option is to be completely outside the system, that our only escape is madness and death. This seems both false to our own experience and to refuse the genuine social criticism in the novel; to rewrite these endings as somehow "happy" is to deny that the society should be changed.

Biography, then, remains the only way to create happy endings for these two fictions. No one discusses "The Yellow Wallpaper" without mentioning Gilman's own triumph over Mitchell's rest cure; very few feminist readers look at *The House of Mirth* without some mention of Wharton's emergence as an important writer. And yet these fictions became central in the "feminist canon" long before others that feature victorious feminine characters. Nineteenth-century novels that feature women who not only avoid the invalid stereotype but become physicians have only come back into print in the last few years; New American Library brought out an edition of Sarah Orne Jewett's *Country Doctor* in 1986, and Elizabeth Stuart Phelps's *Doctor Zay* was reprinted by the Feminist Press in 1987. *Christine*—an openly feminist novel with a triumphant heroine—is not only out of print but still very difficult to find.[27] "The Yellow Wallpaper," on the other hand, was one of the very first volumes published by the Feminist Press in 1973, and Wharton's *The House of Mirth*, of course, has never gone out of print. It is important to our understanding of both the "writing cure" and feminist criticism to evaluate why this has come about.[28]

One important factor in understanding this phenomenon lies in the relation of these texts to women's writing, which, as Helen Papashvily (and others) would have it, is typified by happy endings (the title of her book on the subject is *All the Happy Endings*). "The Yellow Wallpaper" and *The House of Mirth* both belong much more clearly to the mainstream, canonical tradition in American literature—in style, form, and substance—than they do to domestic (or women's) fiction. In other words, they were read by feminist critics at least in part because they were not seen as "feminine" texts. They could be read in the same way and on the same critical ground as "masculine" fiction; they were texts of which feminist critics could be proud because they resisted the "sentimentality" of the happy ending.[29] Gilman and Wharton did in fact, to an extent, reject or revise the basic tenets of domestic fiction. Gilman explicitly rejected the notion that motherhood and managing a household offered women a path to power; like many twentieth-century feminists, she saw the home as a prison for women (as the imagery in "The Yellow Wallpaper" so clearly suggests). Despite her rejection of much of their ideology, Gilman nevertheless has affinities with the previous generation of women writers. Like them, she centers her fiction on female characters, and like them, her work is deeply distrustful of men while it focuses on a community of women. "The Yellow Wallpaper" is atypical of much of her work because it concentrates so exclusively on one woman, but it does so only to reveal how dangerous the lack of "society and stimulus" can be. In Wharton's case, the situation is reversed: she has affinities with domestic ideology—as Elaine Showalter has argued, the warm kitchen scene at Nettie Struther's is symbolic of the feminine community and warmth that Lily has missed and that might have saved her—but she attempts to break with the previous generation of women writers when it comes to structure, style, and narrative outcome. At every point, *The House of Mirth* seems like a novel determined to rebut nineteenth-century women's fictions in which the heroine ends up happy after long years of suffering.[30] In *The House of Mirth*, mistakes only lead to further mistakes, suffering to more suffering.

In contrast to the traditional plot of women's fiction, neither "The Yellow Wallpaper" nor *The House of Mirth* offers the reader the satisfaction of the heroine's triumph over adverse circumstances. Gilman and Wharton are, in fact, relentless about creating fictional worlds in which their heroines have very few options; the narrator of "The Yellow Wallpaper" could, of course, have rebelled against John, but she would only have been "sent to Weir Mitchell" later. Lily could have saved herself by sacrificing Bertha Dorset, or by blackmailing her, but would then have only become a part of the corrupt society Wharton condemns. Both writers therefore reject domestic ideology precisely at the point of suggesting that a happy ending is possible within the structure of existing society. For Gilman, it is the "happy ending" of domestic fiction—wife- and motherhood—that causes the problem in the first place. Wharton's attitude is more complex. In one sense, marriage is the one possibility for Lily's survival and happiness; in another, it is the degradation of husband hunting that is the problem in the first place.[31] Wharton offers the scene of Nettie Struther's happy ending as a foil to Lily's unhappy one but assures the reader that such an ending is impossible for Lily within the world of New York high society. Gilman and Wharton use their heroines as proof that women's lives needed to be changed, that it was the social structure that was really sick.

In both fictions, the woman's defeat is closely linked to her social class. Just as the options that are open to Nettie Struther, the working-class woman, are closed to Lily Bart, so, too, are the chances for "congenial work" closed to the narrator of "The Yellow Wallpaper," a woman who has a nurse, a housekeeper, and a wealthy husband. Both fictions subscribe to the Social Darwinist/Spencerian concept of the world outlined by Gilman in *Women and Economics* (1899): "When man began to feed and defend woman, she ceased proportionately to feed and defend herself. When he stood between her and her physical environment, she ceased proportionately to feel the influence of that environment and respond to it" (61). Gilman theorizes that women's social problems and their unequal standing in the culture are a result of generations of selective breeding in which woman's only value is "sex-attraction" and of being shut out of productive labor. "To be surrounded by beautiful things has much influence upon the human creature: to make beautiful things has more. . . . What we do modifies us more than what is done to us. The freedom of expression has been more restricted in women than the freedom of impression, if that be possible" (66).

Gilman argues that the only hope for women—and the whole human race—lies in women becoming workers, earning their keep, and becoming producers instead of consumers because "to do and to make not only gives deep pleasure, but is indispensable to healthy growth. . . . To carve in wood, to hammer brass, to do 'art dressmaking,' to raise mushrooms in the cellar . . . is a most healthy state" (157).[32] The hope of the race, she argues, lies with the "increasing army of women wage-earners, who are changing the face of the world by their steady advance toward economic independence" (63). The only women who are fit to face motherhood without fear of the "gates of death," she continues, are the "savage woman, the peasant woman, the working-woman everywhere who is not overworked" who is allowed to "mingle in the natural industries of a human creature" (182).[33]

Wharton, too, was influenced by Social Darwinist thought and the new medical theories of inheritance and environmental influence (as the title of one of her story collections—*The Descent of Man and Other Stories*—attests). Like Gilman's *Women and Economics*, *The House of Mirth* maintains that women who have been bred for leisure are not fit for a life of self-sufficiency. Wharton seems to share Gilman's view that there is little hope for a change in this situation, and both writers idealize the "innate" strength of the working class. Nettie Struther is able to overcome tuberculosis, poverty, and the stigma of single-motherhood to find health, happiness, and a good marriage. Lily suffers much less adversity, yet it proves fatal.[34] Wharton goes to great lengths to show that this failure is not Lily's fault but the fault of her upbringing, the weakness she inherits from both her parents, and the society in which she lives; the result is a Social Darwinist argument of survival of the fittest. Lily (and her entire class) proves as fragile as the flower whose name she bears.

The female protagonists of these fictions do not, however, remain blameless; Social Darwinism is not the only important and popular cultural theory to find its way into Gilman's and Wharton's work. In the age of self-help, mind cure, and New Thought, Lily and the narrator of "The Yellow Wallpaper" must necessarily be examined not just as help-less pawns in a capitalist, patriarchal, evolutionary system but as auton-omous creatures in control of their own destinies.[35] Accusation is im-plicit in Gilman's story of the defeat of the woman writer. When the narrator complains that writing "*does* exhaust me a great deal" (4), one can almost hear Orison Swett Marden condemning the weakness that would give in to a little exhaustion; after all, Gilman herself managed to write despite such adverse circumstances.

Throughout *The House of Mirth* is the dream of a better society, Selden's "republic of the spirit," which sounds remarkably like a New Thought paradise. New Thought philosophy advocated a notion of suc-cess in which virtue triumphs over materialism. Selden, in describing his "republic" to Lily, defines it in terms of "success": " 'My idea of success,' he said, 'is personal freedom.... [Freedom] from everything— from money, from poverty, from ease and anxiety, from all material accidents.... That's what I call success.... It is a country one has to find one's way to one's self' " (68). Selden's vision is comparable to Orison

Swett Marden's: "Happiness today, now, is our duty. . . . How contempt-ible mere money-wealth looks in comparison with a serene life,—with a life which dwells in the ocean of truth, beneath the waves, beyond the reach of the tempests in eternal calm" (*The Young Man Entering Busi-ness* [1903], quoted in Gail Parker, *Mind Cure in New England*, 31). While many modern critics dismiss Selden's "republic of the spirit" as hypocritical or faddist and discredit his vision of a better world,[36] it nevertheless seems to be the sort of world Wharton advocates as a remedy to the diseased New York society that destroys Lily, even if Selden proves a poor citizen of it. The kind of methodical character building urged by New Thought writers is the only remedy possible for Lily's degrading attempt to acquire money through marriage. Only in a world that valued people for what they were, rather than what they appeared to be or owned, could Lily have developed less materialistic desires.[37]

"The Yellow Wallpaper" and *The House of Mirth* both illustrate that it is the culture that is more diseased than the woman or, at least, that it is the diseased culture that causes her illness or death. In each novel, nevertheless, the woman is condemned for lacking the strength or fortitude to overcome society's ills. Had the narrator of "The Yellow Wallpaper" continued to write despite her fatigue, she might have recovered, like Gilman herself; had Lily Bart not given in to the physical ease and pleasure seeking she had been accustomed to, she might have stayed alive or married Selden.

One does not undertake a biographical reading intending to under-mine the fiction, of course. Feminist criticism that focuses on the biogra-phy of Charlotte Perkins Gilman and Edith Wharton (as I and many others have done) provides a "recovery" of the happy ending by re-describing the context in which to read the fiction. Such criticism sets out what Michel Foucault calls an "author-function," that is, a way to classify the text, define it, compare it with some texts, and contrast it to others. It allows us to "reveal" or "characterize" the text's "mode of being" ("What Is an Author?," 147). We can then read "The Yellow Wallpaper" in the context of *Herland*, *Women and Economics*, and Gilman's autobiography to find a feminist parable. And we can read Lily Bart's failure in the context of Wharton's own escape from the strictures of New York's "polite" society and in the context of *Custom of the Country* and *Age of Innocence* to define it as a novel of brilliant social criticism. As Annette Kolodny has pointed out, such criticism allows us to appreciate the individual text because we know "the whole in which it was embedded" ("Reply to Commentaries," 590). We can therefore reexamine the figure of the invalid woman against a different ground. Such criticism allows us to read the narrative of feminine defeat within the context of the woman writer's victory and to derive our satisfaction from the fact that Gilman and Wharton managed to avoid the fates that they so eloquently described. But before I close on this happy note, I want to examine the impulse—the ideology—that drives this kind of criticism: why do we continue to read and praise novels of feminine defeat only to reinscribe them in biographical stories with happy endings?

Other feminist critics have tried to answer this question, but so far, none have really resolved the conflict between feminist ideology and masculine aesthetics. One answer to this question is suggested by Myra Jehlen in one of the more interesting feminist works on narrative endings, "Archimedes and the Paradox of Feminist Criticism." Jehlen suggests that the "feminine success story" of domestic fiction may be good ideology but remains bad writing; she suggests that the successful female character makes for neither good fiction nor, she implies, a good subject for feminist criticism. In contrast, she suggests that the novel of feminine defeat (best exemplified by Samuel Richardson's *Clarissa*), while worse ideologically (from a feminist standpoint), is more interesting as fiction.

When the conflict Jehlen foregrounds—that between aesthetics and ideological judgments—is taken up in traditional literary criticism, it becomes an unproblematic denial of feminist ideology's literary value. In *Beneath the American Renaissance*, the only criticism to deal at any length with Bullard's *Christine*, David Reynolds argues that *Christine* manages to be a wonderful novel despite its focus on a mid-nineteenth-century feminist spokeswoman. He claims:

> The real success of *Christine* . . . lies not in its advocacy of women's rights or its portrayal of women's wrongs but in its power as a compelling, taut novel written by a progressive American woman. . . . Here we come upon a central paradox of American women's fiction, indeed of women's literature in general: that is, it most often succeeds artistically when it leaves behind feminist politics. In this sense, it becomes women's *literature* when it refuses to be women's *propaganda*

and asserts its power as an expression of universal themes. (394, emphasis in original)

It is doubtful that Jehlen would agree with Reynolds in his assessment of the "artistic success" of women's literature or in his assertion that great literature discusses "universal themes," thus flattening all questions of gender. But she does conclude that feminist criticism, if it is to find a way to reconcile ideological analysis and artistic analysis, must find a way to deal with this paradox. She suggests that we resolve this paradox through a reevaluation of the epistemology that upholds our aesthetic judgments.

Gilbert and Gubar suggest a different possibility for resolution; in their response to Frank Lentricchia's attack on their work, "The Man on the Dump versus the United Dames of America," they claim that they have "long believed that it is necessary to disentangle political ideology from aesthetic evaluation" (389). Despite a fundamental disagreement on most issues, then, Jehlen and Gilbert and Gubar agree that it is somehow possible to separate ideological and aesthetic judgments. But such a separation is impossible, as the "happy endings" of the critical evaluations of "The Yellow Wallpaper" and *The House of Mirth* show.

Feminist critics who read stories of feminine defeat but embed them in the "whole" that includes the woman writer's dramatic victory over illness and society's strictures are, it seems to me, trying to find a way to sidestep the contradiction in their ideological and aesthetic evaluations. This paradox is configured by traditional (male) standards of literary value on one side (what counts as "good fiction") and by New Thought standards of success on the other (what counts as a "happy ending" for the authors). It is an attempt to find a feminist-ideological justification for an aesthetic evaluation based on traditional literary critical standards, without recognizing that it is a capitalist, patriarchal ideology of self-discipline that informs that "feminist" evaluation in the first place. I do not mean to suggest that the "endings" would have been happier for Wharton and Gilman had they, like their heroines, succumbed to the forces of their society, but we should recognize that the move on the part of feminist critics to "recover" happy endings for these fictions does exactly what the fictions themselves argue against: it provides an individual solution to the problem of societal "dis-ease" without fundamentally challenging the structure or ideology of that society. Like most feminist fictions, "The Yellow Wallpaper" and *The House of Mirth* explicitly challenge societal norms and the power of the individual to overcome them. To then celebrate the individual writer's triumph over those norms is to disavow the social criticism in the fiction. The same feminist critics who value fiction like Wharton's and Gilman's because it, like masculine realist fiction, resists the "happy ending" of domestic novels nevertheless reenact that happy ending in their criticism by subscribing to a theory of individual power.

It would be nice if I could offer a "happy ending," an easy resolution to this dilemma, at this point. But I find that whatever solution I offer has a new set of problems, creates a new kind of unhappy ending of its own.

If we continue to read these unhappy fictions and resist the impulse to add on our critical happy endings, we create two new problems. First, we are left with only a negative feminism, an argument about what the world should not be like, not an argument for what changes we might make. But it also leaves the aesthetic of defeated women in place; the sense that only dead or mad women are beautiful remains unquestioned. If we are to find any way to reconcile ideology and aesthetics, we cannot continue to read merely the same texts.

Of course, we could also revise our aesthetic evaluations entirely and recuperate the lost sentimental tradition; we can urge publishers to bring back into print the sentimental texts we have lost. This is, of course, a project already underway with Rutgers University Press's American Women Writers Series, with the Feminist Press, and with New American Library's Plume Women Writers Series, among others. The problem with this—aside from the need to completely reeducate our aesthetic sensibilities—is that what counts as a "happy ending" for many sentimental fictions—the woman's eventual marriage and her coming into wealth—is not really what we would advocate today as a happy ending. For better or for worse, New Thought philosophy is deeply embedded in the American success ethic today, perhaps especially among feminist scholars who had to will their way through graduate school and into the profession. If one listens to contemporary conversations with an ear for New Thought phrasing, one hears the same self-reliance, determination, willpower, and "stick-to-itiveness" that Gilman urged in the pages of *Success*. Nineteenth-century sentimental fiction advocates a completely different ethic of "success" and has a different notion of what counts as a happy ending. As professional women, feminist critics may be uncomfortable with the wholesale move into a sentimental canon that holds marriage out as the only "happy ending."

We could therefore turn to "New Woman" fictions, where heroines manage to defy social convention, become successful professionals, and sometimes even couple that professional success with romantic success. These novels—like *Dr. Zay, Country Doctor,* and *Christine*—give us an individual who fundamentally changes society: a woman whose success is predicated on a change in the world and who uses her success to help other women. This "solution," though, continues to uphold individualistic, New Thought, capitalist notions of success, at least to a certain extent, while simultaneously forcing us to reevaluate aesthetic judgments. It would not be an easy or trouble-free solution.

Perhaps the best solution is to try to do some of all of the things suggested here: read unhappy endings as social criticism, and read the different kinds of happy endings with a critical eye. We can also search for texts that resist the dichotomy happy/unhappy at all; texts like Zora Neale Hurston's *Their Eyes Were Watching God* can be categorized as neither happy nor unhappy. But we need to foreground the relation between ideology and aesthetics as well as the questions of the uses of aesthetics and of whether one ever "escapes" ideology. We should, I think, work to keep Jehlen's paradox problematized.

Chapter 5

Fighting (with) Illness: Success and the Invalid Woman

"You ain't got no right Melanctha Herbert," flashed out Jeff through his dark, frowning anger, "you certainly ain't got no right always to be using your being hurt and being sick, and having pain, like a weapon, so as to make me do things it ain't never right for me to be doing for you. You certainly ain't got no right to be always holding out your pain to show me."

—Gertrude Stein,
Three Lives *(1909)*

"I am cherishing a host of feminine virtues," replied Yorke, stretching his big dimensions in the little carriage. "I shall make a rather superior woman by the time I get well."

—Elizabeth Stuart Phelps,
Doctor Zay *(1882)*

In Harriet Beecher Stowe's 1871 novel, *Pink and White Tyranny,* the virtuous sister-in-law of the domineering, silly wife who gives the novel its name complains that "a woman, armed with sick headaches, nervousness, debility, presentiments, fears, horrors, and all sorts of imaginary and real diseases, has an eternal armory of weapons of subjugation" (117). As we saw in the previous chapter, the same sentiment would be echoed by Freud more than twenty years later (in the "Dora" case), when he noted that some diseases are the "result of intention" that can be used as weapons (*Complete Psychological Works*, 7:45). The notion that illness could be a weapon—a particularly feminine weapon—was intensified by the ideology of "success" and the New Thought philosophies at the turn of the century, which identified illness as a matter of will; illness, if willful, becomes something one uses to achieve an end. It also comes to represent either weakness, sin, or a resistance to good. This chapter examines the figure of illness as a particularly feminine weapon—a weapon wielded by the sick woman herself or a weapon of divine retribution aimed at her because of her sins. As we saw in chapter 1, the attitude toward illness as either willful or retributive existed in the 1840s; Marie St. Clare typifies the intentional invalid, while Juliette Summers stands as an example of how illness can reinforce moral law. But Edith Wharton's and Ellen Glasgow's uses of this figure are adapted to American culture in the early twentieth century.

Wharton's *Ethan Frome* (1911) and Glasgow's *Barren Ground* (1925) are relentlessly unhappy fictions. Even though *Barren Ground* could best be described as a female success story, Dorinda Oakley's success is accomplished with no joy and little satisfaction and is overshadowed by sickness and death; she finds "peace" and "success" but not love or even human community. In *Ethan Frome*, no one escapes failure, illness, bitterness, and loneliness. In these two novels, invalidism takes on a number of new figures. Zeena Frome and Mattie Silver make invalidism intensely unattractive; Eudora Oakley and Rose Emily Pedlar stand as representatives of an irritating invalidism that, in its self-sacrifice and self-abnegation, seems more pathetic than tragic, more stupid than noble. Rather than offering an occasion for pity or romance, illness in these two novels appears as a weapon of feminine or "divine" retribution. Zeena uses her illness as a weapon against Ethan and Mattie, while they in turn seem to be punished with illness for their infidelity. Likewise, Jason Greylock's wife is punished with madness for stealing Dorinda's lover. These novels also provide examples of men who are punished with illness; here, illness is no longer a strictly female preserve. Ethan Frome is crippled for life by indecision, weakness, or an inability to escape the traps of a bad marriage and "too many winters in Starkfield." Jason Greylock suffers a twenty-year decline because he is too weak to resist his father, the brothers of the fiancée he does not love, or the "broomsedge" that overtakes everything sitting uncultivated in rural Virginia. Finally, illness in these novels is no longer a sign of wealth and leisure, as it had been in so many nineteenth-century fictions. In the early twentieth century, illness moved from drawing rooms and "ancestral estates" to poverty-stricken farms.

Whereas illness once signified excess, "spending" too much energy, and therefore was a sign of wealth, in *Ethan Frome* and *Barren Ground* it signifies want, having too little energy or spirit, and therefore becomes a sign of poverty. As I have shown in previous chapters, for nineteenth-century women, illness represented feminine refinement, wealth, and leisure; it was a condition to which women aspired. But in these novels, women's illnesses are the result of overwork, isolation, or wrongdoing; sickness is represented as an undesirable state, if not a punishment. In the nineteenth century, health was associated with the country and nature, illness with the city and industrialization. In these two twentieth-century texts, country life and nature are opposed to human health, while the city and scientific modernization offer the only means to a rewarding and productive life. Wharton and Glasgow set out a fundamental re-presentation of illness as far as class and geography are concerned, if not (as we will see) as far as gender is concerned, even though the men in these novels are an unhealthy lot.

Why does female invalidism, which had been a mark of bourgeois distinction throughout the nineteenth century, become so unattractive in Wharton's and Glasgow's novels of rural poverty? Even in texts like "The Yellow Wallpaper" and *The House of Mirth*, which challenge many cultural representations of sickness, illness remains the province of the upper middle class and, at least in Lily's case, the beautiful. Illness is no longer sympathetic but either a well-deserved punishment or a means to an abuse of domestic power. Are these novels, therefore, marks of a changing aesthetic—sickliness no longer appealed—or a changing understanding of sickness? Or is the invalid woman's new unattractiveness a matter of class, suggesting that poor women have no right to be invalids? The answers to these questions are complex and originate from Progressive Era challenges to nineteenth-century gender roles and class distinctions as well as to notions of "success" and "intention." Feminists attacked the nineteenth-century ideology of separate spheres, whether domestic, medical, or bourgeois, at the turn of the century; Progressive Era reforms, advances in medical practice, and World War I changed the tone and nature of that attack but intensified it nonetheless. These two texts, through their representations of invalidism, reveal some of the stakes and results of that battle.

In these new representations of illness, Wharton and Glasgow do not "kill the invalid woman." Instead, they punish weak or bad women and men with invalidism. This chapter examines the changing figure of the invalid by contrasting women who in some measure recover from illness—Zeena Frome and Dorinda Oakley—with the men who succumb to it—Ethan Frome and Jason Greylock. I will examine these figures in the context of the political, domestic, and social upheavals of the 1910s and 1920s and the Progressive Era models of success.

Success, Class, and Health

Wharton's and Glasgow's changed representations of illness are not exceptions for their times. The cultural figure of female invalidism generally underwent radical alteration in the early decades of the twentieth century. The image of invalidism changed from delicacy, spirituality, and femininity to carelessness, laziness, and poverty. Changes in women's place, in health care, and in public attitudes toward sickness all contributed to this changed representation, as did the new cultural discourse of advertising. While the woman of the nineteenth century would have accepted illness as her lot in life—and may even have aspired to it—the twentieth-century woman would come to see it as something that not only should be avoided but, with the right products and attention to her health, could be. She came to believe that only those who could not afford health, or who did not care, had to be sick.

Women's lives and health changed a great deal during the first two decades of the twentieth century. On 26 August 1920 women's suffrage became law; the second generation of New Women—those educated by the pioneering women who had established their own colleges and universities—had won the seventy-year battle for the vote and believed that real equality was just around the corner. These women, unlike their nineteenth-century predecessors, wore comfortable clothing and, thanks in part to the physical fitness for girls movement, took active part in sports. Health reforms urged by women's groups since the 1880s became standard practice in many hospitals and clinics. Women were increasingly audacious and independent. During World War I, many women took jobs outside the home, doing work previously thought impossible for women; their lives would never be the same. In 1920, 23 percent of all women worked outside the home, many as professionals (the number of professional women increased 226 percent from 1890 to 1920 [Glenda Riley, *Inventing the American Woman*, 50]). By the 1920s, the "flapper"—the woman who wore short skirts, lived on her own, had a job, probably used birth control, drank, and smoked—was accepted as the modern woman (Lois Banner claims that this acceptance came as early as 1913 [*American Beauty*, 176]). She had "come a long way" from the corseted, sickly homebody of the latter nineteenth century. As Barbara Ehrenreich and Deirdre English put it, "Everyone wanted to be 'on the go,' 'in the swim,' and even the most privileged women were not about to sit out the American Century with a sick headache" (*For Her Own Good*, 128). Of course, the picture was not so rosy for all women; many still worked in menial positions, were underpaid, underclothed, underhoused. In the days before New Deal legislation, the rift between the rich and the poor grew ever greater. Public optimism nevertheless flourished despite widespread hunger, despicable working conditions, and inadequate housing, a phenomenon that was repeated in the 1980s.

Medical practice also underwent enormous changes during the first two decades of the twentieth century. These changes were so widespread and so drastic that popular mythology had a hard time keeping up. After late nineteenth-century discoveries of bacteria, the closed energy medical model gave way to an "invasion" model that was consistent with germ theory. This gave rise to a whole new discourse on the threats to people's health and a whole new image of illness. Advances in public health and hygiene, cleaner drinking water, sanitized milk, better sewage treatment, for example, began to control many kinds of infectious diseases. American life expectancy increased five years during the first two decades of the twentieth century (Peter Conn, *The Divided Mind*, 7). These important advances ushered in a new "golden age" of medicine and significantly increased the authority of the medical profession. But the mysterious microscopic creatures that could invade one's body unseen opened the way for many misunderstandings, myths, and vague, ill-defined dangers.

These dangers were often associated (not entirely without cause) with the poor and the unclean. In the Progressive celebration of American prosperity, power, and success, there was often little sympathy for poverty, weakness, and failure. One would expect the discovery of bacteria to have reformed public conceptions of illness; understanding that microorganisms caused illness should have altered notions of illness as individually idiosyncratic or class affiliated and should have changed popular notions (fostered by New Thought) of illness as willful or sinful. Ironically, "germ theory" (the idea that bacteria cause disease) merely provided a "scientific" basis for much of this ideology. An imperfect understanding of the relation between disease and public hygiene led to an equation of "germs" with "dirt." The pitiful living conditions of the poor were newly understood then, in part accurately, as sinks of disease. Guided by a Social Darwinist understanding of genetics or a New Thought understanding of will, many people became convinced that the poor lived in filth amid disease because they either could do no better or wanted to do no better. Disease and poverty were inextricably linked in the public mind, as were success and health.

Sensational journalists frequently wrote about the horrible and un-healthful living conditions of the poor, as did a whole new generation of novelists. The concern about germs in overcrowded urban slums and about the detrimental effects of poor living conditions led naturalist writers like Theodore Dreiser, Frank Norris, and Stephen Crane to try to expose the forces that kept poor people impoverished and sickly. In "Progressive" America, hygiene and health care in the slums and for the rural poor were indeed abysmal.[1] "The poor lived and died in misery. They skimped on food. . . . Their children suffered from rickets. In general, health, like income, differed along class and racial lines. The life expectancy of a black man was ten years less than that of a white man, a result of inadequate health care and a greater incidence of malnutrition and disease" (John Chambers, *The Tyranny of Change*, 80).

Journalists, novelists, and sociologists writing about these conditions intended to point out the need for reform. The effect, however, was often quite different. Understanding of the new science of bacteriology was imperfect, even among medical professionals. Among the laity, it was still a complete mystery.[2] Therefore, in spite of the journalists' good intentions, the effects of such stories often led not to pity for the poor but to loathing. Guided by a rudimentary understanding of Darwinism, many took the poor health of the poverty-stricken as a sign of their "unfitness." As Robert Bannister illustrates in *Social Darwinism: Science and Myth in Anglo-American Thought*, this response often led to a sense of inevitability, but it sometimes took the more virulent form of eugenics.[3] At the very least, Social Darwinist thought in America fostered the notion that the poor were poor because they were sickly and weak. Popular images of illness remained resolutely the result not of germs but of weakness of will or heredity. Even in the writings of such well-read women as Edith Wharton and Ellen Glasgow, illness is rarely the result of a tangible (or curable) disease but the result of weakness of will, character, or inheritance.[4]

In the early decades of the twentieth century, the quest for health that began at the turn of the century became a national obsession. Public understanding inflated the degree of medical advances; people became convinced that soon all disease and discomfort would be ended. Americans began to actively pursue health with the same drive and fervor they pursued wealth. Jackson Lears argues that between 1880 and 1930, Americans, with the encouragement of new mass media advertising, developed a "therapeutic worldview." The late nineteenth-century medical model based on scarcity of energy (the closed energy model discussed in previous chapters) was replaced in the early twentieth century by a model of abundance; New Thought practitioners argued not that one needed to save energy (as had Weir Mitchell and his fellow practitioners) but that the more energy one spent, the more one would have. These medical models paralleled concurrent economic ones. As consumer culture developed, Americans were encouraged to spend money rather than save it, to believe that spending was the quickest route to further prosperity; they became convinced that the same was true of their health. "Saved" energy was squandered energy, but "spent" energy would bring happiness and would release still more energy. "Mind-curists were brothers under the skin to a new breed of corporate liberal idealogues—social engineers who spoke of economic rather than psychic abundance but who shared the interest of mind-curists in liberating repressed impulses" (Lears, *No Place of Grace*, 54). Advertisers of "cures"—from electric massagers to soaps, patent medicines, and toothpaste—told Americans that they could buy their way to health (Edgar Jones, *Those Were the Good Old Days*). In the early part of this century, good health became the consumer product it remains today.

If anyone could buy his or her way to health, then illness was surely a sign that he or she could not afford to do so. Success manuals and fiction throughout the Progressive Era equated the successful man with the healthy one; Teddy Roosevelt's sporting life signified not only success but manliness. Illness became a sign not just of weakness, then, but of "unmanliness." Sickness was a sign of bad management or malfeasance. The emphasis on "self-control" as a path to health, advocated in the nineteenth century by John Harvey Kellogg (of cornflake fame), became a call to "let go" by the 1910s, but the principle was the same: everyone had "reserves" of energy, and bad psychic management of this "principle" would lead to poor health.

With this reassessment of illness came a change in the public iconography of illness; artists and writers no longer offered the beautiful, romantic invalid as the image of feminine beauty. Tuberculosis lost much of its exotic appeal when it was proven to be the result of a bacillus, not an artistic or spiritual temperament. Sickness became less often an occasion for romance than for pity or scorn. This reassessment did not occur all at once or evenly; in some Victorian fiction—notably, in Charles Dickens's work and in some women's fiction (*Jane Eyre*, for example)—illness is linked quite clearly to poverty. And as late as Thomas Mann's *Magic Mountain* (1924) or Eugene O'Neill's *Long Day's Journey into Night* (published posthumously in 1956), tuberculosis could still be the romantic product of an artistic temperament and a rich spirituality. It is impossible, therefore, to pinpoint a moment when the public image of illness gives up its romance or takes on its association with poverty. As we shall see in the next chapter, Henry James (in 1902) and F. Scott Fitzgerald (in 1934) continue the tradition of considering illness an occasion for romance. But the romantic invalid could not occupy quite the same high cultural position after the discovery of something so unromantic as "germs." (James leaves Milly Theale's illness unspecified, and Fitzgerald relies on the twentieth century's remaining "unexplained" illness—mental illness—to sustain the romanticism of their heroines.)

These new representations of illness were undoubtedly to women's advantage; they no longer had to avoid exercise, wear uncomfortable clothing, or cultivate ill health in order to be fashionable. In the 1910s and 1920s, it grew distinctly less fashionable to be ill. At the turn of the century, magazine artist Charles Dana Gibson's "Gibson girls," who were healthful, athletic, and beautiful, became popular. As Lois Banner illustrates in *American Beauty*, increasingly from the 1890s through the 1910s, health became associated with beauty; "During the Progressive era the natural woman of feminists and health reformers seemingly carried the day" (203).[5] Athletic, energetic women appeared more frequently in popular iconography during the Progressive Era (for examples, see Martha Banta's *Imaging American Women*).

This "progress" was bought at a cost, though. If illness is understood

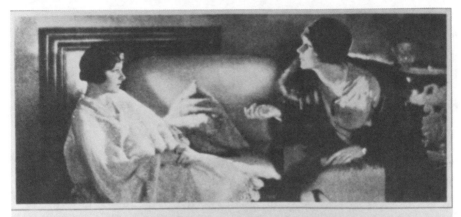

"Why *in the* world do you continue *to* empty *the* filthy contents *of* a cleaner bag

. . . *When Modern Sanitary Methods Are Available in the Air-Way Sanitary System?"*

Grace—"Oh, I'm so sorry you're ill, Anne. I was over to Mother's and she told me about you, so I rushed right over."

Anne—"I'm certainly glad you came. I've been upstairs in bed since last Thursday, but the Doctor said I could come down on the davenport today. It's not so lonesome and I'm feeling better already. I'll be all right in a day or two."

Grace—"I hope so. Where did you get that awful cold?"

Anne—"I don't know unless it was the other day when I was cleaning. I ran the vacuum cleaner around and then went right outdoors to empty the bag. I was warm and didn't think about a wrap. The bag was pretty full and I had to shake it and then turn it inside out and brush it. I stayed out in the cold longer than I had intended. That night I began to cough and here I am."

Grace—"That's probably just where you caught cold. Why in the world do you continue to empty the filthy contents of a cleaner bag anyway? Running out into the cold to shake out the bag! You ought to be scolded. You're so up-to-date with everything. I am amazed that you have not bought an Air-Way Sanitary System.

With Air-Way you never have to empty a bag."

Anne—"Never have to empty a bag? Where does the dirt go?"

Grace—"It's collected and sealed in a Sanitary Dust Container. When the container is filled, just detach it and either burn it or throw it away. Then put in a fresh dust container. I'll use about a dollar's worth of dust containers in a year. It's a dollar invested in my health. No dust blows back on my person or clothing. Really this is the only sanitary way to dispose of the collected dirt that I have ever seen."

Anne—"It sounds wonderful. Just think of not having to shake out that dirt."

Grace—"It is wonderful. You know I had a heavy old cleaner, but I gave it to my laundress when I saw how much easier and better the Air-Way would do my work. It's so light that it's really a pleasure to use. It polishes my hardwood floors, cleans my radiators, mouldings, lampshades, overstuffed furniture—in fact, everything that doesn't have to be washed. And you ought to see how much brighter my rugs look."

Anne—"Did you say it polished floors?"

Grace—"It certainly does. My floors never looked as well. Then there's something else, the Insector. You know how I always dreaded moths. Well, now I use the Air-Way Insector regularly and spray everything with Air-Way Moth Control. It's a dry chemical, not one of those liquid insecticides."

Anne—"I need some of that Moth Control."

Grace—"This Moth Control comes out of the System in a spray of tiny crystals which dissolves into a powerful penetrating gas that seeps into cracks and crevices. It isn't just a surface treatment. It goes very much deeper. I never saw anything like it. I use it regularly, just as directed."

Anne—"Well, I certainly must buy an Air-Way. No more bag shaking for me. Where can I get one?"

Grace—"Look in your phone book under the "A's" for Air-Way Branch. It's always listed that way. They'll send a man out to show you one right here in your home. And you'll certainly be amazed at what it will do. You'll thank me for advising you to get one."

Air-Way
SANITARY SYSTEM
It has raised the standard of sanitation in the home

Illness is the result of the failure to buy the right product in this advertisement from 1929; Anne has caught a cold from the germs in the bag of her vacuum cleaner. (From Edsels, Luckies, and Frigidaires: Advertising the American Way, *by Robert Atwan, Donald McQuade, and John Wright [New York: Dell Publishing Company, 1979], 22)*

as avoidable—something one can buy or will one's way out of—then the person who becomes ill is necessarily lax. The adoration of the pale, fragile maiden reclining on a couch was on the wane. Such figures more often appeared in advertisements for patent medicines, examples of a state that the vigilant woman could avoid. Illness in the Progressive Era became a blameworthy condition.

Advertising in mass circulation magazines simultaneously developed and extended the threat to women's health, emphasizing the woman's personal responsibility for her own and her family's illnesses. Women (and the families they cared for) no longer had to be ill, these ads asserted, if they would only buy the right products. Failure to do so, however, could lead to dire consequences. Ads for products as diverse as mouthwash, toothpaste, incinerators, and vacuum cleaners all assured women that failure to buy their products would threaten their families with "germs" (Edgar Jones, *Those Were the Good Old Days*).

One ad for Scott Tissue illustrates how far advertisers took this threat. As the camera looks up at a surgeon and a nurse obviously at work, the caption warns the unwary housewife that "the trouble began with harsh toilet tissue." Describing the products as "famous health products," which are approved by "Doctors, Hospitals, Health Authorities," the advertiser warns that "surgical treatment for rectal trouble" is the result of using the wrong tissue. Women could prevent this scenario, if they would only buy the right product.

These threats to health became another avenue for controlling women's ever-increasing demands for professional opportunity. One ad, in an attempt to assure women that their "jobs" at home were professional enough, referred to the wife and mother as the "G. P. A." (General Purchasing Agent, that is) (see a reproduction of the ad in Roland Marchand, *Advertising the American Dream*, 169). This new role of "purchasing agent," one physician of the time lamented, had caused untold suffering for poor women, because in that role they became aware of all the beautiful things they were missing. In *The Nervous Housewife* (1920), Dr. Abraham Myerson devotes a chapter to "Poverty and its Psychical Results," in which he blames poor women's nervousness on advertisers: "The most successful commercial minds of America are in a conspiracy against the poor Housewife to make her discontented with her lot by increasing her desires; they are on the job day and night and invade every corner of her world; well, they have succeeded" (125).

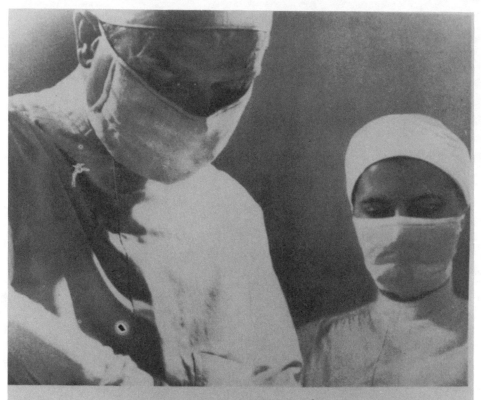

... and the trouble began
with harsh toilet tissue

Doctors, Hospitals, Health Authorities approve **Scott Tissues** for Safety

What is comical to us could well have seemed threatening to women who did not understand the way germs worked; advertisers used that misunderstanding in this advertisement for Scott Tissue from Ladies' Home Journal, *March 1931. It warns against the dangers of "rectal affliction" caused by "impurities" in tissue. (From* Advertising the American Dream: Making Way for Modernity, 1920–40, *by Roland Marchand [Berkeley: University of California Press, 1985], 102)*

Although it is difficult, and perhaps unnecessary, to uncover a "male conspiracy" of industrialists, advertisers, and physicians, such ads worked in conjunction with medical experts' advice and eugenicists' warnings that were aimed at re-creating the "separate spheres" argument on new, "scientific" ground. Jackson Lears agrees: "There is no doubt that many women were victimized in new ways by the leaders of the consumer culture." Advertising was most often directed at women, since they were both the primary readers of mass circulation magazines as well as the primary consumers of products for the family. Ads not only attempted to convince women that material consumption could heal their "dis-ease" with the culture, they also helped to defuse women's political demands into demands for new and better products (Lears, "From Salvation to Self-Realization," 27).

With a variation on the nineteenth-century figure, then, the threat of poor health was once again used to interfere with women's pursuit of personal and political equality. But while the nineteenth-century woman was assured that any variation from the domestic ideal would undoubtedly lead to her own "cancer, insanity and a wasting death" (Carroll Smith-Rosenberg, *Disorderly Conduct*, 23), the twentieth-century woman was assured that it would take all her time and vigilance to guard herself and her family from "germs." Germ theory, Barbara Ehrenreich and Deirdre English argue in *For Her Own Good*, transformed "cleaning from a matter of dilettantish dusting to a sanitary crusade against 'dangerous enemies within'" (143). Women no longer had to stay at home because they were too weak to do anything else but because there was no time to do anything else (128). Housework became a "science" and a war on germs. This change transformed medical separate spheres arguments from vague personal threats to women who pursued extradomestic careers into definite threats of positive dangers to women's families if they did not diligently pursue domestic responsibilities.[6] Women were responsible for their husbands' digestive systems and were at fault if their children did not meet standards of height and weight.

The important difference from the nineteenth-century threat of illness is that in the twentieth century, women were understood to have absolute control over not only their own health but their family's health, too. With the development of the "invasion theory" of illness, women found themselves fighting a constant battle against contagion, vermin, and germs. If these bad forces invaded their houses or bodies, it was

Women's duties extended beyond battling germs to nutrition; they were even held responsible for their husbands' productivity at work in this advertisement for Post's Bran Flakes from Ladies' Home Journal, *July 1931.* This man's constipation is his wife's fault. (From Advertising the American Dream, *by Roland Marchand, 299)*

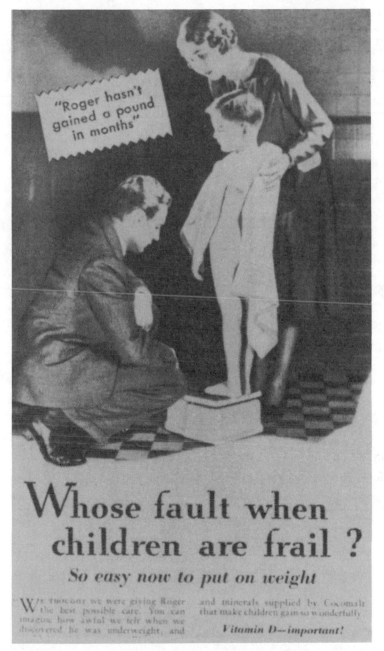

A mother's purchase of the wrong products could threaten her children, as in this advertisement for Cocomalt from Ladies' Home Journal, *January 1928. (From* Advertising the American Dream, *by Roland Marchand, 244)*

because of their lack of vigilance, not nature, as it had been in earlier centuries.[7]

The equation of illness and femininity, established in the nineteenth century, carried on into the twentieth. But the relationship between illness and femininity did not remain the same. Advances in health care, hygiene, dress, and exercise changed how women lived their lives; cultural associations between illness, poverty, and weakness diminished the former social distinction illness had carried. And inflated optimism about new scientific cures meant that illness, even for women, was no longer understood to be even in part *natural* but entirely the result of some fault. What remained, however, was the constant *threat* of illness for women and the assurance that strict modes of behavior could save them.

Neither *Ethan Frome* nor *Barren Ground* describes illnesses attributable to "germs," but both equate poverty, weakness, and failure with illness; both link wealth, strength, and success with health. Glasgow distrusted the therapeutic ethos of the times. Her Scotch-Irish background had taught her fierce self-reliance and to suspect quick fixes. But she was explicitly a Social Darwinist; she claimed to have read *The Origin of Species* often enough to know it by heart and "frequently proposed the relevance of that book to an analysis of her fiction" (Peter Conn, *The Divided Mind*, 171). Like naturalist writers, with whom she has much in common, Glasgow portrays a world in which weakness leads to illness and poverty; only the strong survive and prosper. Wharton, although she was not a Darwinist and was frequently in favor of social reforms, still saw a link between poor health and poverty, as we saw in *The House of Mirth* (see chapter 4). *Ethan Frome* and *Barren Ground* are critical of a crippling, sickening culture, challenging both gender roles and the ideology of the developing consumer culture, but both accede at significant points to those gender roles and to the "therapeutic ethos" of consumerism. The novels question early twentieth-century ideologies, but they also reflect them.

Both *Ethan Frome* and *Barren Ground* contribute to the early twentieth-century ideology that sees a causal relation between ill health and failure, an association that complements the notion of a "writing cure" in tone and substance. In these two novels, men and women who do not "live up to their potential," who do not tap their own "reserves" of energy, who cannot muster enough self-reliance or independence to "hit hard and win" in the battle of life, are "naturally" invalids and are, further, weak or bad people. Reading the "cures" in these novels— Dorinda's stubborn insistence on strength, Zeena's dogged rising to the occasion—and the illnesses—Mrs. Oakley's neurasthenia, Jason's complete collapse, or Mattie's and Ethan's broken bodies and spirits—one recognizes the same ideological motivation that drives New Thought, a "writing cure," and "success" in industry: an individualism that insists on personal responsibility for one's behavior and an ability to change one's world.

In one way, this represents a healthy move for women during the Progressive period; no longer must women succumb to the "natural" imperative to be ill. They can come to believe that their individual efforts will be rewarded and refuse to fulfill the restricted role allowed them in society. On the other hand, it attaches a new stigma to illness because disease becomes a sign of moral and emotional failure, of poverty of the spirit. Failure in these novels is unequivocal. Once someone fails at one thing—work, health, achieving a long-held ambition— they fail at everything. Both novels focus on working unsuccessful farms, on unsuccessful love relationships and marriages, on competition between women and between women and men. Both, therefore, raise questions of what success and "winning" are. In these novels, illness underscores the ugliness of competition; it is a weapon in the battle, the result of the battle, and its final arbiter.

Failing Health

Ethan Frome could be described as the great American failure novel. The ugly, hypochondriacal Zeena Frome is the only character who succeeds at anything, and her victories—keeping her husband, recovering some of her lost health—are hollow ones at best. Ethan, on the other hand, fails at farming, at getting out of Starkfield, at his marriage, at finding a way to run away with Mattie, and, finally, at suicide. And Mattie, whose father was a failure in business, has already failed at bookkeeping, stenography, and shop clerking because the work was too difficult for her, and her health broke (30). We soon find out that she is also a failure at housekeeping; Ethan has to help her with her chores, neglecting his own work. In the age of "Progress," of success stories, and terrific American confidence, Wharton created an American nightmare; instead of freedom, growth, strength, and unlimited capability, she describes imprisonment, weakness, and impotence. Those same nightmarish restrictions formed, as we saw in the previous chapter, the basis of Gilman's story of defeat, "The Yellow Wallpaper." But here, twenty years later, the limitations imposed upon the woman in that story by her physician-husband (as both "cure" for and cause of her illness) are imposed upon an entire family by an unseen hand. The Frome family, from Ethan's parents to his "hired girl," are oppressed by forces as vague as "society" or, as old Harmon Gow would have it, "Starkfield." As in "The Yellow Wallpaper," the result of such oppression is illness. But while "The Yellow Wallpaper" implicitly raises the question of the narrator's responsibility for not resisting her husband (see chapter 3), *Ethan Frome* much more directly examines issues of personal responsibility and of the ability to change one's circumstances. The novel frankly questions whether "Endurance" (the name of Ethan's ancestress, featured in the Frome family graveyard [39]) is a noble quality or a sign of weakness and inability to change.

"Endurance" was a question undoubtedly much on Edith Wharton's mind as she wrote *Ethan Frome*; 1909–11 were years of intense personal upheaval. Her three-year long affair with Morton Fullerton had just ended, and her husband, Teddy, was becoming increasingly difficult; his many illnesses, debts, and infidelities strained his already bad relations with Edith.[8] She was actively considering divorcing him. As R. W. B. Lewis explains, *Ethan Frome* is a quite autobiographical work, in which Wharton casts herself as the much beleaguered Ethan (*Edith Wharton: A Biography*, 308–11). She was far from alone in considering divorce during the early part of the century; during the Progressive period, marriage underwent new and increasing questions about how far commitment could and should go. The divorce rate, which had been one in every twenty-one marriages in 1880, rose to one in twelve by 1900, and one in nine by 1916 (John Chambers, *The Tyranny of Change*, 27, 85). The rising rate of divorce was one result of the shift in cultural values toward self-fulfillment. One speaker at a 1908 symposium on divorce put it this way: "Virtue no longer consists in literal obedience to arbitrary standards set by community or church but rather in conduct consistent with the demands of a growing personality" (quoted in Lears, *No Place of Grace*, 54). In *Ethan Frome*, Wharton illustrates—through Zeena, Ethan, and Mattie—the conflict in American culture between endurance and seeking self-fulfillment, between "obedience to arbitrary standards set by community" and "the demands of a growing personality." Ethan's inability to fully commit himself to either option, Mattie's real lack of options, and Zeena's exploitation of the few options that illness allows her lead to invalidism all around.

In *Ethan Frome* Wharton does not take a consistent or simple stance on either side of the debate between endurance and self-fulfillment, nor does she take a position in the debates over commitment and marriage, the power of self-determination, or the validity of the therapeutic ethos. Throughout the novel, illness is the punishment for making the wrong choice, but there is never a guarantee that the right choice would prove any healthier, nor that it is possible to make the right choice, nor even that there is a right choice. Ethan Frome marries Zeena out of fear of being alone on the farm (35). One can conjecture that he was afraid that being left alone on the farm after his mother's death would cause him to become "queer." After their marriage, however, it is Zeena, rather than Ethan, who has gone "queer" as "women did" (36); within a year of their marriage, she has gone from being an efficient and energetic nurse to being an invalid herself. Ultimately, of course, marriage does not save Ethan either; he eventually finds living with the demanding Zeena as taxing as living alone would have been. And yet Ethan still looks to marriage to save him. His dreams of Mattie Silver are as much dreams of salvation as they are dreams of romance. "Confused motions of rebellion stormed in him. He was too young, too strong, too full of the sap of living to submit so easily to the destruction of his hopes. Must he wear out all his years at the side of a bitter querulous woman? Other possibilities had been in him, possibilities sacrificed, one by one, to Zeena's narrow-mindedness and ignorance. . . . All the healthy instincts of self-defense rose up in him against such waste" (64). Ethan's line of self-defense is, immediately, to remember another man who "had escaped from just such a life of misery by going West with the girl he cared for" (64). So, again, Ethan looks to marriage to save him from a "life of misery."

Throughout *Ethan Frome*, characters look for "quick fixes" to their problems. Zeena relies on her patent medicines, on her new doctor, or on a new hired girl for relief from her ailments, just as Ethan relies on a new marriage for relief from his. On one level, Wharton is critical of this faith in easy cures; Zeena's problems are more profound than those which can be eased by patent medicines, and Ethan's new marriage would create as many problems as it would solve. But on another level, the level on which *Ethan Frome* becomes a novel of social criticism, Wharton subscribes to the same therapeutic ethos she condemns.

Elizabeth Ammons points out in *Edith Wharton's Argument with America* that the social criticism in *Ethan Frome* makes clear that "the American economic system itself" is a prison that lays too much responsibility on men and allows women too few adult freedoms (71). Clearly enough, Wharton illustrates that it is society that has created the Fromes' problems, but running counter to that social criticism is a condemnation of Zeena's (and, to a lesser extent, Ethan's) inability to rise above those constraints. Zeena is too self-concerned to keep up her own house. When Zeena was nursing Ethan's mother, she was the model of efficiency and "seemed to possess by instinct all the household wisdom that his long apprenticeship had not instilled in him" (35), but as a wife, she lets the house deteriorate. In keeping with the warnings of the "domestic science" movement, Zeena does not devote herself to housekeeping and therefore suffers an "invasion" that destroys her husband's health. That it is Mattie who "invades" and not "germs" matters little here because the moral is the same: had Zeena been in her "proper place," doing her "proper work," her household would never have been afflicted with illness.[9]

Such an assessment of blame is at the base of most readings of Zeena as an "unsympathetic character." Even Ammons, who sees her as having been "produced by poverty and isolation and deadening routine" (69), nonetheless calls her "a witch." Zeena is not just a witch, but, Ammons asserts, in this "fairy story" that "ends askew" (67), Zeena is a witch who "wins" (63).[10] Zeena Frome represents an interesting variation in the figure of the invalid woman; she is the invalid produced by the culture who is nonetheless culpable and unsympathetic. Her "triumph" (as Ammons calls it) is at best questionable, as I have already noted, and therefore illustrates the dangers of using illness as a weapon—the only weapon Zeena apparently knows how to use—and the unsavory nature of the competition itself. Zeena's "victory" questions not just the validity of fighting with illness but notions of "success" themselves.

Freud claimed that hysteria, when used as a weapon, was always "leveled at a particular person" (*Complete Psychological Works*, 7:45), an insight that necessitates a complex understanding of psychological weapons.[11] As a weapon, illness is, at best, a double-edged sword: in order to damage another, the ill woman has first to make herself ill. In one of her late short stories, "Roman Fever" (1934), Edith Wharton describes a conflict between two women over a man: a jealous Alida Slade uses a forged letter to try to trick her friend Grace Ansley into going to the Colosseum after dark, hoping that the resulting malaria will keep Grace away from Alida's fiancé long enough for the wedding to take place.[12] The competition in *Ethan Frome*, however, is not so straight-forward. Zeena Frome does not plot to make Mattie Silver ill (even though this is the final outcome). Instead, she uses her own illness to attempt to sever the relation between Mattie and her husband. In "Roman Fever," Alida's plan miscarries; although she "wins" tempo-rarily, she finds out twenty years later that Grace had, after all, won a sort of victory. Alida is, in other words, eventually wounded by her own weapon. In *Ethan Frome*, however, Zeena must wound herself—must work through her own body—before she can have any effect on Mattie. Mattie Silver is the ultimate object toward which Zeena's weapon is aimed, but Zeena must work not only through her own body but through her marriage as well.

Illness here becomes a very peculiar weapon, indeed. To "win," Zeena has to be "much sicker" than anyone thinks (53).[13] To "win" Ethan in this kind of contest will alienate him completely. The real competition, then, as far as Zeena is concerned, cannot be for Ethan's love—she has never had that—but for control over him, for possession of him. Of course, it was "possession" of Ethan in the first place, that is, her disappointing marriage to him, that led to her illness. She had married Ethan thinking that they would not stay on the farm; "She had let her husband see from the first that life on an isolated farm was not what she had expected when she married" (35). When it became clear that the farm was not going to sell, that she would have to remain there, she "developed the 'sickliness' which had since made her notable even in a community rich in pathological instances" (36). Despite Ethan's (and the narrator's) conviction of the "impossibility of transplanting her" because "she would have suffered a complete loss of identity" in the big, impersonal cities (35–36), the narrative suggests that it is the maddening isolation and poverty of country life, results of her marriage to Ethan, that have ruined Zeena. In competing with Mattie for Ethan, then, Zeena sets up a competition that she cannot win because "win-ning" does not accomplish anything positive.

Zeena openly vents her anger at the other woman only after Mattie has broken a pickle dish. Zeena calls her a "bad girl" for having "took the thing I set most store by of anything I've got" (62–63). The central paradox in this novel is that even though life with Ethan has brought Zeena no practical pleasure, as with the pickle dish that she never uses, she finds satisfaction through ownership. The thing possessed, then, makes no real difference, though its absence would; nor does it matter under what conditions the thing is possessed. Possession itself is all. The novel leaves unanswered the question of whether Zeena's illness is caused by the desire of possession or by the threat of loss. Does her illness cause this unregulated "consumption," or is "consumption" her disease? The novel leaves this question unanswered or, rather, affirms both answers. In either case, *Ethan Frome* examines the crippling effects of an overwhelming desire to possess. Wharton therefore to some extent rejects a faith in health (or success) through consumption.

Belief in the therapeutic powers of consuming was an integral part of the novel in both the eighteenth and nineteenth centuries—as *Pamela* or *Madame Bovary*, for example, reveal. Throughout *Ethan Frome*, Zeena represents this belief. Before the narrator meets Zeena, he sees her name on the envelopes Ethan picks up, which bear "conspicuously in the upper left-hand corner the address of some manufacturer of patent medicine," and on the "wooden box—also with a druggist's label on it" (4). Ethan is described as dreading Zeena's trip to the doctor "because of the cost" (32). Zeena believes that she can buy her way to health, that hiring a housemaid will make her well.[14] Zeena's rampant consumption serves two purposes. First, it represents the kind of promised self-fulfillment through consumption and possession described by Lears, which turns out to be false but which is self-sustaining. The fact that she is a "poor man's wife," as Ethan reminds her (56), exacerbates rather than limits her desire to consume. Second, her consumption offers her a weapon to use against her husband.

Even though Zeena's consumption does not cure her, and may even be part of what makes her sick, the expense of her treatments makes it possible for her to turn her illness into a weapon. As the novel makes clear, her trip to the doctor is brought on by Ethan's misbehavior; Zeena's expenses allow her to be always "holding out [her] pain to show" Ethan (as Gertrude Stein puts it in the opening epigraph to this chapter) and then to charge him for it, as well. Zeena can point to her own doctor-certified needs to remove Mattie from the house: "[The doctor] wants I should have a hired girl. He says I oughtn't to have to do a single thing around the house" (54). Beyond that, she can confront

Ethan with his responsibility for her illness to justify her demands; when Ethan asks her if the doctor told her how to pay for hired help, she replies, "No, he didn't. For I'd 'a' been ashamed to tell *him* that you grudged me the money to get back my health, when I lost it nursing your own mother" (55). Since they are poor, Ethan expects her to understand that she has no right to make the demands that she makes. Their poverty makes her medical expenses, then, a powerful weapon. The confrontation between Ethan and Zeena is "as senseless and savage as a physical fight between two enemies in the darkness" during which "their thoughts seemed to dart at each other like serpents shooting venom" (55). Zeena's illness gives her the power to literally make Ethan pay for failing her.

But while the novel questions Zeena's faith in the positive value of consuming, it also affirms it. As I have claimed earlier, the novel upholds the therapeutic ethos precisely at the point at which it becomes social criticism. To blame Zeena's illness on "poverty and isolation" is to concede that more money—that is, a *real* ability to consume—and more opportunities for socializing would heal her "dis-ease." Throughout the novel, we are assured that money would have solved all the problems the Fromes face; had Ethan had more money, he could have finished his education, he and Zeena could have moved to the city, or he could have let Zeena keep the farm while he and Mattie started a happier life out west.

It is not faith in consumption that condemns Zeena, then, but her weakness, her use of that weakness as a weapon, and her willingness to compete with another woman for possession of a man. Just as Wharton would condemn Alida Slade to a hollow victory in "Roman Fever," so here she condemns Zeena. In contrast to *The House of Mirth*, in which Bertha Dorset's ruthless competition with Lily accomplishes her intended purpose, most competition between women in Wharton's fiction ends badly. Sandra Gilbert and Susan Gubar argue in *No Man's Land* that early twentieth-century fiction is typified by "battles between the sexes,"[15] a view shared by Joseph Boone in *Tradition Counter Tradition*.[16] But in *Ethan Frome*, although Ethan and Zeena's battles are venomous, the real deadly battle is between two almost powerless opponents for very limited stakes. In their attempts to "win" Ethan, Zeena—through her use of her illness as a weapon—and Mattie— through an attempted double suicide that would allow her to "never have to leave [Ethan] any more" (81)—reveal the pathos and futility of their competition. Its outcome, the invalidism of all three of them, questions the validity of the competition itself.

While *Ethan Frome* is a novel of the American nightmare, *Barren Ground* could be called the novel of the American businesswoman's dream. Dorinda Oakley overcomes a childhood of poverty and isolation, takes over the family farm, and becomes rich and successful. Her success is the result of determination and hard work, not luck or a fortuitous marriage. But Dorinda is not a success at everything: her early love affair is a disaster, and afterward she swears off love, declaring herself "finished with all that" at barely twenty. Her success at farming, her failure at love, and the failing health of almost all the women around her offer us a second look at how a woman writing in the earlier part of the century envisioned the relations between success, failure, competition, and illness.

Just as Wharton wrote *Ethan Frome* shortly after the end of a love affair, Glasgow, too, wrote *Barren Ground* just after her break with Henry Anderson (see Linda Wagner, *Ellen Glasgow: Beyond Convention*, 78–79, and Julius Raper, *From the Sunken Garden*, 79–100). And just as *Ethan Frome* represents Wharton's attempts to work out questions of "endurance" and personal fulfillment, *Barren Ground* represents Glasgow's attempts to envision a productive and successful life for a woman that does not depend on love and marriage. In this novel, Glasgow illustrates one possibility for a woman's success that is far different from the traditional success accorded to women in novels— marriage to a good (and wealthy) man. Glasgow takes Dorinda out of woman's "proper sphere" and makes her a success in a man's world, thereby raising the question of what happens to women who challenge tradition and of what happens to those who do not. Unlike earlier texts, in which women who stepped out of their proper roles were punished with invalidism and death, here it is the women who stay in their "place" who become ill.

Early in the novel we learn that in Dorinda's family, failed love affairs can have devastating effects. Her mother tells her that "those feelings have always gone hard in our family": "There was your great-aunt Dorinda, the one you were named after. . . . When she couldn't get the man she'd set her heart on, she threw herself in the mill-race. . . . Then there was another sister, Abigail, who went deranged about some man she hadn't seen but a few times, and they had to put her away in a room with barred windows" (80). Dorinda does not heed her mother's warning and falls in love with a young doctor, Jason Greylock. Like Ethan Frome, she believes that her marriage will save her from the deadening poverty, isolation, and illness that she sees all around her. Instead, she finds herself pregnant and alone after Jason marries another woman. At first, like her great-aunts, she loses her mind and tries to kill Jason. Recovering from that, however, she goes to New York City where, suffering from fatigue and nausea brought on by poverty and loneliness, she steps out in front of a carriage and is run over. After a miscarriage and several months of invalidism, she finally recovers, only to pronounce herself "finished with all that" business about love (183). When she returns to Pedlar's Mill, she finds that the woman Jason married, Geneva Ellgood, has gone insane. As far as Dorinda is concerned, the message is clear: love leads to illness. She never allows herself to succumb to that "weakness" again.

Dorinda has had plenty of evidence that love and marriage lead to illness. All the married white women in the novel are sickly. Rose Emily Pedlar and Eudora Oakley both stand as exemplars of a wife and motherhood that sacrifices everything—beauty, dreams, and health— to serve the family; they are examples to Dorinda of the suffering she will never force herself to endure. Rose Emily, dying of tuberculosis, is too poor and too devoted to her family to afford treatment; instead, she maintains pathetically that she will be better the next day. Dorinda admires her courage but recognizes that it is based on a "heroic illusion" (17). Tuberculosis here is not the romantic figure of the nineteenth century but one of pathos, representing self-abnegation and poverty.

At home, Dorinda witnesses her mother's sacrifice to an unaware and undeserving family. Mrs. Oakley is a type of the overworked neurasthenic; she is "a tall, lean, angular woman, who had been almost beautiful a little while forty years before . . . [but whose] face was so worn by suffering that a network of nerves quivered beneath the pallid veil of her flesh. . . . She had worked so hard for so many years that the habit had degenerated into a disease" (31). The lesson Dorinda eventually learns is not simply that failed love relationships are unhealthy but that love relationships, themselves, represent weakness and are therefore unhealthy. She also learns that "unproductive" work, that is, housework, the work that women have traditionally done, is unhealthy. The only healthy women Dorinda meets are single, black, or live in the city.

Glasgow sets Dorinda out as an exception to the rule that white farm women all suffer a great deal of sickness, pain, and invalidism. But black farm women—those who earn their own living—are uniformly healthy. This representation evokes the myth of the strong black woman—a myth we now recognize as racist—but it also reveals Glasgow's attitudes toward women and work. The women who work in Dorinda's dairy, who come to milk the cows at sunrise and again at sunset, and her companion, Fluvanna, never suffer a moment. Glasgow's position as a privileged white southern woman is revealed in these figures; she seems unable to imagine that black women could suffer as white women do.[17] In her representation of black women, Glasgow falls back on the nineteenth-century stereotype of working-class women as naturally healthy; because *she* has never seen their suffering, she assumes it does not exist. Even as she tries to liberate her heroine from a stereotypical female invalidism, she perpetuates a stereotypical assurance that hard work is good for the "lower races." Glasgow makes a clear distinction between black women and middle-class white women (and distinguishes both from "poor whites," who are lower, because lazier, than either). For the white women, whose husbands own their own farms, work is always without tangible reward and proves debilitating. For black women, who work for wages, work is a "natural" part of life. Dorinda's mother works herself to death on a poor farm but dreams of having led a successful life as a missionary in Africa. The black women in *Barren Ground* are not allowed such dreams—or even such failures.

For Dorinda, work—man's work, running her own farm and turning out a product for the marketplace—is the key to health. Dorinda embodies the Protestant work ethic and becomes a successful Progressive hero; she works honestly, long, and hard. Work insures her health because it leads to success, wealth, and control of land and workers. Glasgow, more directly than Wharton, associates work and success with health.

In *Barren Ground*, Glasgow rewrites the traditional female success story by reevaluating the place of competition in a woman's life. She contrasts two kinds of competition. One kind, business competitiveness between Dorinda and all the other farmers in the region, she holds out as healthy and life-giving. Even when Dorinda eventually buys Jason's farm—when he has gone bankrupt—Glasgow depicts her purchase not as an empty act of revenge but as one of satisfying triumph: Dorinda finally buys for herself the farm that was denied her when Jason married another woman. Competition between women over a man, however, brings results as disastrous in *Barren Ground* as in *Ethan Frome*.

For Glasgow, competition between women for a man is in itself sickening, and a "victory" is a guarantee of eventual defeat. Early in Jason's courtship, he tells Dorinda to "beg, borrow, or steal" a blue dress. When Dorinda finds out from the dressmaker that Geneva Ellgood, the local rich girl, is to have a fine new outfit for Easter, Dorinda decides to spend her savings on a dress rather than on a new cow for the farm. The competition between Dorinda and Geneva over Jason is straightforward and, as far as Dorinda is concerned, amounts to open warfare: "For an instant Dorinda held her breath while a wave of sickness swept over her. At that moment she realized that the innocence of her girlhood had departed for ever. She was in the thick of life, and the thick of life meant not peace but a sword in the heart. Though she scarcely knew Geneva Ellgood, she felt that they were enemies" (54). Such competition deflowers as well as sickens. Men may take women's virginity, but women corrupt each other by competing for men. Further, the competitive urge is not merely a high-spirited involvement with life but is warlike; it brings a "sword in the heart." Unlike the battling couples Gilbert and Gubar describe in *No Man's Land,* consistently composed of men and women fighting each other, here two women war with one another. Dorinda does not find happy communities of women intruded upon by men; she finds instead women ready to sacrifice each other for the sake of marriage.

But if female competition here is sickening, degrading, and warlike, "victory" is much worse. After Dorinda returns to Pedlar's Mill from New York City, Geneva stops Dorinda's carriage, babbling incoherently about being "blissfully happy" and claiming that Jason had killed her baby. Looking at her, Dorinda thinks, "This is what marriage to Jason had brought" (279). Each of Geneva's appearances in the novel is more pathetic than the last. Both she and Jason are ruined by Geneva's victory in the competition.

The start of this competition is marked by spending money and by buying clothes. Glasgow continually questions the therapeutic ethos of consuming or of expecting any "cure" from material goods or other people. For example, after Dorinda has spent all her money on a new blue outfit, Jason barely notices. As does *Ethan Frome, Barren Ground* questions the belief that consumption, romance, or "success" will bring happiness or satisfaction. Dorinda's possession of the blue dress proves as empty as Geneva's possession of Jason. But Glasgow does not simply reject consuming altogether; it is, instead, reliance on consumption alone for happiness that she rejects. Dorinda's guilt lies not in spending her money but in buying a dress for herself rather than a cow for the farm; significantly, her later success is based on running a dairy—that is, on eventually buying a whole herd of cattle. In Glasgow's reckoning, Dorinda is as guilty of mismanaging her emotional "capital" in loving Jason, rather than depending on her own strength of will to sustain her, as she is of mismanaging her money in buying a dress.

Glasgow indicts other forms of consumption, as well, in a way that recalls and rewrites Gustave Flaubert's *Madame Bovary*. Dorinda's early vulnerability is the result of having been "nourished on the gossamer substance of literature" (10), which keeps her from seeing Jason for what he is—a weakling. As does Emma Bovary, Dorinda attempts to live her life like the romances she has been reading; she expects to be "saved" from the boredom and poverty of Pedlar's Mill by Jason. And like Emma, Dorinda is a country girl who sees being a physician's wife as a chance to live a more exotic life. Jason represents for Dorinda a romance that provides a "kingdom of the spirit" through which she believes she can escape poverty and desolation (22). But Jason, like Monsieur Bovary, is a doctor who cannot help himself, much less Dorinda. *Barren Ground*, Linda Wagner explains, "successfully breaks down the stereotypes of 'romance'" (*Ellen Glasgow: Beyond Convention*, 74). Dorinda violates the "vein of iron" within her, is untrue to her inner principles, and mismanages her emotional and monetary "principals"; illness is a weapon of divine retribution for these "sins," and her recovery a sign of having learned her lesson.

While Glasgow sets herself against the therapeutic value of consuming, she nonetheless acquiesces in an ideology that equates health and success and accedes to the therapeutic value of investment. As does Wharton, Glasgow seems to base her evaluation of consumption either on scale or on results. She does not condemn consuming itself; the mark of Dorinda's success is that she can become a consumer, and the way to that success was through wise investment in farming equipment.[18] But she does disapprove of "foolish" consumption by the poor. Dorinda's faith in marriage as salvation, like Ethan Frome's, is condemned; her hopes for happiness from the blue dress, like Zeena's hopes of relief from her pharmacists' boxes, are likewise shown to be false. Ultimately, Dorinda is the only healthy white woman in the novel because she is the only successful one, and once she is successful, Glasgow's representation of her excessive expenditures changes. When Dorinda buys Jason's farm even though she does not need the extra land, buys expensive and fashionable clothes, keeps the best car in the county, and renovates her farmhouse, Glasgow presents such purchases as a right that she has earned.

Barren Ground reevaluates the place of competition and the meaning of success and failure in a woman's life. Traditional female success, like traditional female competition, leads to invalidism and death. Early in the novel, Mrs. Oakley tells Dorinda, "Marriage is the Lord's own institution, and . . . a good thing as far as it goes. Only . . . it ain't ever going as far as most women try to make it" (81). Dorinda does eventually marry, but she marries a man who will be more business partner than husband, a man she respects but does not love. Glasgow tries in this novel to reform the standards for a successful life, setting up standards that do not depend on marriage. After Jason's death, Dorinda faces a crisis when she realizes that she has only felt love for a few short months. For a time, she feels the weight of her defeat when reckoned conventionally but decides that there are other things worth having: "Though in a measure destiny had defeated her, for it had given her none of the gifts she had asked of it, still her failure was one of those defeats, she realized, which are victories. At middle age, she faced the future without romantic glamour, but she faced it with integrity of vision" (408). Glasgow redefines female success and failure, but she does not bring it into accord with healthy relations with other people. Dorinda does not ever allow herself to love another person fully; the only other person she ever loves in any way is her stepson, John Abner, who evokes her sympathy and compassion because he was born lame. Men are only sympathetic in *Barren Ground* when they are wounded or ill—that is, when they do not threaten women's health and happiness.

Invalid Men and the Ideology of "Separate Spheres"

Neither Glasgow nor Wharton identified herself as a feminist, but both women were deeply interested in the condition of women and wrote about them often. Both had to reconcile their femininity with their professionalism; both lived unconventionally, despite their often very conventional attitudes toward tradition and resistance to modernity. *Barren Ground* and *Ethan Frome* are difficult texts for the feminist reader, in part because the women in them raise disturbing questions about the roles of work, power, and love in women's lives. Dorinda Oakley, a strong, independent, and successful woman, could well be a feminist heroine, but she is a strikingly joyless one. Zeena Frome is the very image of everything feminists have complained of in male writers' representations of women; at the 1987 Modern Language Association panel on "Edith Wharton and Women," none of the panelists (all feminist critics) would respond to a question about Zeena, except to note that she was certainly Wharton's most unlikable woman. To talk about either of these novels as "feminist" texts, then, causes problems for the feminist critic. Neither Glasgow's vision of the failure of human community nor Wharton's portrait of the self-centered, weak, and cruel wife offer themselves as typical feminist narratives; it is almost impossible to recover a "happy ending" to either one. But at the heart of both novels are questions of gender and of the crippling, sickening effects—on both sexes—of late nineteenth-century separate spheres ideology. While "The Yellow Wallpaper" and *The House of Mirth* each question the notion of "separate spheres" on one level, rejecting some aspects of it but also accepting it to some degree (as I argued in the previous chapter), *Ethan Frome* and *Barren Ground* meet that belief and its attendant problem of gender head on.

Wharton and Glasgow question gender-constructing ideologies from several directions. Nineteenth-century medical writers, as we saw in chapter 1, maintained the "natural" health of rural life and of working people, condemning the harmful effects of cities and too much leisure; here, Wharton and Glasgow present the poverty, strain, and loneliness of those "naturally healthful" farms. Those same Victorian medical authorities asserted that men were necessarily healthier and stronger than women; Glasgow and Wharton question that assumption as well. Domestic ideology explicitly affirmed the importance of the home and implicitly endorsed a woman's right to fight to preserve the sanctity of that home; Wharton and Glasgow dispute, to some extent, the importance of the home and strongly challenge the rightness of female fighting, when it is a fight over a man. These two novels turn a distinctly twentieth-century feminist consciousness onto questions of woman's "proper sphere."

Nonetheless, Wharton and Glasgow do not maintain simple ideological positions. Women should not fight over men, they suggest, but, at least as far as Glasgow is concerned, fighting for land is different. And even though their men are not naturally stronger than their women, that does not mean that women are uniformly strong, either. More importantly, while Wharton and Glasgow challenge nineteenth-century medical and domestic conventions, the ideology of individual success which informs that challenge often creates more disturbing problems than it solves. Where earlier writers could accept failure as a result of "natural" physical weakness, these two women must confront failure as something intentional, the result of a weakness that is moral as well as physical. Further, neither woman reconciles her distrust of capitalism's promise of therapeutic consuming with her implied equation of wealth, success, and goodness.[19]

In addition, for Wharton and Glasgow, illness is still a "feminine" role, even though these novels offer striking examples of sickly men— both Ethan Frome and Jason Greylock end up invalids. Ethan is ineffective and lame; Jason becomes an alcoholic and eventually a consumptive. Dorinda's father also ends his life as an invalid, after suffering a paralyzing stroke. There are a number of "causes" for male illness in these two novels; failure, betrayal, poverty, and loneliness cause male as well as female invalidism. But illness seems to strike men harder in these novels than it does women. In *Ethan Frome*, the narrator expresses little or no sympathy for Zeena or even Mattie but regards Ethan's disability—which is less severe than Mattie's—as a tragedy. In *Barren Ground*, Jason is eventually defeated in every way he can be; his illness leaves him in the poor farm and eventually mentally absent. Male invalidism does not merely defeat these men, it *unmans* them.[20] It thereby reveals the tensions inherent in Progressive challenges to the ideology of separate spheres for the sexes.

I have argued that men in these texts figure as a commodity in a competition between two women, a competition that proves devastating for the women involved. But it proves just as devastating for the men. Ethan ends up an invalid, just as Zeena and Mattie do; Jason ends up utterly defeated by illness and poverty. In the end, however, both writers use male invalidism to cast doubt on the validity of the entire competition. The invalidism of men figures in these novels to question the validity of the struggle between women—men are not acceptable objects for female warring. Male invalidism accompanies failure—at farming, at relationships, at careers—and is a sign that these men are not really valuable commodities at all, not worth the degradation of female competition.[21] But male invalidism in these novels does not merely question Ethan's and Jason's value as commodities; it also questions their value as men.

In his study of magazine biographies during the late nineteenth and early twentieth centuries, *America's Heroes*, Theodore Greene claims magazines equated success, manliness, and health. "Physically the Progressive heroes in all occupations were models of the strenuous life. . . . Only the reactionary villains appeared with flabby physiques" (259). Almost always in these magazine success stories, ill health for men was a sign of failure or evildoing. In addition, during World War I, shell shock was interpreted as evidence of weakness; at first, doctors regarded this weakness as hereditary, but as the war progressed, they began to regard shell shock as a form of resistance to and escape from the war. According to Elaine Showalter, "All signs of physical fear were judged as weakness" and "alternatives to combat—pacifism, conscientious objection, desertion, and even suicide—were viewed as unmanly" (*The Female Malady*, 170–71). By extension, any illness, or failure, was also a sign of "unmanliness" (that is, femininity).

Post–World War I literature features a number of wounded and maimed male characters; usually, their injuries are specifically sexual ones. Jake Barnes, Clifford Chatterley, Ford Madox Ford's "Good Soldier" all suffer wounds in the war that are literally and figuratively castrating; T. S. Eliot's J. Alfred Prufrock, "Fisher King," and "hollow men" are emblematic of weakness and impotence. Gilbert and Gubar claim that "maimed, unmanned, victimized [male] characters are obsessively created by early twentieth-century literary men" (*No Man's Land*, 36). Gilbert, in "Soldier's Heart," notes that "gloomily bruised modernist anti-heroes churned out by the war suffer specifically from sexual wounds, as if, having traveled literally or figuratively through No Man's Land, all have become not just No Men, nobodies, but *not* men, *un*men" (423, emphasis in original). These men are certainly threatened by women (as Gilbert and Gubar argue), but they are also threatened by militarism—the "unmanning" nature of the war—and the new industrial complex in which they are seen as faceless machines. They are men who go out into the world and are defeated by its violence and cruelty, its ruthless competitiveness, and their anonymity in it.[22]

Ethan Frome and *Barren Ground* represent those same "maimed, unmanned and victimized" men, but they are created by literary women rather than the literary men Gilbert and Gubar discuss.[23] Wharton's and Glasgow's invalid men do not, however, go out into the wider world and encounter a harsh force that cripples them. Instead, it is staying at home, staying on the farm, particularly, that ruins them. Harmon Gow tells the narrator of *Ethan Frome* that Ethan's real malady was that "he's been in Starkfield too many winters" (5), and Old Matthew Fairlamb tells Dorinda that Jason is "a bit too soft" to withstand life in rural Virginia and warns that he had better "git away before the broomsage ketches him" (14). Whereas male modernist writers envision their heroes' invalidism as a result of too much contact with an impersonal, urban, and violent world, revealing an implicitly nostalgic longing for a simpler, preindustrial rural life, Wharton and Glasgow envision male invalidism as the inability to stand up to the harshness of nature, the isolation of rural life, and the disappointment of frustrated ambitions.[24]

In *Ethan Frome* and *Barren Ground*, men become invalids because they stay at home, as women traditionally have. These invalid men serve to suggest that if men were denied the opportunities that women have been denied, they, too, would become invalids. Glasgow makes this point quite straightforwardly in *Barren Ground*. In the very first chapter, she describes the demographic changes that provide the backdrop for the novel: "With the end of free labour and the beginning of the tenant system, authority passed from the country to the towns. The old men stayed by the farms, and their daughters withered dutifully beside them; but the sons of the good people drifted away to the city, where they assumed control of democracy as well as of the political machine which has made democracy safe for politics. An era changed, not rudely, but as eras do change so often, uncomfortably" (5). *Barren Ground* counteracts this demographic reality. Here, the old men who stay on the farms do indeed wither, but at least one daughter who is left behind does not wither dutifully beside her father, nor do all the sons get away to rule in the cities. Instead, Jason, the son who stays behind on the farm, is quickly overcome by the force of nature, while the daughter, Dorinda, harnesses all the power of scientific farming to become the richest and most successful farmer in the county. Even though her father could never do anything with the farm, despite working himself to death trying, Dorinda transforms it within just a few years into a showplace. Meanwhile, Jason's farm, which is, in itself, a better place than Dorinda's, deteriorates completely under his management.

Wharton's novel does not offer such a positive vision of rural success to counter Ethan's failure; no one in the novel—male or female—is strong enough to win the battle against nature in "Starkfield."[25] All they can do is withstand it. The narrator, during his one winter there, comes to understand "why Starkfield emerged from its six months' siege like a starved garrison capitulating without quarter" and why "most of the smart ones get away" (6).[26] "Getting away" is the one chance that is offered to Ethan, and he misses it, first because he cannot sell his farm and later because he cannot imagine leaving without any money.

Both Ethan and Jason dream of better lives in the city. Ethan got away once, to school, where he studied engineering; the narrator discovers that Ethan is still interested in science. But he was called home to take care of his ailing parents and later had to take care of his ailing wife. He never got away again. Jason, who was trained as a doctor and practiced for a while in the city, also was called home to care for an ailing parent. He, too, planned to go back to the city as soon as his father died. But his father lingers on for years, leaving Jason on the farm long enough to ruin him. Again, Wharton and Glasgow put these two men in a position usually filled by a woman: stuck at home tending an ill parent, unable to pursue their own lives, they themselves fall ill.

Male modernist writers imagine men literally "unmanned" as a result of their contact with the violent outside world. These two women writers, however, imagine men put into women's place, feminized, and therefore ill. Ethan and Jason are metaphorically castrated. Not only do Ethan and Zeena have no children, but his lameness is the archetypal symbol for castration. Nor does Jason father any children; his wife's madness even takes the form of accusing him of killing her baby. Glasgow is ruthless in Jason's unmanning; he loses his farm, loses his country medical practice (because of his alcoholism), and ends up at the poor farm. In his final illness, he is not merely unmanned, he is no longer really human. Dorinda nurses him through this final illness and realizes, as she looks at him, that he suffered from "an emptiness of spirit. He was silent because there was nothing left in him to be uttered. . . . His figure, bowed under the rugs, seemed to her to become merely another object in the landscape" (397).

Although these texts (and other modernist writings) feature invalid men, the men live conventionally "feminine" lives—even though these conventions were themselves changing. The invalid is trapped in a routine and unstimulating home, unable to escape, with all options closed off by family ties. And the invalid is described as, if not feminine, certainly not masculine; he is unmanned and therefore ill. This is a very different representation of illness than that offered by male writers in the early twentieth century and one that very clearly comes from woman's experience of Victorian social mores. Neither Wharton nor Glasgow here describes a world where the "outside world" is threatening or cruel; the horror they imagine is at home, on the farm. Illness is figured in the domestic arena, transformed by the ideology of success, advertising, war, and industrial development.

Wharton and Glasgow therefore react against and challenge domestic ideology, which, by centering women's power in the home, keeps them there; they challenge medical ideology, which argues for the healthfulness of home life. Both authors depict women's traditional role in the family as powerless and illness inducing to indicate that modern women cannot follow in their mothers' footsteps. Both writers suggest that the way of the older generation led to illness: Ethan's mother and, we are led to believe, the other Frome women in the graveyard all "went queer"; Dorinda's great-aunts and her mother all suffered from nervous diseases. But Wharton and Glasgow also challenge the very premise of domestic and medical ideologies by illustrating that the two "spheres" are not really so separate: the competition that exists between women and the stress of housework do not allow them peace or serenity; instead, their lives are as full of strife as male warfare or business.

Chapter **6**

Economies of Illness: Working the Invalid Woman

Like Alice James, writers who have chosen to write about illness have often been deeply interested in exploring the worth of the invalid woman. All of the fictions I have discussed so far have focused on, in Alice's words, the "value" of the invalid, the question of whether the invalid has "productive worth." They have all centered on the relation between illness and leisure, work, or money: does illness come from too much work? from too much leisure? Does one "earn" illness? Can one work or buy one's way out of it? In E. D. E. N. Southworth's *Retribution*, Juliette finds a way to "work" Hester's illness for personal gain and, thereby, "earns" her own later illness and death; in Bullard's *Christine*, Annie cannot make an honest living for herself and degenerates into consumption. Washington Irving and Mrs. Davidson, in *Biogra-*

phy and Poetical Remains of the Late Margaret Miller Davidson, attempt to find the value of Margaret's death. In Poe's and Hawthorne's
tales, women's illnesses are spawned by the conflict men feel about
whether woman's value is as an object for male "production" or as a tool
for "reproduction." The very notion of a "writing cure" suggests that one
can work one's way out of illness; in "The Yellow Wallpaper," Gilman
illustrates the "dis-ease" that results when a woman is denied meaning-
ful work, and in *The House of Mirth*, Wharton offers Lily Bart as a
warning against not preparing women for productive life. In *Ethan
Frome*, Wharton goes on to set up Zeena Frome as the example illustrating that when "woman's work" is neglected, the household falls
ill. Glasgow, perhaps more than any of the other writers in this study,
explicitly connects work and health; Dorinda Oakley is the epitome of
the woman working her way out of and away from illness.

In Henry James's *The Wings of the Dove* (1902) and F. Scott Fitzgerald's *Tender Is the Night* (1934), the relation between illness and work is
again brought into focus. Here, unlike the texts we have seen in the
previous two chapters, illness is reassociated with leisure, riches, and
beauty. Milly Theale and Nicole Warren Diver are not just two of the
most canonical invalid women in American fiction, they are two of the
richest ones. More emphatically even than any of the other texts in this
study, *The Wings of the Dove* and *Tender Is the Night* focus on making
illness *pay*, on discovering the "worth" of the invalid woman. Kate Croy,
Merton Densher, and perhaps even Milly herself all seek ways to make
Milly's illness profitable, to turn sickness directly to financial and social
gain. Dick Diver's profession is dependent on making a profit from
wealthy people's illnesses, and it is partially the tension between his
work and Nicole's leisure that eventually destroys their marriage and
his health.

Both *The Wings of the Dove* and *Tender Is the Night* focus on a man
who is involved with an invalid woman and who gains (or stands to gain)
in some way from her illness or her death. Each text is concerned
centrally with issues of work and leisure, spiritual and material gain,
human "value" and "success." In this chapter, following the previous
chapter's discussion of women writers' responses to the ideology of
"success," I will explore male writers' reactions to the same ideology.
Chronologically, these novels envelope *Ethan Frome* and *Barren
Ground* and so, of course, do not deal with identical cultural forces.
James's novel is poised between nineteenth- and twentieth-century

fictions; his female figures are shaped by Victorian customs and restrictions, while his economic and social world is colored by turn-of-the-century priorities and proprieties. Fitzgerald's novel is set in the period after World War I and was written during the last years of the boom of the 1920s and the early years of the Depression; his women are "flappers," his men postwar "hollow men." But James's and Fitzgerald's novels are shaped by many of the same questions of gender roles, power, and "success" that influenced Wharton and Glasgow.

This chapter will examine these novels in two related contexts: first, in light of conventional representations of invalid women as we have seen those conventions defined in the preceding chapters. Both James and Fitzgerald employ several "standard features" of the invalid; we shall look at how they work out their variations by examining their figures in comparison with earlier appearances. In particular, we will look at how these writers use, respond to, and revise the conventions established in woman-authored texts like E. D. E. N. Southworth's *Retribution*. Second, this chapter will examine *The Wings of the Dove* and *Tender Is the Night* against the background of the different "economies" within which they make sense. These novels question the "value" of the invalid, a value that we can measure only within the context of their economies, the systems through which they establish worth and on which they base human exchange and interchange. Ultimately literary and economic values in these texts become troublingly intertwined.

Willpower

One's interpretation of *The Wings of the Dove* depends on the definition of Milly Theale's "willpower," centering on the question of whether she is an innocent who is victimized because of her power to control money (through her last will and testament) or whether she is a willful invalid whose death represents a sort of retributive renunciation of the social world she finds in Europe. James obscures her illness, treatment, and death so that the only views of them available to us come through the filters of other characters' interpretations—interpretations that are subject to their own needs, desires, and prejudices. But obscurity on this point—the role of "willpower" in Milly Theale's narrative—leaves unclear what *kind* of narrative *The Wings of the Dove* is and what kind of value Milly represents. She may be the traditional heroine of nineteenth-century fiction, whose self-sacrifice represents love and forgiveness, but she may also be a twentieth-century invalid whose illness, if not entirely willful, is at least manipulated to render the greatest reward. Clearly, Kate Croy and Merton Densher try to make Milly's illness "pay," but James leaves unclear whether or not Milly does so as well. Only by considering the literary and economic contexts in which Milly's illness could "pay" can we sort out a resolution to these interpretive questions.

One way to begin to sort out these interpretive questions is to consider Milly Theale in the context of the other literary invalids we have seen. The invalid with whom she has the most in common is Hester Grey in *Retribution*. In fact, the plot of *The Wings of the Dove* is remarkably similar to Southworth's novel. As in *Retribution*, a beautiful but poor woman (Juliette Summers/Kate Croy) plots to gain an invalid woman's (Hester Grey/Milly Theale) great wealth and persuades the man who loves her (Ernest Dent/Merton Densher) to help. Since, of course, this wealth cannot be passed on easily from woman to woman, Juliette/Kate contrives to marry Dent/Densher who will inherit the money after the invalid's imminent death. (In Southworth's novel, Dent is already married to the invalid; in James's, Densher must court her, even though already engaged to Kate.) In both novels, the couple whose schemes have wrung both life and money from the invalid woman eventually come to distrust one another, and they are unable to enjoy the profits from their deceit. That James's retribution is more immediate than Southworth's matters little: what his gains from swiftness and intensity, hers makes up in duration and the totality of the eventual defeat. Like Southworth, James imagines a structure of retribution that is implicit in the guilty act and represents the forces of innocence and corruption allegorically in the two women.[1] In both texts, the "bad" woman is carefully drawn so that her misdeeds are, if not excusable, at least understandable, and her great beauty and privileged upbringing do not fit her financial status; the innocent invalid, on the other hand, is an heiress but is plain, has simple tastes, and has few material desires. What Elizabeth Allen claims of James's novel is true for Southworth's as well: "Materialism is another name for spiritual potential. . . . It makes morality/spirituality possible. Kate's potential for integrity is eroded by the sheer economic squalor of her circumstances" (*A Woman's Place in the Novels of Henry James*, 150). Finally, in both novels, the man's chief sin is his weakness in agreeing to participate in the beautiful woman's scheme, and he eventually repents, realizing only too late the moral value of the woman who has died.[2]

Critics have historically cited Hawthorne as the great influence on James, but we see here a little-recognized influence, that of the women writers of the nineteenth century.[3] When such comparisons *are* noted, they are usually derogatory, either to James or to his female models.[4] My comparison of the two texts is meant to do neither. *The Wings of the Dove* and *Retribution* are both absorbing novels. James's novel is not really "better" than Southworth's; the "master" has taken as many lessons as he has given. James does not go "beyond" Southworth in envisioning a richer, more complex world or situation. The character-ization, the psychological insights into motivation, are not any keener in one or the other. Their language is certainly different, but the quality of that difference is a matter of taste or maybe even mood; the jury is still out on James's style, and when a "jury of her peers" judged South-worth's, it pronounced hers worthy.[5] But there *are* important differ-ences of emphasis between the novels, differences that will tell us much about the changed conceptions of women and invalidism between 1849 and 1902. The illness itself, the situation of the invalid does not really change, but the economy for figuring illness—and for valuing it—does.

While Southworth leaves her reader in no doubt about Hester's inno-cence (Hester's only mistake is to love her husband and her friend too much to doubt them, to love other people too much to properly attend to herself) or the disease that kills her (tuberculosis), James leaves pre-cisely these two points obscure in his representation of Milly Theale. And while Southworth allows Hester to die happy, even if betrayed, James subjects his invalid to the pain of full knowledge of her betrayal before her death. Hester dies in peace, but Milly, we presume, dies in misery (again, the deathbed scene is unseen; while Southworth openly represents Hester's death, all we know of Milly's is that she "turned her face to the wall"). While Southworth is clear about her heroine's re-sponsibility for her own illness (it is a result of too little self-interest), James never makes it clear how much responsibility Milly Theale must bear. Southworth makes no secret of the fact that Hester is too selfless to properly guard herself against the onslaught of tuberculosis and too trusting to suspect Juliette and Ernest. James never makes it clear what kills Milly, what she could have done to "live," as her doctor advises her, nor whether she keeps herself alive by willpower or whether she wills herself to die after Kate's and Merton's betrayal. These differences can be traced to a difference in the conception of the kind of power that an invalid can wield, a difference rooted in two different "economies."

In *Retribution*, Hester is invested with a great deal of power: the power to be a moral exemplar. And her example eventually proves effective. Her daughter grows up to be a good person; her husband comes to realize Hester's value and to honor her goodness. Hers is the Christian power to save others through self-sacrifice, a power little connected to material life and one that transcends earthly concerns. That the exercise of this power is accomplished by her death does not diminish the fact that it is a kind of power, because it is purely altruistic. Hers is the kind of "sentimental power" Jane Tompkins describes in her discussion of *Uncle Tom's Cabin*, the power to influence other people's moral lives after one's death (*Sensational Designs*, 122–46). Hester is clearly a moral exemplar for the reader, a model of the unselfish, and therefore spiritual, life.

Hester's power is based on what could be called a "domestic economy," that is, an economy in which ethics are consistent with domestic ideology and the household is the model for human exchange and value. Within this economy, the community is foremost and Hester's sacrifice makes sense because it can benefit the entire community (not just through the example she sets for her husband and child but also through the freedom she tries to grant her slaves). Since the household is its model, this economy is rooted in the material world, but its force is felt at the spiritual level. That is, it is based on a work ethic that has as its goal the benefit of the entire household but that also has the effect of purifying the individual of selfish, material desire. Woman's work in such an economy is not for her own individual improvement or enrichment but for the comfort, pleasure, and improvement of the entire family; nonetheless, it has the effect of enriching her spiritually, of laying up treasures in heaven. Hester's death, within such an economy, is valuable to her successors not because of the wealth she leaves behind but because of the example she sets in devotion to community, rather than personal, good. For example, she keeps herself alive solely by will until her twenty-first birthday simply so she can sign the manumission papers of her slaves. Such an exertion of "willpower" (both volitional power and the power of her bequest) is purely for the good of others, enacted at great physical pain to herself. While Hester bears some responsibility for her own illness, the blame she bears is the guilt of being too innocent.

James seems to want to represent the same kind of moral power in Milly Theale. She is one of the "meek gentle *doves*," as Helen Papashvily describes them in *All the Happy Endings*, who characterized women's novels in the 1840s and 1850s. But by 1902, it was impossible for him to maintain such confidence in the innocence of the invalid woman. Reassessments of willpower in illness and cure made it virtually impossible to represent Milly as unambiguously blameless. Not only was the cultural discourse on illness shifting so that illness came to represent a failure or perversity of will (see chapter 5), but Henry's personal experience with Alice's doctors brought him assurances of the necessity of an individual's complicity in sickness. He wrote to his brother William that Alice's "disastrous, her tragic health was in a manner the only solution for her of the practical problem of life" (*The Letters of Henry James*, 215), a comment that suggests that he believed her illness to be willful. That comment could also be applied equally well to his representation of Milly Theale's dilemma. Virginia Fowler claims in *Henry James's American Girl* that "Milly's disease becomes a refuge from active participation in the world; in effect, Milly takes up her illness as a source of self-definition and security" (97). Although James claims in the preface that the novel is about a young woman's fight with her coming death, the novel itself never makes it clear whether Milly eventually loses her will to live, to fight her illness, or whether she wills herself to die as a way to cope with Kate's and Merton's betrayal of her.[6] James's celebrated obscurity here is not simply a literary device for heightening the mystery or pathos of Milly's death; it represents a fundamental inability to envision an invalidism in which willfulness is not a significant part.[7] He therefore leaves Milly's illness, her death, and her complicity in them open to conjecture.

By 1902, the therapeutic ethos of individual consumption had seriously undermined the possibility of maintaining a "domestic economy." Women writers, as we saw with Wharton and Gilman (in chapter 4), would later openly challenge the domestic economy and its effects on women. But here James does not challenge the ethos of the domestic economy; instead, he examines its efficacy in a much-changed world. To do this, he puts a typical heroine from a domestic novel into a situation in which her ethics and value(s) will no longer work—a fiercely competitive economy of consumption. In so doing, he does not condemn the domestic economy of writers like Southworth; in fact, his effort may be to condemn the consumer economy into which Milly Theale is thrust. James raises the question of whether the exclusively domestic sphere and system of value is possible any longer. He simultaneously identifies with and rejects a female tradition of writing.

In "Male Vision and Female Revision," Carolyn Karcher argues that James represents the woman writer in *The Wings of the Dove*, Susan Shepherd Stringham, as monstrous. Mrs. Stringham is not only a social, but an authorial, parasite: "She attaches herself to Milly Theale . . . with an excitement that 'positively [makes] her hand a while tremble too much for the pen,'" and she "confesses an inclination to 'put Kate Croy in a book and see what she could so do with her'" (229). Karcher is right about the satire of James's representation of the woman writer, but it is not a representation that he offers entirely as the opposite of himself. Like Susan Shepherd Stringham, it is James who puts Milly and Kate into a book, who must decide whether to "chop [them] up fine or serve [them] whole." In other words, James here represents *himself* as the woman writer, however "monstrous" he/she may be.[8] James himself is the one who profits from an invalid woman's drama. When we remember that James used his beloved cousin, Minny Temple, and his sister Alice as models for Milly Theale, then we see further that it is James, himself, who is the social observer, who puts his friends into books to see what he can do with them.

Like the women writers of the nineteenth century, he represents a world in which men are moral invalids: Lionel Croy, Lord Mark, and Merton Densher are exceedingly weak men. And women suffer physically for men's moral failings: Milly's illness is worsened by Lord Mark's revelations and Merton's betrayal, and Kate and her sister suffer because of Lionel's misdeeds. But the world in which James's characters act out their drama is no longer a nineteenth-century world, no longer influenced by a domestic economy in which gifts like Milly Theale's bequest to Merton Densher can be understood to represent a clear moral viewpoint.

James sets out three "entrances" into the text of *The Wings of the Dove*, portals that delineate the economy of the novel. The frontispiece to the 1909 edition is a photograph of a large wooden door with the caption, "The Doctor's Door." The act of turning the page metonymically represents the opening of that door. Viewed this way, to physically

This photograph by Alvin Langdon Coburn was the frontispiece to the 1909 edition of Henry James's The Wings of the Dove, *where it bears the caption, "The Doctor's Door." (Courtesy of the Houghton Library, Harvard University)*

enter James's text, we must go past that door into the doctor's arena, an arena in which one may find a cure for illness but in which profit is made from illness, whether or not there is a cure.

For the New York edition of the novel, James added a preface, which, like the photograph of the doctor's door, alerts us to the fact that we are entering a sphere in which illness and economic transactions are to be our subjects. Describing his decision to pursue the subject of a young woman's battle with death, James notes that he had been reluctant to undertake it because the subject "might have a great deal to give, but would probably ask for equal services in return, and would collect this debt to the last shilling" (3). Describing his "economy of composition" (13), James explains that he "was to find it long since of a blest wisdom that no expense should be incurred or met, in any corner of picture of [his], without some concrete image of the account kept of it, that is of its being organically re-economised" (15). His preface signals our entry into a world of accounts, exact reckonings of worth, and reciprocal obligations.[9]

Our third "entrance" into the text, in the first chapter, is through the "vulgar little room" in a "vulgar little street" that belongs to Kate Croy's father. In this shabby room, a testament to the "failure of fortune and of honour," we are introduced to the fierce economic competitiveness that will characterize all human relations in the novel, to the undisguised appraisal of people's worth, and to the ruthless use of illness as a weapon in this competition. Kate has been called to her father under the pretext that he "was ill, too ill to leave his room" (I, 1, i, 23),[10] only to find him, in fact, out. When he returns, ostensibly from a visit to the chemist, he tells her that he is still "exceedingly unwell" and has called her to him "that you may see me as I really am" (I, 1, i, 24). What she (as well as the reader) sees is that he is not "exceedingly unwell" but faking illness in an attempt to gain sympathy—and probably money—from Kate. To that end, Lionel Croy urges Kate to accept her aunt's offer (to "do" for her, if she will forsake her failed father) and to "work it." He even offers his "illness" and failure as potential bargaining chips: "I'm not, after all, quite the old ruin not to get something *for* giving up" (I, 1, i, 29). When Kate refuses to agree to the bargain, her father quips, "Do you know, dear, you make me sick?" (I, 1, i, 31). The first chapter turns on the value of Kate as a potential commodity on the marriage market and the value of a "sick" father in dealing with her aunt. John Vernon argues that this world of the "sordid and predatory" is always to be found in James as a "subtext of leisure" ("Labor and Leisure," 185). Its sordid setting and crass evaluation of the extent to which others can be "worked" establishes the tone of interactions among nearly all the other characters in the novel.

These three entries into the text tie economic individualism to health and human relations. In this competitive consumer economy, an exact account of every expense is kept, and every condition can be "worked" and turned to advantage, including illness. Illness can be conjured up to change the balance of power in an economic competition or used as a bargaining chip to increase one's value. Illness can become a tool, an asset in trading practices, or, when taken behind the doctor's door, the basis for the economic exchange between doctor and patient. Typical of other novels of James's late phase, *The Wings of the Dove* represents a world in which "the middle and upper classes are workers in disguise" (Vernon, "Labor and Leisure," 187), but "the only things [these workers] actually produce are effects" (Jean-Christophe Agnew, "The Consuming Vision of Henry James," 84).

"Work" in this novel is a kind of social stock speculation. Everyone makes an investment in their relations with other people; everyone speculates on what that relation might be worth. When Kate tells Merton that Milly "won't have loved you for nothing," she is merely openly representing the underlying relations that have existed between all the other characters, including Sir Luke Strett.[11] Even Milly, the character most exempt from the economizing of human relations, admits to Densher that she is leaving London in deference to this social accounting: "Well, it's a kind of economy—I'm saving things up. . . . Though your *account* of it's fantastic—that I'm watching over its *future* . . . I want—in the *interest* itself of what I've had and may still have—not to make stupid mistakes" (II, 6, v, 231, emphasis added). James's consumer economy, in contrast to Southworth's domestic economy, has as its model for human relations not the household, where everyone works to mutual benefit, but the marketplace, where everyone works for individual, personal gain. Maud Lowder, in the character of "Britannia of the Market Place" (as James describes her), is, as Millicent Bell claims, "the mythic divinity of the book, the representative of the great hidden force underlying its events" ("The Dream of Being Possessed and Possessing," 101).

Every character exists within a relation to Milly Theale that depends on what that person can gain from her. Milly is, in one sense, the victim of all this greed; as "dove," she is both innocent and an easy prey for predators. She is the only character who is, at least initially, free of the financial economizing of human relations. But after a season's exposure to the consumer ethics of human valuation, Milly reveals how she has internalized the novel's market economy, even as she recognizes the vulnerability of her position:

> What value did she now have? It throbbed within her as she knelt there that she had none at all; though, holding herself, not yet speaking, she tried, even in the act, to recover what might be possible of it. With that there came to her a light: wouldn't her value, for the man who should marry her, be precisely in the ravage of her disease? *She mightn't last, but her money would.* For a man in whom the vision of her money should be intense . . . any prospective failure on her part to be long for this world might easily count as a positive attraction. Such a man . . . would make the best of her, ill, damaged, disagreeable though she might be, for the sake of eventual benefits. (II, 7, iv, 267–68)

Milly comes to think herself valuable only to the degree that she can be gotten rid of or will disappear in time—an attitude that Southworth's Hester Grey could never have held. Milly assumes that the only value she can have for a prospective suitor is monetary and that her monetary value is enhanced for a prospective suitor by her illness. Jean-Christophe Agnew, in "The Consuming Vision of Henry James," claims that in his representation of consumer culture, James is "wholly critical *and* wholly complicit" (84), an attitude we can see revealed in this ambiguous representation of Milly Theale. As the one character who might resist the market economy of the novel, the one character whose representation as "magnificent" is consistent with a domestic economy, she nonetheless sets her own value in consumer-economy terms. Like the Bronzino portrait to which she is compared, Milly's value is as a priceless—and dead—object. As Alfred Habegger has noted, even the "magnificent" gesture of her bequest exists within the "universe of reciprocal obligations" ("Reciprocity and the Market Place," 463) as a payment to Densher for his kindness.[12] In Milly Theale, James represents how pervasive the worldview of the marketplace had become.

Milly Theale is not James's first invalid woman whose value is directly proportionate to the "ravage of her disease." Other Jamesian men have been able to recognize the "value" of a woman only after her death. In

Daisy Miller (1878), Winterbourne is unable to grasp Daisy's worth as an unspoiled "American girl" until after she dies of the Roman fever, and John Marcher, in "The Beast in the Jungle" (1903), only discovers May Bartram's value to him at her grave. But in Juliana Bordereau's relation to a morally in-valid man in *The Aspern Papers* (1888), James offers his clearest portrait of profit seeking through illness and death. Placing the figure of Milly Theale against that of Juliana Bordereau reveals some of the economic tensions in *The Wings of the Dove*. In *The Aspern Papers*, as in *The Wings of the Dove*, a young man (the unnamed narrator) wants something desperately (love letters here rather than money), something he can only get after a woman dies. His betrayal of her trust, like Densher's, hastens her death. But in *The Aspern Papers*, the narrator cannot plot to marry the invalid woman and quickly there-after inherit her possessions; instead, he must spar first with the invalid woman and then with her niece. Each woman has her price: for Juliana, who is near death, the letters from her former lover represent a way to raise money (which she will leave to her niece as a bequest), while for the niece, Tita, they represent a way to get married.

In Juliana Bordereau we see the invalid woman at her most perverse; she clearly suspects early on what our narrator wants from her and, at least in the version he provides us, teases him with hints and samples in order to extract more money from him. Indeed, the "green eye-shade" she always wears in his presence recalls an accountant's eyeshade, suggesting that her once poetical eyes have been weakened by her too intense concentration on money matters.[13] In contrast to Juliana's phys-ical invalidism, the narrator is a moral invalid, a man dying to steal a dying woman's most prized possessions. Still, the ill woman is not much better; her trading with the narrator is meant to benefit her niece rather than herself and to exploit one who would exploit her, but she is none-theless trading on past love and using her weakness to improve her bargaining position. The narrator sees Juliana as a fierce competitor, a ruthless tradeswoman, who pushes to see how much money she can extract from him while providing him the least satisfaction.

Traces of this antagonistic relation between an invalid woman and other people remain in *The Wings of the Dove*. In focusing on various kinds of competition—between Kate and Milly, between Merton Den-sher and Lord Mark, even between Densher and Kate and Densher and Milly—the novel questions who "wins" and what "winning" would mean in such a context. As do *Ethan Frome* and *Barren Ground*, James's novel asks how much power and what kind of power an invalid woman can have, and how her illness can be used to gain power over her.

In the preface to *The Wings of the Dove* and in his notebook, James is entirely sympathetic toward Milly.[14] But toward his other invalid women he maintains the double view of the invalid woman that we have seen in other representations since the 1840s: sympathetic though these women are, they nonetheless either bring on or contribute to their own illness (like Daisy Miller) or relentlessly exploit it (like Juliana Bordereau). In *The Wings of the Dove*, again, James maintains this same double vision. How we read Milly depends on whether we assume that she is the completely innocent victim of her body and her "friends," or whether she, like everyone else in the novel, has learned to "work" her situation for what it is worth. James writes, "She worked—and seemingly quite without design—upon the sympathy, the curiosity, the fancy of her associates" (I, 3, i, 83). But in the context of the others' "working" each other, in the context of Milly's own sense of her value, and in the context of James's other invalid women, we cannot take his "seemingly" too lightly. In this novel in which upper-class women "work like niggers and navvies" (II, 6, v, 231), even the working of Milly's illness cannot be an entirely innocent activity. Nor can her disease be simply reckoned within the domestic economy; since Milly is influenced by the consumer economy in which she lives, we can never be sure her illness is unrelated to a desire for personal gain.

In his notebooks, James refers to her illness as "consumption, heart-disease, or whatever" (*The Notebooks of Henry James*, 169), but in the text, it is never specified. Although diagnosing Milly Theale has been something of a critical sport, Milly's illness remains mysterious, doubtful; its origins are unclear, its treatment obscure.[15] In fact, the only direct references to her illness in the text are Sir Luke's assertions that she is not ill at all. He claims that she can live if she wants to; he tells her simply "to live," to be active, to "see all she can" (I, 5, iii, 149–51). When Sir Luke calls her a "capital case" (I, 5, iii, 149), Milly interprets his remark as a death sentence, despite his repeated disclaimers. She believes he is putting up a brave front in order to spare her. She, however, is "too subtle" to fall for such ruses: "She either mattered, and then she was ill; or she didn't matter, and then she was well enough" (I, 5, iv, 155). Milly's "subtlety" turns on the fact that "she had been treated—hadn't she?—as if it were in her power to live; and yet one wasn't treated so—was one?—unless it had come up, quite as much, that one might die" (I, 5, iv, 152). Milly's subtlety makes her illness itself suspicious. Virginia Fowler notes that Milly's death is, "perhaps unconsciously, to some extent self-willed" (*Henry James's American Girl*, 89).

The novel suggests that Milly's illness may be willful, the result of her "secretly romancing . . . all over the place" (I, 5, iii, 146). Milly, whose thoughts are "like the secrecies of a little girl playing with dolls when conventionally 'too big'" (I, 5, i, 132), plans to present herself in an expected role, contrives to be what others want her to be. In the first mention of Milly's illness, Susan Stringham asks her if she is feeling unwell; Milly's response is, "I don't know—haven't really the least idea. But it might be well to find out" (I, 3, ii, 90). When she thinks she has "found out" that she is ill, Milly senses that her role has changed: "The beauty of the bloom had gone from the small old sense of safety. . . . But the beauty of the idea of a great adventure . . . had been offered her instead" (I, 5, iv, 152). She can only have this "great adventure," then, by being ill.

Later, after she and Susan have both seen Sir Luke and, apparently, he has told them nothing, we see more of Milly's "romancing." She suggests that Susan and Sir Luke could "quite fall in love" and therefore "make . . . no end of a good thing of me." She elaborates her medical romance into a kind of recreation of her lost nuclear family: "We'll be— the three of us, with whatever others, oh, as many as the case requires, any one you like!—a sight for the gods" (II, 7, i, 240–41). Throughout the novel there are suggestions that Milly is creating for herself a very romantic (or melodramatic) illness indeed. She tells her suitor Lord Mark that she rented the Venetian palace because she would like to die there (II, 7, iv, 269) and then, we are left to presume, times her death for Christmas Eve.[16] None of these instances are proof that Milly wills the illness itself, but they suggest that, at the very least, she "works" her illness to its greatest advantage. In *A Woman's Place in the Novels of Henry James*, Elizabeth Allen calls Milly a shape-shifter because of her ability to "transform and control the way she appears" (153), depending on her observers and what they expect. If she can be at will "a dove," "magnificent," or an "American girl," why not an invalid woman, too?

The problem with such a question is that no one would *want* to be an invalid woman. But as we have seen (in other chapters), the invalid role has many uses. It not only offers itself to Milly as a "great adventure," but, more importantly, it allows her an opportunity to exploit her "value" to men. Since Milly realizes, as we saw above, that her value is proportionate to her nearness to death, she might see a way to use that illness to attract Densher. Virginia Fowler points out that "since Milly seems to believe that she cannot compete with Kate for Densher's love as a normal woman, then her way of 'making it up' to Kate perhaps constitutes an effort to change the grounds of the competition. Kate could not, certainly, compete with a dying girl" (*Henry James's American Girl*, 96). Such an interpretation certainly explains why Milly, after her first visit to Sir Luke, feels as if she has taken up a weapon:

> It was as if she had had to pluck off her breast, to throw away, some friendly ornament, a familiar flower, a little old jewel, that was part of her daily dress; and to take up and shoulder as a substitute some queer defensive weapon, a musket, a spear, a battle-axe—conducive possibly in a higher degree to a striking appearance, but demanding all the effort of the military posture.
>
> She felt this instrument, for that matter, already on her back, so that she proceeded now in very truth after the fashion of a soldier on a march—proceeded as if, for her initiation, the first charge had been sounded. (I, 5, iv, 152–53)

What remains unclear is whether she is a soldier in the struggle against illness or whether illness is her weapon in some struggle. But if it is the latter, then one could claim that Milly finds a way to use illness to achieve an unfair competitive edge. In the consumer economy in which most of the characters in the novel operate, it is assumed that if Milly could marry, she would get well. Susan Shepherd Stringham tells Maud Lowder that the doctor has as much as told her that Milly should be in love; the two of them decide that it should be with Densher (II, 7, i, 247–48). In other words, they decide that Milly's acquisition of Densher would cure her (an acquisitiveness that resembles Maggie and Adam Verver's in James's *The Golden Bowl*). While we never get as direct a rendering of Milly's understanding, it seems clear that she (like Ethan Frome) at least hopes that love and marriage will cure her and perhaps uses her power over Densher's sympathies to attract him. She can therefore use illness as a weapon in the battle of love at the same time that she uses love as a weapon in the battle against illness.

Vern Wagner, in "Henry James: Money and Sex," argues that in the most diabolical construction of this situation, Milly realizes that her money alone is not enough to attract Densher and so uses her illness and its promise of soon-to-be-inherited wealth as a lure. He suggests that *The*

Wings of the Dove is possibly the "next to the 'wickedest' story James ever wrote," because if Milly's illness is willful, then her death is, too, since it becomes a weapon directed against Kate Croy and Merton Densher. "Her death therefore is her final victory, for it cools the plot against her, wins her the man, and defeats the other girl" (225). But as we saw in the previous chapter, illness is a very peculiar weapon, and "victories" won by its means are mixed at best. In Wagner's version, Milly's only chance to "win" is to die. The "victory" Wagner sees is an entirely negative one: she "defeats" Kate but does not win anything for herself. In the material economy of the marketplace, the only economy in which such a competition could be staged, such a victory can make no sense because it offers Milly no material reward. Wagner therefore confuses the potential for "sentimental power" that Milly's death offers (that is, the power to spiritually improve Kate and Densher by her sacrifice) with her "consumer power" to purchase Densher with her great wealth.

This confusion is not Wagner's alone. James leaves obscure which economy drives Milly's actions and Densher's reactions. By not revealing the contents of Milly's last letter, James manages to make impossible a confirmation of whether her bequest to Densher is a sign of forgiveness or retaliation; all James makes clear is that she did leave Densher a great deal of money. After reading the letter from Milly's lawyers, Kate tells Densher that the bequest is "worthy of her. . . . [It is] stupendous" (II, 10, vi, 402). Milly is, to the end, a "girl who couldn't get away from her wealth" (I, 3, i, 86), whose *worth*iness is measured at her death by her money. Like Wharton's Lily Bart, her intentions are left to be read only through her last economic transaction.

James's novel differs from the novels written by women in the nineteenth century in his attitude toward women's power in society. In the domestic novel, as Mary Kelley points out in "The Sentimentalists: Promise and Betrayal in the Home," the ills women suffer are caused by men. She claims that this suffering is most often caused by male materialism; "Novel after novel, story after story, repeated the melodramatic tale of man's obsessive quest for wealth and social position" (440), a quest that threatened women's lives and health. Women's novels were therefore challenges to a world corrupted by men, which women have the potential to change for the better. In *The Wings of the Dove*, though, all the men are amazingly weak, and it is women who embark on the "obsessive quest for wealth and social position." Lionel Croy, Lord Mark, and Merton Densher all cause women much pain and make matters worse, but those matters are determined by women. James follows the domestic tradition in setting Lionel Croy at the opening of the novel, illustrating his disastrous effects upon Kate, and in making Lord Mark the instrument of Milly's eventual demise. But the real power in the novel is centered in Maud Lowder; it is she who controls the "circle of petticoats" in which Milly's drama is played out and who represents the marketplace. Kate, too, is the real instigator of Milly's betrayal, not Densher; she has the power to influence him when she gives in to her aunt's sordid material quest. James therefore distances himself from the tradition of women's novels by examining women's manipulation, competition, and acquisition.

In a move similar to Wharton's and Glasgow's (as we saw in chapter 5), James describes the domestic world as identical to the business world and thereby challenges the stereotypical gender distinctions of the nineteenth-century novel. But James equivocates in ways that neither of these women writers do. Wharton and Glasgow, however problematically, set up a new economy of earned illness and health with which they replace the domestic economy of self-sacrifice. James does not offer any new working economy in which to understand Milly's sacrifice, her gift, or Kate's and Densher's renunciations. He condemns the consumer economy but stops short of affirming another. The ending of the novel offers no assurance that Kate and Densher will have benefited from Milly's sacrifice or from their own, nor does it affirm Milly's "value" to them or to the reader. Milly's final message—whatever its intent—never gets through. Her "will" is never accomplished.

James's novel therefore represents the end of the domestic economy but does not fully move into the consumer economy. Milly Theale's illness becomes a lens to focus James's scrutiny of both economies but, as such, remains itself unclassifiable. James leaves us unable to measure the worth of his invalid woman, unable to calculate her value— perhaps suggesting that, after all, measurements of human worth are inappropriate. But by obscuring the economic forces that make illness "pay," he leaves them essentially untouched by his critique.

Clinical Ethics and the Invalid Economy

In *Tender Is the Night*, F. Scott Fitzgerald, unlike Henry James, does work out a new economy to replace the domestic—one in which the invalid woman is able to accomplish her will absolutely. James, Wharton, and Glasgow all leave open the possibility that consuming could lead to health (Zeena Frome might have been well if she had had enough money to live in the city, as might Jason Greylock; Milly Theale might have recovered had either she or her wealth really attracted Densher), but Fitzgerald takes such speculations to their logical conclusion. His American heiress, Nicole Warren Diver, whom Fitzgerald characterizes by her "wholesale buying," eventually recovers from hysteria, presumably at the cost of her physician-husband's own health. Here, at least as far as health is concerned, the rich *are* different. But Fitzgerald's therapeutic economy of consumption is not the same as that in Wharton's *Ethan Frome* or Glasgow's *Barren Ground*, where *commodities* could hold the key to health. Instead, Fitzgerald offers the clinic as a new economic model, representing a *service* economy based on treatment and release. But even though such a "service economy" bears a resemblance to the earlier "domestic economy" where women offer their services or sacrifices for the good of others, the services offered here are strictly for sale, the sacrifices ineffective and unacknowledged.

As does James, Fitzgerald represents a clash of ethics with the prevailing economy. Our reading of the novel depends on our interpretation of the various characters' complicity with the economic system that the novel attacks. In contrast to James, Fitzgerald does not question whether his invalid woman is at odds with the world around her; instead, it is the doctor, Dick Diver, who is out of touch with prevailing economic realities. In Fitzgerald's world, the woman's recovery comes at the point when she accepts the clinical economy; the man's failure comes when he can no longer function within it. We can better understand this "clinical economy" and how it establishes and fails to establish the "value" of the invalid woman by looking at Fitzgerald's representation of the relation between the ill woman and her doctor in the context of other, earlier, representations. Many of the earlier figures of invalidism—some of them entirely contradictory—appear in *Tender Is the Night*, worked into this new economy.

Unlike James, Fitzgerald envisions a world in stark contrast to the one that appears in nineteenth-century novels written by women. In *Tender Is the Night*, Fitzgerald appropriates the domestic economy but moves it to a male realm—his model for social relations is no longer the household but the clinic—and thereby redefines the social/sexual spheres of the sexes. Such a redefinition necessitates several realignments. Ruth

Prigozy argues in "From Griffith's Girls to *Daddy's Girl*" that during the 1920s and 1930s the sentimental power of women was finding new life in the film industry. The new heroines of the silver screen were American "child-women" whose virtue defied the corruption of their fathers. Fitzgerald parodies these films and the sentimental power of women in his description of Rosemary's movie, *Daddy's Girl*. His nightmare image of the father-daughter relation—in Nicole's victimization by her father—directly disputes the notion that such child-women can reform their fathers. In Fitzgerald's novel, women have none of the "sentimental power" that they had in nineteenth-century women's fiction or in twentieth-century cinematic simplifications of it. Instead, the male doctor becomes the representative of morality and self-sacrifice to community good.

Fitzgerald uses the morality that informs nineteenth-century women's fictions and the films that developed from them, but he completely inverts it. Here, as in domestic novels, illness is suffered because of the sins of others, but Fitzgerald enacts a transformation of that system: Nicole is originally made ill by her father's violation of her, but as she recovers, Dick takes on the role of sufferer. Here, as in domestic fiction, illness becomes a sign of value, but it becomes a *male* value. Like nineteenth-century women writers, Fitzgerald idealizes work, expresses a disregard for material gain, and advocates an ethic of self-sacrifice. But Fitzgerald directly challenges the woman-centered ideology of domesticity by representing such virtues in a man rather than a woman. Fitzgerald appropriates and inverts domestic ideology, rejecting as in-valid the detachment and distance necessitated by clinical ethics. Oddly enough, in this economy based on a clinical model, it is ultimately the doctor who must suffer, who must sacrifice himself, in part because he cannot reconcile the domestic morality on which his ideology of service is based with an economy where service is for sale.

Whereas earlier writers saw the feminine values of the household as enriching, the guidance of women as improving the race, Fitzgerald maintains that such values and guidance have weakened the American man: "The American Woman . . . [possessed] the clean-sweeping irrational temper that had broken the moral back of a race and made a nursery out of a continent" (232). In Fitzgerald's understanding, it is the "Gold Star Muzzers" who send their sons to war, not the war-loving acquisitive fathers represented in women's fiction. Fitzgerald represents a world made invalid by women, where one man's efforts to

maintain the honest virtues of hard work, love, and caring are foiled by
an invalid economy that denigrates his sacrifice. *Tender Is the Night* is
clearly a reactionary novel—reacting against the ideology of domesticity that represents moral values as feminine. As Judith Fetterley
argues in "Who Killed Dick Diver?: The Sexual Politics of *Tender Is the
Night*," "The enemy in the text is the American woman and the text does
a job on her" (114).[17]

Whatever Diver's own faults, Fitzgerald represents him as a man corrupted by women. In this novel, gender roles are completely switched;
women control the family finances while Dick controls the social sphere,
arranges dinner parties, and "takes care" of other people. Rosemary's
initial impression of Dick is of someone who is "kind and charming—his
voice promised that he would take care of her" (16), and, of course, his
profession, as doctor, is to "take care" of others. As Fetterley rightly
argues, "The world Nicole inhabits, . . . the world Rosemary falls in love
with, is the creation of Dick Diver and it is a woman's world" (115). Even
though Dick creates this world, it is nonetheless supported and controlled by Baby and Nicole Warren's money; it is not just paid for but is
dictated by them. Baby and Nicole determine what style of living the
Divers will maintain; Dick's "job" is to make that life as pleasant as
possible. In direct contrast to virtually every other text in this study, here
it is women who determine the family's social standing, who dictate life-
style to men.[18] Dick stays entirely out of Nicole's money matters, preferring to leave such business decisions up to Baby, even when it concerns
his own professional life. Ultimately, Dick's failure is this acquiescence to
women.

The "obsessive quest for money and social position" that, Mary Kelley
argues, characterizes men in much nineteenth-century women's fiction
and that is transferred to women's domestic dealings in Henry James's
fiction, is represented in *Tender Is the Night* as typical of women.
Women have taken over the business world entirely, and men like Dick
have given up the pursuit of money. Fitzgerald claims that in Dick "a
desire for money [was wedded] to an unacquisitive nature" (201), a
characterization that could apply to all the men in the novel. None of
them are really concerned with money, nor are they involved in business. Dick is a physician-writer, more in love with his profession than its
potential for financial gain; Franz Gregorovius is also a physician and
also apparently unconcerned with great wealth; Abe North is a musi-
cian. Even Tommy Barban, the mercenary warrior, fights more for the

love of fighting than for the financial reward it offers. Businessmen in the novel are unsavory or criminal: Nicole's grandfather, the origin of the Warren money, was a "horse-trader," her father a committer of incest.

Despite the fact that few men in James's *The Wings of the Dove* work, there is no direct condemnation of acquisitive work there. In fact, the men in *The Wings of the Dove* who do not support themselves or their families come in for scorn. Lionel Croy's dependence on his daughter's support is the source of James's and the reader's distaste for him, and Lord Mark's all but invisible ambition for either work or government raises questions about why Maud Lowder is attracted to him. In *Tender Is the Night*, though, working for the sake of money alone flies directly in the face of the novel's ethics.[19] The oddness of *Tender Is the Night* is its glorification of work when almost no one does any. Despite Nicole's claim, in the section of Book 2 written in her voice, that "you've taught me that work is everything and I believe you" (161–62), neither she nor Dick end up following that belief. The one "worker" in the novel— Rosemary, the actress—makes her appearance in the Divers' world because working has made her ill; she caught the grippe while making a film, necessitating her vacation in Europe (17). In contrast to James's world, in which members of the upper class are disguised as "workers," here even work is disguised as leisure. Like Dick's "work" on the beach with the rake and shovel, his real work—his always incomplete writing, his periodic visits to the clinic—always appears more as avocation than vocation.

In *The Wings of the Dove*, the driving economic force behind characters' "working" is accumulation, if not of money itself—as in Kate Croy's and Merton Densher's "working" of Milly—then of social prestige and status. In the world of *Tender Is the Night*, however, the accumulation of money occurred in the past; it is something Nicole's grandfather did. The economy of *Tender Is the Night* exists to provide enjoyment of that accumulation. In his provocative essay, "Money Makes Manners Make Man Make Woman," Richard Godden describes the difference between Henry James's and F. Scott Fitzgerald's economies: "What one witnesses between 1900 and 1930 is a shift in economic emphasis from 'accumulation' to 'reproduction.' . . . Put crudely—by 1900 the accumulated capital exists; the real issue is how to produce sufficient profit to support that accumulation" (19). He argues that this necessitates a shift from manners to fashion, from taste to style, and that the world Fitzgerald represents is one in which such a shift has been accomplished. For Godden, this shift is represented in *Tender Is the Night* by Rosemary and the emerging mass culture industry; Rosemary becomes a mechanically reproducible commodity, promising fulfillment but never delivering it. She represents the perfect consumer product: able to be had anywhere but never really had (29).

There is another way to understand the shift of economies represented in *Tender Is the Night*; in Fitzgerald's economy, the goals of consumption have changed. For this changed economy, the clinic is a better model for the attitude toward consumption Fitzgerald reflects than is the film industry. The prevailing mode of the novel is not merely the pursuit of the freedom from pain; Fitzgerald's characters seem to want oblivion in their pleasure seeking. In *The Wings of the Dove*, James remarks that "Europe was the great American sedative" (I, 3, i, 82). In *Tender Is the Night*, Fitzgerald portrays the society of Americans that develops in the intervening thirty years, a society of wealthy Americans who used Europe as a drug (and who use drugs in Europe). In this sense, Fitzgerald's invalid woman, Nicole, represents her class because it is she, specifically, who is brought to Europe to be "cured." In James's novel, the model for social relations is stock speculation, but in Fitzgerald's, it is therapeutic treatment. Fitzgerald's characters are motivated by a desire for relief from pain. When Dick discusses Rosemary with her mother, her value to him becomes that of a drug: "She had come to possess all the world's dark magic; the blinding belladonna, the caffein [*sic*] converting physical into nervous energy, the mandragora that imposes harmony" (164). When Nicole considers whether or not she should have an affair with Tommy, she bases her decision on the possible effect on her health: she "honestly thought that such an experiment might have a *therapeutic value*" (291, emphasis added).

This "clinical economy" seemingly has much in common with the commodity-based consumer economy we saw in *Ethan Frome*, but it would be more accurate to describe it as a *service* economy. Just as Zeena wants to own Ethan, Nicole wants to own Dick; just as Ethan envisions a life with Mattie as the resolution to his problems, Nicole envisions a life with Dick as the solution to hers. But in *Tender Is the Night*, the focus is not as much on ownership, on accumulation, as it is on the service that one person can offer another. Ownership alone is not enough; Nicole leads "a lonely life owning Dick who did not want to be owned" (180). While Zeena wants to own Ethan but never use him—

like the pickle dish she keeps on the top shelf—Nicole wants to make use of Dick's strength, his ability to create a safe haven for her, his stability and kindness. Perhaps Nicole simply expects more for her money, since she obviously makes a much larger investment, but the difference between Zeena's and Nicole's attitudes toward their husbands is better described in terms of the difference between a commodity and a service economy. Value is calculated not by ownership but by use.

The rudiments of such a clinical economy can be seen in *The Wings of the Dove*, but in most cases, such relations are overtly professional, like Milly's relation to Sir Luke or to Eugenio, or they are abortive, such as Maud Lowder and Susan Shepherd Stringham's plan to heal Milly by involving her with Densher. But by the time Fitzgerald writes *Tender Is the Night*, the figure for *all* social relations has become the clinical model: treatment, payment, and release. When someone no longer amuses, as Dick no longer amuses by the end of the novel, their usefulness—their value—is depleted and they are dropped from society and by their spouses. The payment for remaining useful, according to Mary North Minghetti, is "nourishment." She tells Dick, "All people want is to have a good time and if you make them unhappy you cut yourself off from nourishment" (313). The paradox of *Tender Is the Night* is that the only character who does not seem to recognize this social pattern, who does not thrive in this clinical economy, is the doctor.

It would seem that Dick Diver, a physician himself, would find a clinical economy congenial. It is Dick, however, who has the most difficulty with it, because such an economy demands a truly clinical detachment that Dick cannot maintain in either his personal or his professional life. The social world in which he involves himself is constructed on principles of detachment; people here do not get involved. Like Baby Warren, they keep accounts of whether or not people have "been paid" for their services; if the account is clear, those who are no longer useful are dismissed. Dick tries but cannot settle into this economy. As he bids good-bye to Mrs. Speers, after telling her he is in love with Rosemary, Dick "once more accepted the fiction that he shared Mrs. Speers' detachment" (164). But Fitzgerald's portrait of Dick is of a man with no detachment at all. Dick's failing health comes as a result of his inability to maintain the detachment necessary within a clinical setting or a clinical economy. In this novel where people are admired for being "hard," Dick Diver is irredeemably "soft."

Even in his professional contact with people, Dick is unable to remain emotionally uninvolved with his patients. While treating the woman who is his "most interesting case," the woman with the "nervous eczema" who turns out at her death to have been suffering from neurosyphilis, Dick's response to her is more emotional than clinical.[20] "In the awful majesty of her pain he went out to her unreservedly, almost sexually. He wanted to gather her up in his arms, as he so often had Nicole, and cherish even her mistakes, so deeply were they a part of her" (185). Later, a "scene" occurs after Nicole receives a letter from a former patient who accuses Dick of seducing her daughter. Even though Dick recognizes it as "the letter of a maniac," an accusation of which he is innocent, we see in his admission that he had kissed the daughter (187) that he is guilty of overstepping the proprieties of a clinical setting. But Fitzgerald represents such "improprieties" on Dick's part as virtues. Like his father—a minister—Dick does not attempt to separate his care for his patients from caring for his patients. But such emotional involvements clearly put him at odds with clinical ethics and with the clinical economy at work in the leisured world of Americans in Europe. He is initially successful in this society because he is so intent on "curing" other people, on taking care of them, but he fails in the long run because he is unable to maintain the detachment that they expect to accompany that kind of care.

Nicole Diver, on the other hand, thrives in such an economy. Fitzgerald represents her as *the* archetypal consumer, in a passage reminiscent of Lawrence Selden's evaluation of Lily Bart in Wharton's *The House of Mirth* and James's characterization of Maud Lowder as the divinity of the market: "Nicole was the product of much ingenuity and toil. For her sake . . . chicle factories fumed and link belts grew . . . men mixed toothpaste in vats . . . girls canned tomatoes quickly in August or worked rudely at the Five-and-Tens on Christmas Eve; half-breed Indians toiled on Brazilian coffee plantations. . . . These were some of the people who gave a tithe to Nicole, and as the whole system swayed and thundered onward it lent a feverish bloom to such processes of her as wholesale buying" (55). Here it is not *products* that Nicole consumes, however, but the *services* of people all over the world. Nicole is the capitalist exploiting the labor of workers all over the world; these people give "a tithe" to the woman who is the goddess of the new capitalist ethic. Nicole is able to buy her way to health because she knows how to make use of others' labor, how to turn it to her own good. In contrast to Lily Bart, whose health fails as does her ability to consume, Nicole's consuming fails with her health. Describing Nicole's massive luggage, Fitzgerald notes that concern with material goods can signal "a superabundance of interest, and, *except during flashes of illness,* Nicole was capable of being curator of it all" (258, emphasis added). Her loss of interest in possessions, then, is a sign of Nicole's illness.

Richard Godden argues that Nicole in the end is not cured but simply made into the perfect consumer ("Money Makes Manners Make Man Make Woman," 27). But as we have just seen, Nicole's health *is based* on consumption. She really does recover because in this clinical consumer economy, consumption is health. But Fitzgerald questions the price of that recovery and whether an invalid woman is worth it. Nicole is represented, therefore, not merely as the capitalist exploiting anonymous workers' labor but as someone who even exploits her husband for her own therapeutic ends. Fitzgerald represents a service economy that works, but only for the rich or the sick—categories that, after all, are not so different in the novel. Healthy workers, like Dick, are used up by it, made ill by it. As do Gilman (in "The Yellow Wallpaper") and Wharton (in *The House of Mirth*), Fitzgerald represents illness as a healthy resistance to a sick society, but he represents that society as a female one that oppresses men. The clinical economy, he argues, is an in-valid economy—diseased and fit only for invalids.

Dick is "corrupted" by Nicole because her cure necessitates his contact with the American rich. Unfortunately, the world that cures Nicole is deadly for Dick. The image of the beautiful young man, poisoned by his too-prolonged contact with a beautiful but tainted young woman is a familiar figure in this study, derived from Hawthorne's "Rappaccini's Daughter." The woman is corrupted by her father—the symbolic incest in Hawthorne's fiction becomes literal in Fitzgerald's—and she passes that taint on to her lover; that taint is figured as money here. Brian Way, in *F. Scott Fitzgerald and the Art of Social Fiction*, rightly claims that "of all the acts of self-betrayal which contribute to [Dick's] ruin, the abandonment of this *proper* work is probably the most serious in its effects" (137, emphasis added). Nicole and the seduction of her money tempt him to abandon that work; "her income . . . seemed to belittle his work" (170). Like Beatrice, Nicole is the guilty innocent, who through her love for Dick unwittingly taints him with her father's poisonous wealth.[21]

Nicole does not have to die at the end of the story to prove her true value, but Fitzgerald does not necessarily imagine a better economy than Hawthorne's, nor does he envision a better figure for the invalid. Nicole thrives as Dick declines—the worse he becomes, the better she is. In other words, Fitzgerald represents her as a vampire, sucking the life from Dick. At one point, Fitzgerald offers an image that suggests that all American women are vampiristic; Nicole asks Tommy to kiss her on the lips, to which Tommy replies, "That's so American. . . . When I was in America last year there were girls who would tear you apart with their lips . . . until their faces were scarlet with the blood around the lips" (295). The vision of women sucking the lifeblood from strong men suggests that Nicole is just such a woman, one who has already drained Dick of his strength, beauty, and health. In the "economy" Fitzgerald envisions, one competes not just for commodities, or for money, but for life. Judith Fetterley argues that "Nicole can become well only at [Dick's] expense. . . . Fitzgerald's imagination cannot transcend the economic imagery which dominates it. In such a metaphoric system, the interests of men and women inevitably are oppositional, for given a limited quantity of sanity, integration, creativity, if one gets more, the other must get less" ("Who Killed Dick Diver?," 127). Fitzgerald, in some ways, reinstates the nineteenth-century closed energy model, but on a social level.

In *The Wings of the Dove*, wealth is governed by an economy based on the scarcity of wealth—for Kate Croy to get more money, Milly Theale must give hers up—but in *Tender Is the Night*, it is health that is governed by this economy. In this way, then, Fitzgerald's novel owes as much to Henry James's *The Sacred Fount* as to *The Wings of the Dove* or to Hawthorne. Nicole and Dick are yet another couple from James's country-house party; Nicole drains the life and youth of her husband, just as the narrator of *The Sacred Fount* suspects Mrs. Brissenden of doing. In *Tender Is the Night*, Fitzgerald carries the emotional vampirism so common to James's work to the physical level. Even though Dick is only five years older at the novel's close than he was at its opening, he has lost his youth, his career, and his ability to heal people. Even though he is only thirty-eight, Fitzgerald writes, "he was not young any more with a lot of nice thoughts and dreams to have about himself" (311).

Finally, Dick is the invalid figure here, made to suffer because of women's wrongdoings. Like Edith Wharton in *Ethan Frome* and Ellen Glasgow in *Barren Ground*, Fitzgerald imagines a world turned around, in which women survive and men are feminized and therefore ill. But unlike the women writers, who see illness and health alike as being earned, Fitzgerald depicts a world where health can be bought and consumed. As does Henry James, Fitzgerald depicts the destruction of nineteenth-century standards of morality and virtue by twentieth-century consumerism, but here his symbolic representation of that destruction is a man, not a woman. In an invalid economy, both male authors claim, only the sick survive. Unlike female authors, though, both suggest that this economy is directed by—and for—women.

> *This is a vast commonplace of*
> *literature: The Woman copies the*
> *Book. In other words, every body*
> *is a citation of the "already-*
> *written."*
> *—Roland Barthes,*
>   S/Z *(1974)*
> *The women one meets—what are*
> *they but books one has already*
> *read?*
> *—Henry James,*
>   The Wings of the Dove
>   *(1902)*

Conclusion:

Invalidism

and the Female

Body Politic

To conclude my discussion of the figure of the invalid woman in American fiction and culture, I want to focus on two very different representations of feminine illness. One is from Tillie Olsen's *Yonnondio: From the Thirties,* which, though not published until 1974, was nonetheless written during the 1930s, and the other is from the 1939 film *Dark Victory.* I will not analyze these two "moments" from the 1930s. Instead, I want to let them stand, schematically, for two extremes in the political figuring of invalidism.

The first figure: Anna Holbrook, in *Yonnondio,* lays in "the blood on the kitchen floor, the two lifeless braids of hair framing her face like a corpse, the wall like darkness behind" (75). Suffering from the poverty, malnutrition, and heat exhaustion brought on by living in an urban slum and by too much childbearing, she has a miscarriage, enters a semicoma for two days, and spends weeks in apathetic lethargy, unable to tend her house, her children, or herself. "A gaunt Anna who could not understand this body of hers that tired so quickly and quivered like a naked nerve; this stranger self. One minute her old competence and strength; the next: addled, brutal, lost" (91). She may never be the happy and healthy woman she was when the Holbrooks worked their own farm on the Plains. When the bank took their farm, it took her health, too. With indomitable spirit, though, she begins to recover, struggles back to something like health and strength, and puts her house and children back in order. As the novel closes, she wakes her husband, telling him, "The air's changin', Jim" (132).

The second figure: Judith Traherne, an American heiress played by Bette Davis in *Dark Victory*, is dying. She has known that the "glyoma" in her brain would kill her eventually. Her doctor, whom she has married, has told her that "she'll seem well and normal like everyone else. . . . There may be a moment, toward the end, when her sight may not be quite as good as usual, a dimming of vision, in a few hours, perhaps three or four . . ." As she plants bulbs outside the country cottage/laboratory where she and her husband moved after their marriage—leaving her mansion, palatial estate, and horse barns for a simpler way of life—her eyesight begins to fail. She and the audience know the end is near. For the next sixteen minutes of the film, she bravely faces death, refusing to tell her husband what is happening because that would selfishly keep him to herself and away from the important medical meeting he is on his way to attend. Her illness has taught her the proper perspective on her own importance; before, she was a spoiled pleasure seeker, but now she humbly recognizes her own unimportance when compared to the work her husband does and the unimportance of her money. Shortly before her death, she asks, "Why do people complicate their lives so? . . . All those horses and that house. . . . Here we have nothing and yet we have everything." When she finally bids him goodbye, she goes upstairs to her room to face her "dark victory" alone. As the final scene fades, we see her in her flower-filled bedroom, aesthetically draped across her four-poster bed, the image of holy death.

Throughout this study I have argued for a *politicized* understanding of the representation of illness in American fiction and culture; political, economic, and social emphases are more important in figuring disease than are any "realities" of "actual illness." In the two figures above, we see two radically opposed images that presumably come from the same culture at the same time. In one, a working-class woman sickens be-

Judith Traherne (played by Bette Davis) dies a romantic—and sixteen-minute-long—death in the 1939 film, Dark Victory. *(Courtesy of Turner Entertainment and the George Eastman House; © 1939 Turner Entertainment Co., all rights reserved)*

cause she is worn down by the harshness of Depression life for the poor. In the other, a mysterious, inexplicable illness arbitrarily strikes a woman who has everything to live for: wealth, beauty, energy. But both of these differing views come from the "same" cultural situation, and both respond to and derive from the historical figuring of feminine illness. They do, however, reflect radically different political agendas.

Tillie Olsen, a 1930s Socialist, advocate of workers' rights, and member of the working-class herself, consciously enters a discourse of politicized illness (as she does again in her famous short story of the 1950s, "Tell Me a Riddle"). Her Depression-era story portrays the injustice of workers' lives and the impossibility of remaining forever strong in the face of ever-increasing strains and hardships. *Dark Victory*, on the surface, is not intentionally political, but it must be viewed as a Depression-era film, a film about loss, about the power of loss to spiritually redeem, and about the unimportance of wealth when considered in the context of lost health and happiness. While *Yonnondio* urges readers to rebel, to resist the capitalist power that keeps them poor, undereducated, underfed, and overworked, *Dark Victory* urges acceptance of one's lot and concentration on spiritual rather than material good and suggests that the rich are not really different—they suffer as much as workers do.

It is tempting for a feminist, leftist reader to characterize the difference between *Yonnondio* and *Dark Victory* as a difference between realism and propaganda, just as the capitalist might well characterize *Yonnondio* as socialist propaganda (since, he might claim, we know that there are no hungry in America). But, of course, both are political fictions; however true or "realistic" they may be, both represent the causes and results of physical suffering in ways that have specific social and economic agendas, which are, however, not simple. For while *Yonnondio* asserts the strength, honesty, and blamelessness of the poverty-stricken invalid, it nonetheless extends the figure of the working class as sick and therefore potentially sickening. And while *Dark Victory* asserts the arbitrariness of disease and the unimportance of money, it nonetheless develops the historical connection between spiritual goodness, material wealth, and illness, suggesting again that a wealthy woman's illness is somehow more important than anyone else's.

Both representations therefore come out of conventional representations for feminine illness in American fiction. *Yonnondio* belongs to the "tradition" we saw as early as *Retribution*, in the slave-heiress Minny Dozier whose maltreatment and forced labor brought on her illness, but that we found much more clearly in Wharton's *Ethan Frome* and Glasgow's *Barren Ground*. In *Yonnondio*, as in Wharton's and Glasgow's novels, harsh, unrelenting, and fruitless work leads to illness and pain, but such work also builds the strength of character it takes to resist such adversity. And, as in these earlier texts, the assumption on which *Yonnondio* is based is that money could cure Anna Holbrook's ills: just enough money to buy adequate food, pay rent on a decent house, and buy sufficient clothes for her children would make all the difference to Anna's health. Wharton and Glasgow, though, represent relative poverty, a poverty that is as much spiritual as material; in *Yonnondio*, we see absolute material poverty joined to spiritual and imaginative wealth. Where Wharton and Glasgow couple illness and personal, individual blame, Olsen resists; in her world, illness is neither arbitrary nor the fault of the individual but is caused by an unjust system. Illness is, however, still feminine. As have other writers in the United States since 1840, Olsen represents a world in which women suffer political injustices directly in their bodies.

Dark Victory, on the other hand, comes from another tradition that we see in *Retribution*—in Hester Grey—and that we have followed through to *The Wings of the Dove*. Judith Traherne is young, beautiful, wealthy, and, except for a few weeks when she believes she has been betrayed, always kind to other people. She, like Hester and Milly Theale, has much to live for, and she learns what Hester and Milly already knew—that material wealth is the least important kind of value. Like Hester, she realizes her own relative unimportance in the face of her husband's work. Like so many other invalid women, she rises to the occasion of her illness and reveals her better self. Finally, as we have seen in *Retribution*, in Hawthorne's tales, in Wharton's *House of Mirth*, and in James's writings, to prove her goodness, she has to die. We must see her figure, finally, arranged aesthetically on her deathbed to understand her real virtue and true value.

The Political Representation of Feminine Illness

In his essay, "Depicting Disease: A Theory of Representing Illness" in *Disease and Representation*, Sander Gilman suggests that illness is always represented as "Other," a theory relevant to my discussion of American fiction's gendered figuring of illness: "It is the fear of collapse, the sense of dissolution, which contaminates the Western image of all diseases. . . . But the fear we have of our own collapse does not remain internalized. Rather, we project this fear onto the world in order to localize it and, indeed, to domesticate it. For once we locate it, the fear of our own dissolution is removed. Then it is not we who totter on the brink of the collapse, but rather the Other. And it is an-Other who has already shown his or her vulnerability by having collapsed" (1). Therefore, for him, "the images of disease, whether in art or literature, are not in flux, even though they represent collapse. They are solid, fixed images that remain constantly external to our sense of self" (2). He goes on to argue that "the image of all disease, the very face of the patient, is a continuous one" (3) and that the structure of representing illness is based in difference. Although some groups may come to internalize this difference, by their illness they are still recognized as "Other." Even when illness and health switch positions, when illness comes to represent the positive and health the negative, Gilman claims, the representation of illness is still "the glorification of difference" (8).

Gilman's theory of the representation of the ill person as Other seems, in one sense, to accord with my own assertion that in American fiction, illness is understood to be female—that is, Other in a male world. His thesis that the representation of disease is unchanging seems to agree with my claim that figures of illness in the 1930s follow conventions established in the 1840s. But there are important differences in our positions and our findings.

As I argued in the Introduction, although the figure may retain the same outward shape, it often represents something very different; like the signifier, what it signifies can often be dramatically contradictory. Gilman's theory depends on a stability of signifiers, an absolute difference between illness and health, that I do not accept. His study finds similarity in the representations of different illnesses "from madness to AIDS" (as his study is subtitled) and between male illness and female illness. In other words, though it mentions both historical and gender differences, this study devoted to the explication of difference nonetheless elides difference: women, the insane, and homosexuals with AIDS are the same—they are *all* Other. He further assumes a clear difference between health and illness, doctor and patient, writer and reader, or artist and viewer. My study shows the difficulty of maintaining such clear distinctions.

For example, is the narrator of "The Yellow Wallpaper" sane or not? Does Charlotte Perkins Gilman privilege health or illness? Not only does the story refuse an easy answer to such questions, it refuses an easy resolution of difference; in the end, John, the doctor, has fainted after his "treatment" by the woman locked in the room, who both is and is not his wife/the woman in the wallpaper. By the same token, *Retribution* figures illness as the result of both pure goodness and pure evil. *Ethan Frome* figures it as too little power to consume as well as an overinterest in consuming. The representations of illness in *Yonnondio* and *Dark Victory* represent neither a "continuous" image nor a safe indulgence in the "glorification of difference" to assure ourselves of our own self-control. Self-control is represented as elusive; we are subject to the whims of nature, social and economic forces, our own bodies. Even in texts like "The Yellow Wallpaper" and *The House of Mirth*, which seek to explore self-control and to make illness Other, that Otherness is not stable; Gilman and Wharton figure invalids who are not so different from themselves—so even if they succeed in making the *illness* Other, they do not make the *ill woman* Other.

Throughout this study, I have argued that figures of feminine illness develop as responses to or revisions of particular ideologies. But such representations also shape ideology, if one defines it as "a complex and contradictory system of representations . . . through which we experience ourselves in relation to each other and the social structures in which we live" (Judith Newton and Deborah Rosenfelt, *Feminist Criticism and Social Change*, xix). Hawthorne's Zenobia *contributes to* a belief that one should not develop both mind and body as much as she is *shaped by* that belief.

The figure of the invalid woman shapes an ideological response to women as somehow not valid, as, in the words of Margaret Atwood that opened this study, "one who has been invalidated." This figure's political importance, however, lies not in its stability but in its historical variation. Even though the *shape* of the figure remains relatively constant in American fiction—that is, women are continually threatened with invalidism, and illness remains a feminine experience—what that figure signifies is kaleidoscopic, shifting to suit the political needs of its user. It is, therefore, impossible to pin down a simple representation of illness or the ill woman as "Other" and refute it on any political grounds. Both E. D. E. N. Southworth and Nathaniel Hawthorne agree that illness is the result of male abuse of women, but the political import of that contention is very different in their texts. Southworth asserts the need for a woman-centered morality and family, while Hawthorne suggests that perhaps women's lives are just the price men must pay for knowledge. Thus, too, can F. Scott Fitzgerald appropriate Southworth's figures of abused women and guilty men but invert her ideology into a condemnation of feminine morality and turn the abused woman into a Typhoid Mary who passes her disease on to the innocent man who loves her and tries to help her.

Sander Gilman's understanding of the representation of illness as continuous further normalizes it. If illness is always represented as our worst fears of lack of control, it is a normal reaction to a normal condition, not an embodiment of ideology. If it always represents difference, and difference will always remain with us, then we can understand our reactions to it, but we cannot change the representation. In my view, by contrast, if the representation is always political, if it is always constructed according to particular circumstances and situations, it can be materially affected. The effect may not always be "positive" or "progressive"—in fact it may sometimes be, as with Fitzgerald, politically regressive and reactionary—but it can still be changed. In other words, if our goal is a changed politics of illness, then understanding that illness has often been represented as Other is a useful first step. It is not, however, either the only or the final step. That realization informs Charlotte Perkins Gilman's own *changed* representation of illness. She maintains the same outward figure she had seen in Edgar Allan Poe's work—a woman driven mad by her intellectual needs—but she adapts that figure to serve entirely different political ends. Rather than asserting that women have no right to such intellectual yearnings, as Poe does, she presents the urgent necessity of allowing women to pursue their own productive needs.

Sander Gilman's theory of representation is important to the extent that it can be used to draw lines of difference between those who have the power to define illness, those who must accept their definition as ill, and those who have the power to materially change the experience of it; but it is limited insofar as it assumes a certain amount of immutability within those categories. The representations of the power to define illness and the necessity of accepting that definition are as different in *Yonnondio* and *Dark Victory* as are the figures of the invalid women I have presented. *Yonnondio* is a revolutionary text, urging resistance to capitalist abuses of workers and embodying the failure of that system in the suffering of one woman. *Dark Victory*, on the other hand, is a hegemonic text, urging acceptance of one's lot, since physical life is unimportant in comparison to the spiritual one for which it is merely preparation. In *Yonnondio*, suffering becomes a way of life but not a natural one; in *Dark Victory*, physical suffering disappears, leaving spiritual distress as the really important force. In Olsen's text, the power to resist belongs to the workers; in the film, only the hero-doctor has a chance to make any real difference. It is significant, in these days of cuts to subsidies for medical care, that one of the supporting actors in *Dark Victory*, Ronald Reagan, would go on to become a shaper of the public policy on health issues.

Whatever their differences, in both texts feminine illness figures the social dis-ease of Depression-era loss. Representing cultural unrest as physical disease is the one constant among the texts of feminine illness in this study. Different though the sources of societal unease may be, they are nonetheless diverted into an image of physical pain. One of the workings of cultural power, then, is to divert political dis-ease into an overwhelming attention to the individual body and away from the body politic.

Such invisible power distracts us from the abstract, sociopolitical suffering of oppression to the concrete, bodily suffering in illness; it discourages our focusing on exterior sources as the cause of misery, encouraging us to direct our energies inward. It prevents our seeing suffering as collective by making it individual. Such cultural power makes us "docile bodies" (to use Michel Foucault's term) precisely by making us *bodies*. We are physically, and therefore psychically, culturally, and politically, separate from others, unable to see our own individual suffering as part of a larger suffering. It is because women have had more cause to be uneasy in our culture than men that illness is figured as feminine—not just because women are more typically seen as "Other." We can see, then, that at moments when masculine privilege seems threatened—as in *Tender Is the Night*—the figure of dis-ease shifts to male illness. And as such power erodes in the second half of the twentieth century—as the "second wave" of feminism increasingly threatens patriarchal tradition and as nuclear weapons make individual power seem ever more out of reach—illness is figured more and more often as male. But my examination of these post–World War II changes will be the subject of another study.

We need to reevaluate our attitudes toward illness and toward the literary representation of it, lest we allow the "Infection in the sentence" to breed the "Malaria" of women's oppression. We must choose "not to suffer uselessly" and not to allow others to suffer so. We must reexamine all representations of illness to understand when the literary figures are genuinely resistant to oppression and when such figures support the cultural drive to distract us from it.

Notes

PREFACE

1. For several discussions of the critique of the National Institute of Health, see Purvis, "A Perilous Gap"; *The Progressive* 54 (October 1990): 24–27; *Newsweek* 116 (December 1990): 60; and Milani, "Women in Waiting."

2. Most of the elderly are women because women live longer than men and because women usually form slightly more than 50 percent of the population. Elderly women's health is further complicated by a poverty that is often a direct result of Medicare and Medicaid policies. See Myrna Lewis, "Older Women and Health: An Overview."

3. For more discussion of women's health and poverty, see "The Politics of Women's Health," in the Boston Women's Health Collective's *Our Bodies, Ourselves*.

4. In *The Birth of the Clinic*, Foucault describes the nineteenth-century categorization of illnesses that led to the separation of one illness from another and, eventually, to the isolation of sick people from their families—into hospitals—and then from each other within the hospital. Scarry, in *The Body in Pain*, examines how pain (in her discussion, specifically the pain of torture) isolates and destroys all reality except that of the pain itself.

5. The AIDS epidemic may be changing our understanding of illness and ideology, however, since public policies governing the dissemination of information and the funding of research are so clearly products of ideology and have such a direct effect on the spread and possible cure of the disease.

INTRODUCTION

1. Studying the literary figure of the invalid woman involves understanding the representation in a specifically rhetorical sense—something with political intent and effect that is constructed, not natural. My use of the rhetorical term "figure" is therefore strategic; "figure" can be used as both noun and verb. It refers specifically to a "figure of speech" and more abstractly to an empty form or to a repeated pattern. Despite this emptiness and malleability, though, figures can take on a life of their own within discourse; figuring is an act of giving shape, giving form, creating resemblance.

2. In "Desire and Power: A Feminist Perspective," MacKinnon claims that "female power" is a "contradiction in terms" (110), a position with which I disagree. Along with Willis, whose response to MacKinnon is printed at the end of MacKinnon's essay, I would argue that a feminist position dedicated to social change cannot accept powerlessness or weakness as constitutive of the female position without reverting to a "politics of despair" (117).

3. On the inadequacy of the terms "power" and "weakness" in this context, see Janeway's *Powers of the Weak*.

4. I discuss the implications of Gilbert and Gubar's argument at more length in chapter 4.

5. For more on the antipsychiatry movement, see Rose's *Sexuality in the Field of Vision* and Turkle's *Psychoanalytic Politics*.

6. Agnew points out the changed meaning of "consumption" in "The Consuming Vision of Henry James" and discusses its significance to James's fiction and to early twentieth-century culture.

7. Belsey suggests that this resolution of conflict is the role illness offers women in today's world ("Constructing the Subject, Deconstructing the Text," 50).

8. Hall charts out a sort of history of cultural studies and describes two models of it—the "cultural" and the "structural." The cultural is represented by Raymond Williams's *Culture and Society* and *The Long Revolution*, Richard Hoggart's *The Uses of Literacy*, and E. P. Thompson's *The Making of the English Working Class*; these three writers share a "foregrounding of the questions of culture, consciousness, and experience, and its accent on agency" ("Cultural Studies: Two Paradigms," 58). The structuralist paradigm is more varied, but he identifies it with Claude Levi-Strauss, Lacan, and Althusser; it is marked by more concern for "ideology" than for "culture."

9. The mediation I describe here is precisely that which Scarry uses to define a "materialist conception of language"; she argues that its two central assumptions are that "language is capable of registering in its own contours the contours and weight of the material world" and that "language itself may enter, act on, and alter the material world" (Introduction to *Literature and the Body*, xi).

10. It is at this point that the idea of figuration becomes powerful. When the background varies, the figure does not remain constant, and when the figure changes, the background is altered; even though the components may not be new, their combinations can be, and those combinations can effect change. Hall argues that the power of cultural studies will come at the point when it attempts to examine both parts of the equation—the subject at work in culture and the culture at work in the subject: "The fact that 'men' can become conscious of their conditions, organize to struggle against them and in fact transform them— without which no active politics can even be conceived, let alone practised— must not be allowed to override the awareness of the fact that, in capitalist relations, men and women are placed and positioned in relations which constitute them as agents" ("Cultural Studies: Two Paradigms," 67).

11. Poovey has also addressed the charges that post-structuralism cannot be useful to political and cultural criticism. In *Uneven Developments*, she discusses at length how discourse—or, rather, the linguistic tendency to binary oppositions—does have very real, material effects. She argues that "whatever their differences, . . . almost all the participants in the mid-nineteenth-century battles for social authority assumed and reinforced [a] binary model of difference articulated upon sex" (6). This "articulated" difference, she shows, affected how

women were treated in the birthing room and in the courts, and sexual difference came to efface all other kinds of difference (including those differences
between women and between classes); in other words, she shows how the
discourse of difference made a difference in women's lives. In "Cultural Criticism: Past and Present," she goes on to show that much of what was problematic in earlier cultural studies is its overlooking crucial insights made by both
feminism and post-structuralism about *difference*: those differences both
within the culture and within the individual. That approach resonates throughout my study, as I examine how the difference between male and female was
often translated into the difference between well and sick. That difference,
again, had real effects on women's lives—in how they could understand their
place in the culture.

12. For more on how the radical split in the self could lead to a revolutionary
politics, see Kristeva's "Women's Time."

13. I use here Macherey's definition of "condition" as "not that which is initially given, a cause in the empirical sense; it is the principle of rationality which
makes the work accessible to thought" (*Theory of Literary Production*, 49).

14. The dilemma here is, of course, the ways in which my own ideological
purposes are themselves undercut. For a long discussion of the problems of a
dialogic theory of discourse for the feminist critic, see my "Dilemmas of a
Feminine Dialogic."

15. There is a fourth narrative alternative: the woman can just remain sick.
But if the narrative is *about* her illness, then such an outcome is a resistance to
resolution; if nothing happens in regard to her illness, then there is, by definition, no story. For there to be narrative about the *illness*, illness cannot be an
ontological state. Even for Milly Theale, the woman in this study who comes
closest to being ontologically defined as an invalid, for the story to "work," there
must remain the narrative tension between whether she will die or get better (if
not well).

16. Chapter 5 and the Conclusion, however, examine representations of
working-class invalid women.

17. Barrett argues in "The Place of Aesthetics in Marxist Criticism" that
reducing the aesthetic simply to the ideological is a politically dangerous move
for Marxist critics. I believe that the same is true for feminist critics.

18. Later, this economic need would be met by a political need for finding a
medical basis for women's inferiority when men found themselves threatened
by feminists.

19. For more discussion of the 1840s and the rise of the middle class, see
Smith-Rosenberg, *Disorderly Conduct*, 79–89.

CHAPTER ONE

1. The invalid woman also became a standard feature of British fiction; see,
for example, women in the novels of Samuel Richardson, Jane Austen, Char-

lotte and Emily Brontë, Charles Dickens, and George Eliot. In an attempt to establish some consistency, this study examines only American texts, but certainly many of my arguments could apply to British texts as well. There were some marked differences in the United States, however, especially in the history of medicine. The divisions among American doctors were based more on medical philosophies than on class, while the British medical system was distinctly class marked. The establishment of the American Medical Association and the policies it propagated led to some developments in medical attitudes in the United States that were distinctly different from those in the United Kingdom.

For studies that examine British representations of illness and women's bodies, see Showalter, *The Female Malady*; Michie, *The Flesh Made Word*; Poovey, *Uneven Developments* (in particular, chapter 2, "Scenes of an Indelicate Character: The Medical Treatment of Victorian Women"); and Homans, *Bearing the Word*.

2. For example, see Irving's *Biography and Poetical Remains of the Late Margaret Miller Davidson* (1841) (discussed in chapter 3) or the religious pamphlets published by the American Tract Society (described by Tompkins in *Sensational Designs*).

3. Douglas Wood acknowledges in a footnote the possibility that "there are many diseases and ailments which, in the absence of sufficient medical know-how can become chronic and make their victim's life a torment without ending it" (" 'The Fashionable Diseases,' " 27 n. 4), but only after she joins her sources in a "satire" on women "who never expected to live through the next year and survived into their eighties and nineties."

4. I examine and define the differences among competing medical theories later in this chapter.

5. In *Fashion and Eroticism*, Steele argues that reports of corset wearing and tight lacing have been exaggerated. Her findings indicate that the average waist measurement was not as small as twenty inches; she suggests that women habitually claimed that their waists were smaller than they genuinely were. Based on clothing measurements made by Annette Carruthers at the Leicestershire Museum and Art Gallery, Steele claims that the average waist measurement was 23.2″ in 1856–81, 22″ in 1881–1900, and 21.9″ in 1900–1910 (163). Present-day sizing indicates just how tight such lacing would nonetheless be—extra-small (size 4) fits a 24.5″ waist; large (size 14) fits a 30.5″ waist.

6. Of course, not all women physicians were reformers, but many reforms were instigated by these pioneering practitioners. See Morantz-Sanchez's "Doctors and Patients: Gender and Medical Treatment in Nineteenth-Century America" in *Sympathy and Science* for a close study of differences between male and female physicians.

7. For more information on the advantages of illness for the nineteenth-century woman, see Douglas Wood, " 'The Fashionable Diseases,' " 34–35. Such ploys often backfired and only made the physician hostile toward the patient. Smith-Rosenberg, in "The Hysterical Woman" in *Disorderly Conduct*, describes how such doctor-patient relations often became power struggles.

8. For a detailed description of the horrors of the treatments for women's diseases, see Douglas Wood's " 'The Fashionable Diseases' " or Poirier's "The Weir Mitchell Rest Cure." E. H. Dixon recommended that physicians who suspected a woman was faking an illness come up with treatment of a "disagreeable character" (*Woman and Her Diseases*, 140). Morantz offers a "corrective" to some of Ann Douglas Wood's assertions in "The Perils of Feminist History."

9. Hysteria is difficult to define, especially for this period in history. E. H. Dixon notes that there are no set symptoms that describe all cases of hysteria but suggests that he knows it when he sees it, and he claims that it is confined to women of childbearing years (*Woman and Her Diseases*, 131, 134). In general, hysteria was distinguished from ordinary "nervousness" by the presence of seizures. (I discuss hysteria and nervousness at more length in chapter 4.)

10. Mark Nichter, a medical anthropologist working among families in India, confirms the possibility of illness used as a "language" to respond to social situations. Nichter calls this language an "idiom of distress," arguing that "illness [may be] an idiom in which symptoms are symbolic as well as somatic constructs" ("Negotiation of the Illness Experience," 5).

11. For a thorough discussion of the distinctions between medical theories in the mid-nineteenth century, see Rothstein, *American Physicians in the Nineteenth Century*, and Starr, *The Social Transformation of American Medicine*.

12. See Jeffrey Berlant, *Profession and Monopoly*, and Starr, *The Social Transformation of American Medicine*, for extensive discussions of the consolidation of power made possible by the formation of the American Medical Association.

13. A Philadelphia doctor, William Shippen, is credited with being the first professor in an American medical school to teach obstetrics and one of the first in this country, in the 1760s, to attend at an ordinary birth. Prior to Shippen, physicians only intervened when mother and/or child were likely to die (Leavitt, *Brought to Bed*).

14. In "The Lesser Man" in *The Physician and Sexuality in Victorian America*, Haller and Haller describe these studies at length. Anthropometry (judging human characteristics based on weights and measures of bodies and body parts) was a popular science throughout the nineteenth and into the twentieth century, finally reaching its zenith in the "scientific" researches performed during the Third Reich. Arguments among nineteenth-century craniometrists turned on issues of absolute weight versus proportional weight of brains and whether or not there were qualitative differences of brain material among the races and sexes.

15. Smith-Rosenberg and Haller and Haller discuss the transposition of religious into scientific faith at length. See especially Smith-Rosenberg, *Disorderly Conduct*, 23, 178–79, and Haller and Haller, *Physician and Sexuality*, chapter 2, "The Lesser Man."

16. Barker-Benfield carries this analysis further in *The Horrors of the Half-Known Life*, arguing that the pressures on nineteenth-century men to regulate

their own lives would lead to their desires to regulate women's lives and the birth of gynecology as a specialty. I return to his argument in chapter 3.

17. Smith-Rosenberg (following other medical historians) explains in *Disorderly Conduct* that the "closed energy" model of human anatomy affected men as well and was the basis for the Victorian campaign against male masturbation; physicians feared that men who wastefully directed energy to their reproductive organs were depriving their brains of vitality. This model also influenced the Victorian word for orgasm, "spending."

18. I've chosen one exemplary text to illustrate what is confirmed in the extensive studies of medical tracts done by Haller and Haller, Smith-Rosenberg, Rosenberg, Degler, and Douglas Wood. Since Dixon's text went through ten editions, one can be reasonably sure that this was a popular work, indeed. Dixon was a fairly prolific writer as well as a well-respected physician. He edited the quarterly journal *Scalpel*, an "expositor of the laws of health and abuses of medicine" that was "caustic, diffuse, philippic, and curiously addicted to poetry" (*Dictionary of American Medical Biography*) from 1849 to 1864. He was also a pioneer in genito-urinary surgery in New York and developed a pessary that was widely used throughout the century.

19. *Daisy Miller* will not be a major focus of this study, but it is interesting to note here that there are frequent injunctions against going out after dark in nineteenth-century medical works, especially for women. Daisy's illness and death are caused by both her independence and her heedless going about at night.

20. Dixon warns that a woman must allow her physician to determine how long she should nurse her child because premature weaning leads to breast cancer, consumption, and apoplexy (*Woman and Her Diseases*, 237); she must consult her physician at any sign of early, late, or painful menses because these are almost always signals of uterine cancer or barrenness (87–88).

21. Dixon was not alone in assuring women of their personal responsibility for illness. Health authorities and advice writers who believed in women's natural healthfulness began to turn illness into a matter of personal blame. (I explore that blameworthiness at more length in chapter 5.) As Cogan notes in *All-American Girl*, "Many advice writers, in fact, offer more than the suggestion of a frown to those young women who are 'invalids,' that is, either unable or unwilling to walk two or three miles before breakfast, bowl, yacht, ice skate, or ride a horse, or who complain of languidness and weakness. Such 'weakness,' advice writers indicate, is probably the result of either personal perversity or moral degeneracy" (31). She quotes one writer, Dr. Dio Lewis, an ardent early supporter of physical fitness for women, as claiming that "sickness is selfish" (31). When one reads such authors along with those who, like Dixon, claimed that illness was natural, when one places their urgings to exercise against others' warnings against such "unladylike" activities, one sees more clearly the contradictions facing the nineteenth-century woman's expectations of what she should—or even could—be.

22. This concurrence is discussed at length in chapter 5.

CHAPTER TWO

1. In Caroline Lee Hentz's novel, *The Planter's Northern Bride* (1854), a young woman falls seriously ill when her father does not allow her to marry the man of her choice; she recovers, but only when her father gives in to her wishes (Papashvily, *All the Happy Endings*, 91). Augusta Jane Evans's heroines uniformly attempt to rise above their lowly birth by their own efforts through ceaseless work; each of these young women "as a kind of unofficial graduation ceremony" "succumb[s] to brain fever" (ibid., 158). Evans's heroines, "if . . . not actually dying, . . . 'wasted, yet beautiful,' [nonetheless] . . . gave that impression" (167). Nina Baym, in *Woman's Fiction*, describes novel after novel in which a mother, sister, or friend of the heroine is an invalid, or in which the heroine is, for a time, an invalid herself. See, for example, Ellen's mother in Susan Warner's *Wide, Wide World* (1851), sickly female relatives in Maria McIntosh's *Two Lives* (1846) and *Violet, or the Cross and Crown* (1856), the sickly female friend in Louisa Tuthill's *Reality, or The Millionaire's Daughter* (1856), and the major role illness plays in Sarah Josepha Hale's *The Lecturess, or Woman's Sphere* (1839).

2. Jehlen's "The Family Militant" is one of the strongest exceptions to my claim, in her focus on Stowe's participation in material politics.

3. I am reading against both Romero's and Spillers's interpretations of Eva as symbolically postpubescent here (see Romero, "Bio-Political Resistance in Domestic Ideology," and Spillers, "Changing the Letter"). While I find their suggestions provocative (especially Spillers's sense of Eva's expression of desire), I also find them to be quite ahistorical. To understand the cultural work of Stowe's figures of the invalid, we cannot read them only through a twentieth-century interpretive filter.

4. It is significant that Eva's wishes contradict the values of the dominant culture's; this willfulness is a likely "cause" of her death. It is also important that she dies when still a child—that is, before the culture can make a "proper" lady out of her.

5. Recent interest in domestic novels has resulted in some attention for Southworth. She is among the twelve authors discussed by Kelley in *Private Woman, Public Stage* (she summarizes but does not discuss *Retribution*), by Baym in *Woman's Fiction*, by Bardes and Gossett in *Declarations of Independence* (they examine *The Discarded Daughter*), and by Susan Harris in *Nineteenth-Century American Women's Novels* (she discusses *The Deserted Wife* at length).

6. Not all reviewers agreed, however. Many noted flaws of plot and style; but, as Baym points out, as Southworth's popularity grew, her style came in for less criticism, until finally she was one of only three authors in Baym's study—with Charles Reade and Charles Dickens—whose individuality of style was frequently cited as a strong point (*Novels, Readers, and Reviewers*, 134–35).

7. The similarity of this plot to Henry James's *Wings of the Dove* will be discussed in chapter 6.

8. The subplot of the novel involves a quadroon, Minny Dozier, whom Dent buys as a maid for Hester to save her from the traders who would make her a prostitute. Minny did not even know that she was a slave until her father's death, when she was sold by his presumed heirs and separated from her infant daughter. Her misfortunes come about because the papers that declare her freedom and establish her inheritance are in the possession of her husband, who is in Paris. Minny falls into hysterical fits and paralysis, until she is treated by a woman doctor who makes her body well by dulling her mind. Hester and Ernest Dent try to track down her husband, who finally sees an inquiry in a Cuban paper and comes to Virginia to retrieve Minny.

9. As the phrenological analysis shows, Juliette, on the other hand, is literally *unheimlich*, un-homely, uncanny.

10. "Phallic mother" is a Lacanian/Kristevan term used to describe the pre-oedipal child's understanding of its mother's power. Literally, the term refers to a woman with a penis, but in a Lacanian framework, the term "phallus" is used figuratively, to refer to the possession of cultural power. For a good discussion of the value and danger of this idea, see chapter 8 in Gallop's *The Daughter's Seduction*.

11. Southworth is vague about what Juliette did. She claims that "the story is well known" and that Juliette "condensed in her short life of forty years more crime than ever blackened the soul of a Borgia" (247). Earlier, she explains that Juliette managed, through political intriguing, to bring a lover who spurned her to the chopping block, so we are left to assume that her "crimes" have to do with this event.

12. Baym does not mention *Christine* in *Woman's Fiction*; when it is mentioned, as in Reynolds's *Beneath the American Renaissance* or Bardes and Gossett's *Declarations of Independence*, it is only briefly summarized.

13. Laura Curtis Bullard bought Elizabeth Cady Stanton and Susan B. Anthony's suffragist magazine, *The Revolution*, in 1870 and edited it for two years; she was also one of the first biographers of Cady Stanton, publishing a brief sketch of her in *Our Famous Women* (1886). Oddly enough, her fortune was made in the patent medicine business, on Dr. Winslow's Soothing Syrup.

14. For a complete discussion of Harriet Beecher Stowe on the woman question, see Boydston, Kelley, and Margolis, *The Limits of Sisterhood*.

15. See Donovan's discussion of Cady Stanton in *Feminist Theory* for more on the relation between early feminism and domesticity and Griffith's *In Her Own Right* for more on Cady Stanton's uses of matriarchal values in her style of feminism.

16. For an excellent discussion of how nineteenth-century women novelists intervened in public debates, see Bardes and Gossett's *Declarations of Independence*.

17. For more details on the life and career of Mary Gove Nichols, see Cayleff, *Wash and Be Healed*, 111–15.

18. On the work of these intervening narrators in women's fiction in the nineteenth century, see Warhol, *Gendered Interventions*.

19. Illness figures prominently in the marriage plot between Christine and Philip Armstrong. When Christine discovers that he has betrayed her with another woman, she falls ill of a severe brain fever but recovers and becomes stronger than ever. She and Philip are finally reunited at *his* deathbed, where he asks her to be his wife before he dies. After the ceremony, Christine nurses him through a miraculous recovery, and they become reformist as well as domestic partners. In yet another contrast to *Retribution*, Philip clearly suffers more for his crimes than does Christine, but that is as far as the contrast goes. The woman with whom Philip has an affair, a poor orphaned seamstress, drowns herself in the village pond, proving once again that it is women who really suffer from domestic disruptions. (I discuss the representation of drowned women as ill in chapter 3.)

CHAPTER THREE

1. Irving, in fact, writes that he has "digested and arranged the following particulars [from Mrs. Davidson's notes], adopting in many places the original manuscript, without alteration." He goes on to note that the biography is, in fact, "almost as illustrative of the character of the mother as of the child" (*Biography*, 11).

2. Sontag has written extensively on the damage done by the metaphors associated with tuberculosis in *Illness as Metaphor*. My argument in this book will follow a different track from Sontag's. While I agree that the figures of illness are often detrimental to the real human beings who suffer from the illness, I do not believe, as Sontag seems to, that one can ever stop that metaphorizing process. It seems more fruitful to explore and examine the metaphors than to urge a halt to metaphoricity.

3. Since I cannot deal with all of Poe's and Hawthorne's fiction in this chapter, there are some significant omissions here. I do not, for example, deal directly with the much healthier Hester Prynne or Phoebe Pyncheon. My argument is not meant to apply to all of Hawthorne's women but to those particular instances in which narrative dilemmas are settled by or at the woman's death. For discussions that do deal more exhaustively with Hawthorne's depiction of women, see Baym, *The Shape of Hawthorne's Career* and "Thwarted Nature: Nathaniel Hawthorne as Feminist," and Person, *Aesthetic Headaches*.

4. These assertions are explained at length in Barker-Benfield, *The Horrors of the Half-Known Life* (3–61). He points out that by the end of the century, this resistance would be crystallized by Huck Finn's unwillingness to be adopted and "civilized" by Aunt Sally.

5. For a theoretical fleshing out of the place of mind and body in romanticism, see Kaplan, "Pandora's Box." For the history and two views of this association of woman with nature and the body rather than culture and the mind, see Griffin, *Woman and Nature*, and Irigaray, *Speculum of the Other Woman*. For two excellent anthropological discussions of the relation between the trope of

woman as nature and the oppression of women, see Ortner, "Is Female to Male as Nature Is to Culture?," and Ardener, "Belief and the Problem of Woman."

6. In *The Lay of the Land*, Kolodny discusses how American attitudes toward landscape and physical nature were shaped by notions of gender; she points to the repeated trope of nature as a woman. Jehlen discusses other American attitudes toward nature and the land in *American Incarnation*. For a thorough discussion of the trope of woman as nature, see Griffin, *Woman and Nature*.

7. See Hull's "'Scribbling Females' and Serious Males" for a discussion of Hawthorne's private attitude toward women writers and artists. Both Baym in *The Shape of Hawthorne's Career* and "Thwarted Nature" and Person in *Aesthetic Headaches* offer a rereading of Hawthorne's relation to women, arguing that he was much more sympathetic than has been suggested up to this point.

8. Early and important feminist theorists like Mary Wollstonecraft and Margaret Fuller attest to the connection between romantic thought and the woman's rights movement. Romanticism was, at least in its earliest stages, ideologically connected to the idea of revolution and equality for all, an idea traced by Bartlett in "Liberty, Equality, Sorority," by Donovan in *Feminist Theory*, and by Tims in *Mary Wollstonecraft*. That notable romanticists did not agree with women's equality does not negate the influence romanticism may have had on early feminist thinking.

9. Ardener, in "Belief and the Problem of Woman," describes this same intermediacy as ambiguity, because women are subsumed under the title "mankind" (defined against its opposite, "the wild") but also opposed to "man" (14).

10. Baym makes a similar point: women, "though made to suffer as bodies, . . . are denied existence as mind." She uses this observation as the basis for arguing that Hawthorne "is suggesting . . . that the male inability to deal with woman's body is the *source* of all the abstract formulations that function as so many defenses against, and diversions from, the truth" ("Thwarted Nature," 66).

11. Chapter 5 takes up the problem of how the mind/body relation was addressed when the closed energy model finally crumbled at the end of the century.

12. See Barker-Benfield, *The Horrors of the Half-Known Life*, chapter 3, for more information on the nineteenth-century conception of "man's work."

13. This doubled attitude toward nature is explored in detail by Kolodny in chapter 4 of *The Lay of the Land*.

14. Ortner argues that the polarization common to feminine symbolism makes inversions of polar equations like woman = nature, man = culture, easy ("Is Female to Male as Nature Is to Culture?," 86). She cites several other historical instances in which woman have been equated with culture and men with nature.

15. Person points out that Poe "anticipates the artist-scientists" of Hawthorne in the narrator's refusal to see what effect his art is having on his bride and in his preference for the "aesthetic version of woman" (*Aesthetic Headaches*, 44).

16. Bonapart argues that "The Oval Portrait" expresses Poe's feelings of guilt

that two women's deaths had been the models for so much of his own art (*Life and Works of Edgar Allan Poe*, 259).

17. Poe's confidence in the sickly woman's absolute power was probably due in large part to episodes from his life. Bonapart draws detailed analogies between Poe's portraits of powerful, though dying or dead, women and the characteristics of both his sickly mother and his dying wife to argue that all these women represent an infantile confidence in maternal omniscience and a childish wish/fear that his all-powerful mother could return to life (ibid., 218).

18. Poe's tale of Madeline's breaking free of her tomb and Berenice's being buried alive may be more realistic than has been previously thought. Dixon, in his discussion of hysteria, cites "numerous cases" of hysterics being buried only to reveal, upon exhumation of the body, "indubitable appearances of resuscitation." He chides the American public for the "rapidity with which we hurry our dead to the grave," arguing that to foreign visitors, "it looks like, and too often is, evidence of a want of affection" (*Woman and Her Diseases*, 141).

19. Jordan, in *Second Stories*, reads "Ligeia" in sequence with "The Fall of the House of Usher" and the three Dupin detective tales to conclude that "Poe saw the danger—to art and to culture—of the androcentric tradition . . . and he was indeed experimenting with the idea of a radically different consciousness, one that would be capable of imaginative revision" (150). Jordan's argument is persuasive; however, I am not trying to make any final conclusions about all of Poe's tales in this chapter.

20. Dayan, in *Fables of Mind*, reads Ligeia's reembodiment as resurrection: "Poe thus takes on the idea of resurrection and defines it expressly as a resurrection of the *body*" (177). This suggests a different way to read Ligeia as a Christ figure against domestic heroines who function, though very differently, as Christlike.

21. Since the mid-nineteenth-century word for psychiatrist was "alienist," we are to understand that our narrator also suffers from temporary bouts of insanity, which is yet more reason to doubt him.

22. See Dayan's reading of this story, "The Intelligibility of Ligeia," in *Fables of Mind* for a different point of view. She argues that "The point, of course, is not whether 'Ligeia' is a story of 'real magic' or one 'of remorse and hallucination' by a psychopathic killer or bookish dreamer, nor to entertain other supernaturalist explanations, but to look at the transaction between Ligeia and Rowena as an epistemological problem to be solved" (178).

23. The name "Beatrice" also suggests sexual abuse. It is usually understood, as Hawthorne hints in the tale, to refer to Dante's Beatrice, but several years later, in *The Marble Faun*, Hawthorne repeatedly calls attention to Beatrice Cenci, who was raped by her father. The "Beatrice" of this story likely has her origin in both of these earlier figures.

24. The question of why Baglioni's "antidote" kills Beatrice has been addressed by Uroff in "The Doctors in 'Rappaccini's Daughter'" as an allusion to the nineteenth-century conflict between allopathic and homeopathic medicine. No one in the nineteenth century, no matter their medical philosophy, had much

understanding of why medicines worked as they did; allopathy and homeopathy represented two different theories of how drugs operated in the system. Uroff maintains that the Hawthorne story is an antidoctor allegory, upholding neither the allopathic nor the homeopathic theory; he argues that it illustrates the devastating effects of both medicines. In "'Rappaccini's Daughter' and the Nineteenth-Century Physician," Gross agrees and argues further that the story exemplifies the deep distrust of doctors among the nineteenth-century public. Hallissy, on the other hand, maintains in "Hawthorne's Venomous Beatrice" that Baglioni, an allopath, does not understand that Rappaccini, a homeopath, has created Beatrice not as a poison but as an antidote to poison. While these are very interesting theories about the intersection of literature and medicine, they do not solve the metaphysical question of Beatrice's innocence or guilt or why the antidote kills her.

25. Had Hawthorne's story been written a few decades later, it could almost have been considered realism. Arsenic became an important cosmetic in the late nineteenth century, and there were reports (perhaps apocryphal) that women who regularly used it had killed their husbands with kisses (Haller and Haller, *Physician and Sexuality*, 144).

26. This second entry also describes Dr. Rappaccini himself and "The Bosom Serpent."

27. According to the *Oxford English Dictionary*, "poisoner" can mean either one who or that which poisons, so "poisoner" is not always an active role. It is, however, most commonly used to refer to one who poisons, while noxious substances are most often described as "the poison" or "poisonous." In any case, this reading of "the Beautiful Poisoner" does not depend on Beatrice's intent but on the fact that it is she who poisons Giovanni. Hawthorne writes, in the active voice, that it is she who "instilled a fierce and subtle poison into his system" (1051).

28. The term *empoisonneuse* also refers, in colloquial usage, to a woman who is in the way, who obstructs desires, who is a nuisance.

29. This is more or less in line with Person's reading of the story. He reads it as the challenge that the acceptance of a woman's right "to define herself in her own words" brings; he argues that when Giovanni finally refuses to allow Beatrice her own self-definition, "Beatrice is vicitmized by a male imagination that cannot overcome its own fear of woman" (*Aesthetic Headaches*, 117–18).

30. I am borrowing the term "homosocial desire" from Sedgwick's *Between Men*.

31. In *The Interpretation of Dreams*, Freud notes that flowers can frequently symbolize female sexuality, specifically with reference to defloration. "The dream had made use of the great chance similarity between the words 'violet' and 'violate'—the difference in their pronunciation lies merely in the different stress upon their final syllables—in order to express 'in the language of flowers' the dreamer's thoughts on the violence of defloration" (*Complete Psychological Works*, 5:376). (One notes the coincidence that Beatrice's favorite flower is purple.)

Freud explains with reference to a different dream that flowers can serve as a double symbol of sexual purity and corruption: "[Dreams] show a particular preference for combining contraries into a unity or for representing them as one and the same thing. . . . The same blossoming branch (cf. *'des Madchen's Bluten'* ['the maiden's blossoms'] in Goethe's poem *'Der Mullerin Verrat'*) represented both sexual innocence and its contrary" (4:318–19).

32. Baym herself reads the story as a troubling allegory of faith—troubling because it is antithetical to Hawthorne's usual critique of "visionary delusion." She concludes that it is also an "allegory of sex," in which "Giovanni is a type of the sexually confused Victorian male, struggling between his wish to accept sex as a beneficent part of life and his strong conviction that it is unnatural and evil" (*The Shape of Hawthorne's Career*, 109). This is largely the same conclusion to which Person comes in *Aesthetic Headaches*.

33. For examples of the criticism that does read Hawthorne's women within the light-dark symbolism, see Carpenter, "Puritans Preferred Blondes"; Rahv, "The Dark Lady of Salem"; and Birdsall, "Hawthorne's Fair-Haired Maidens."

34. For a good discussion of the homoerotic element of *The Blithedale Romance*, see Lauren Berlant, "Fantasies of Utopia," 36–37.

35. Hawthorne interestingly shifts the gender of the innocent here and adds an element of homosocial desire between women, too; this is, perhaps, part of the overall suggestiveness about free love (see Lauren Berlant, "Fantasies of Utopia," for a discussion of the role of love in *The Blithedale Romance*). There is also a critical question of Priscilla's innocence; she, too, seems to embody the ambiguity of innocent/guilty. For a reading of Priscilla as a sexually experienced, reformed prostitute, see Lefcowitz and Lefcowitz, "Some Rents in the Veil."

36. Baym argues that Zenobia's "Legend of the Silvery Veil" illustrates the problem of the mind/body imbalance; she suggests that Zenobia's tale points to the contrast between Zenobia's physicality and Priscilla's spirituality as evidence that "a crude equation has been made between spirit and lack of body" that finally results in "an abnormal sex indeed, in which young, frail, immature girls become objects of sexual interest while fully sexed adult women are experienced as frightening, corrupt, or repellent. The ideal is diabolic" (*The Shape of Hawthorne's Career*, 197).

37. Jordan does not address *The Blithedale Romance* in *Second Stories*, but she argues that in other Hawthorne fictions he represents the eruption of the female voice.

38. Baym argues that Zenobia "unites sex, art and nature in one symbol" (*The Shape of Hawthorne's Career*, 190).

39. Lauren Berlant argues that the failure of love and the language of love finally destroys the utopian experiment of Blithedale: "Love acts as a thread that travels through the various elements that constitute the manifest and buried historical sites on which individuals negotiate their lives in this narrative: ultimately the novel questions the language of love itself, exposing love's inability truly to mediate, to merge, to illuminate, to provide a clarifying model of anything, whether utopian or tragic" ("Fantasies of Utopia," 33).

40. Schriber argues in "Justice to Zenobia" that Zenobia is murdered. Bauer also comes close to this position: "Hollingsworth has effectively willed Zenobia to death, for he has insisted that she either succumb to his patriarchal system of reform or lose her place to her rival Priscilla" (*Feminist Dialogics*, 45).

41. The history of attitudes toward and laws about suicide seems to coincide between England and America at this time. Anderson in *Suicide in Victorian and Edwardian England*, Kushner in *Self-Destruction in the Promised Land*, and Gates in *Victorian Suicide* all cite different evidence but come to much the same conclusions.

42. The notebook entry on which Zenobia's death is based also cites melancholy as the cause for suicide: "On the night of July 9th, a search for the dead body of a drowned girl. She was a Miss Hunt, about nineteen years old; a girl of education and refinement, but depressed and miserable for want of sympathy— her family being an affectionate one, but uncultivated. . . . She was of a melancholic temperament" (Hawthorne, *American Notebooks*, 112).

43. Hawthorne's mad men—Aylmer, Rappaccini, and Hollingsworth—all suffer from the nineteenth-century mental disease monomania, defined as a morbid fixation on one particular thing. For an extended argument on male madness in mid-century American fiction, in particular in Herman Melville's "Bartleby the Scrivener" (1853), and the harshness of mercantile life, see Gillian Brown's "The Empire of Agoraphobia" in *Domestic Individualism*.

CHAPTER FOUR

1. While sickliness was thought "romantic" for men as well, it did not acquire the same cultural status for men that it did for women. For an extended discussion of male nervousness at the turn of the century, see Lutz's *American Nervousness, 1903*; he discusses the careers and "cases" of such nervous men as Theodore Dreiser, Theodore Roosevelt, William and Henry James, Hamlin Garland, Frank Norris, William Dean Howells, and W. E. B. Du Bois. Lutz also addresses Gilman's and Wharton's nervousness but looks at their writings about houses as well. I discuss the figure of the sickly man in chapter 5.

2. See Walsh, *"Doctors Wanted,"* 120–32, for more detail on the Clarke controversy and its aftermath.

3. Gubar argues that Lily's body is "converted completely into a script for [Selden's] edification" (" 'The Blank Page,' " 251).

4. "Specific etiology" is the theory of disease that developed when germs were discovered, maintaining that every disease has a particular cause (etiology) and particular germs cause specific diseases. One cannot catch malaria from being exposed to tuberculosis germs, for example. It replaced the older "closed energy" model (discussed at length in chapter 1), which held that all illnesses were the result of an imbalance of energy in the body.

5. See chapter 1 for definitions of homeopathy, hydropathy, Grahamism, and eclecticism.

6. Stage, in *Female Complaints*, discusses the patent medicine business and its relation to women's health.

7. Hale points out that contemporary theorists, because of their understanding of heredity and the passing on of acquired attributes, feared that illnesses caused by the environment in one generation would be passed on to future generations. The pessimistic "degeneracy theory" contributed to a fear that contemporary abuses would lead to a weakened race and the demise of civilization (*Freud and the Americans*, 76–78; see also Haller and Haller, *Physician and Sexuality*).

8. One of Freud's most revolutionary contributions to the theory of hysteria was that men could suffer from it, too.

9. "Neurasthenia" could be making a comeback in the late twentieth century as "Chronic Fatigue Syndrome" (CFS, or, by the skeptical, "Yuppie's Disease"). As with neurasthenia, almost anything can be a symptom of CFS and the diagnoses of it are strongly class marked, but (a sign of progress?) they are much less strongly gender marked.

10. According to Hale, one of the major causes of the crisis in psychiatric treatment was the idiosyncrasy of diagnoses; what counted as "mania," or "neurasthenia," or "hysteria" varied from doctor to doctor and country to country (*Freud and the Americans*, 84).

11. For more detail on the New Thought movement, see Braden's *Spirits in Rebellion* and Parker's *Mind Cure in New England*. For more on the relation between transcendentalism and New Thought, see Stewart Holmes, "Phineas Parkhurst Quimby."

12. Mark Twain's excoriation of Mary Baker Eddy (in *Christian Science* [1907]) was sparked as much by his distrust of her sentimentalism as by his suspicion of her profiteering (Parker, "Mary Baker Eddy").

13. For discussions of "The Yellow Wallpaper" in terms of the rest cure, see Poirier, "The Weir Mitchell Rest Cure," Berman's chapter on Gilman ("The Unrestful Cure") in *The Talking Cure*, Treichler's "Escaping the Sentence," and Lutz's chapter in *American Nervousness*, "Women and Economics in the Writings of Charlotte Perkins Gilman and Edith Wharton." Lutz also reads the story in terms of a nineteenth-century prejudice against patterned wallpaper.

In "The Empire of Agoraphobia" in *Domestic Individualism*, Gillian Brown takes a different tack on Gilman's representation of the rest cure. She reads Gilman's critique of the enforced immobility of the rest cure as intimately linked with issues of mobility and immobility in the late nineteenth-century marketplace: "The aim of the rest cure, then, is not to limit market mobility but to reinforce a domestic stillness, to underscore the healthy function of the stationary. In restricting women to bed, the rest cure in a sense demobilizes the domestic in order to recharge it for reproductive service to the market. . . . Gilman . . . used immobility to parody and protest against domestic confinement, to withdraw from household business" (175).

14. Lewis claims that March–July 1898 marks the beginning of Wharton's real career, and she did not undertake the rest cure until October–December. Since my subject is not where or when Wharton learned to write but the

relationship between her adoption of the writer's role and her refusal of the invalid's role, this distinction is not really important for the purposes of my argument.

15. Haller and Haller identify drug abuse as one of the chief women's health problems in the nineteenth century (*Physician and Sexuality*, 271–304). They use Lily Bart as their example of the widespread use of drugs (287–88).

16. It seems striking that Gubar does not count quilt making, needlework, pottery, and other domestic art forms as "available" media for art. Her distinction between "masculine" and "feminine" art forms clearly privileges the traditionally masculine.

17. It seems important that this appears in French in Alice James's *Diary*; it is, I think, the only passage in the diary written in French. The alien language may, therefore, suggest her desire to keep the sentiments it expresses separate from herself. I have not been able to identify the "philosophical angel" she is quoting (if in fact she is quoting). The passage translates: "Under that inspiration [suffering] the most humble existences can become works of art more superior to the most beautiful symphonies and the most beautiful poems. Are not the works of art that are realized in one's self the best? The others, which one tosses out [of oneself] onto canvas or paper, are nothing but images, shadows. The work of life is a reality" (my translation).

18. Gilbert and Gubar's claim in *Madwoman in the Attic* that writing was a "masculine" form has come under attack from Frank Lentricchia in "Patriarchy Against Itself." The statistics on writing, especially novel writing, in the United States do not bear out their claim that writing was a male bastion (see Baym, *Novels, Readers, and Reviewers* and *Woman's Fiction*, and Davidson, *Revolution and the Word*).

19. Lutz, in *American Nervousness, 1903*, offers examples of numerous writers who took up writing as part of a cure for nervousness.

20. Gilman had two mind curists in her family. Wharton refers in some of her letters to popular mind cure poet Ella Wheeler Wilcox, and Dale Bauer has reported finding a number of Elizabeth Towne's pamphlets among Wharton's papers (personal communication). According to Parker, "Anyone who read a daily newspaper or subscribed to a popular magazine or belonged to one of the major Protestant denominations would have been aware of the fact that respectable people—neighbors, friends, relatives—were apparently being healed every day without drugs" (*Mind Cure in New England*, 152).

21. I discuss these psychoanalytic theories and their relation to the woman writer in " 'The Writing Cure': Charlotte Perkins Gilman, Anna O., and 'Hysterical' Writing."

22. Derrida discusses the use of writing to "stand in one's absence" or to take one's place in "Plato's Pharmacy" and *Of Grammatology*.

23. Bauer's reading of *The House of Mirth* in *Feminist Dialogics* appeared after I had finished the original version of this chapter. Although our conclusions are remarkably similar, she does not consider the novel in either a medical context or in the context of turn-of-the-century painting.

24. Bazin in "The Destruction of Lily Bart," Dimock in "Debasing Exchange," and Shulman in "Divided Selves and the Market Society" all discuss different aspects of Lily as an object of exchange in a capitalist marriage market.

25. R. W. B. Lewis notes that Walter Berry introduced Wharton to Zola's work in 1898 (the year of her breakdown and treatment at Weir Mitchell's). Although he maintains that Zola's work "exerted no influence upon [her] early development" (*Edith Wharton: A Biography*, 85), we can see here that Albine, as well as the genre of paintings to which her death belongs, may well have influenced the ending of *The House of Mirth*.

26. Parker discusses Gilman's distrust of "mind-meddling" and mind curists at length (*Mind Cure in New England*, 87–93). Gilman's version of mind cure was intensely individual and self-reliant; she was distrustful of the aspect of mind cure that involved "letting go" or confessing intimate details to someone she did not know.

27. *Christine* is available on microfilm in the *Wright American Fiction, 1774–1900* series, but the end of the novel is missing from the microfilm.

28. Kate Chopin's *Awakening* is also standard reading and fits much of the argument in this chapter. Even though I do not examine that text here, many of the same figures we have seen in other texts are repeated in Chopin's novel: the woman's defeat, her ambiguous ending (drowning again), the linking of abundant sexuality and intellect with illness. One positive feature of Chopin's novel is that the heroine's body disappears rather than becoming a beautiful or edifying object.

29. This attachment to canonical style may help to explain why *Christine*, which is ideologically very much attuned to contemporary feminism but stylistically sentimental, has not yet been "recovered."

30. Lambert argues that Wharton plays on the traditional expectations of women's fiction to "trap" and "frustrate" her reader ("*The House of Mirth*: Readers Respond," 79). Showalter argues that Wharton's work goes back to the early tradition to "render it ironic" ("The Death of the Lady (Novelist)," 137). For a different view, see Karcher, "Male Vision and Female Revision," which argues that *The House of Mirth* is a revision, not of women's fiction, but of James's *The Wings of the Dove*.

31. The belief that husband hunting is degrading for women and is responsible for the degradation of the race is central to Gilman's *Women and Economics*.

32. It is precisely this devotion to production that Michaels, in *The Gold Standard and the Logic of Naturalism*, identifies as the problem in "The Yellow Wallpaper."

33. Gilman idealizes working women in precisely the same way that E. H. Dixon does. (His ideas are discussed in chapter 1.)

34. This same opposition between the pampered woman who dies from some adversity and the strong working woman who can survive almost any hardship exists in *Christine* between the socialite Annie Murray and the farmer's daughter Christine Elliot, but it is less well developed.

35. Bazin's, Shulman's, and Dimock's articles on Lily as an object in a market society are all quite good, but they tend to make Lily completely a dupe of patriarchal capitalism. None allow for the sentiment that Wharton and her audience would have held—surrounded as they were by New Thought and "success" philosophies—that Lily could have resisted these degrading forces had she wanted to badly enough. In "Highbrow-Lowbrow Revisited," Tompkins has criticized much Marxist-influenced denunciation of mass culture for exactly this tendency to treat the subjects of the industrial-capitalist power structure as "ignorant, passive masses" with no individual choices or experiences. To read Wharton's novel as making a clear class-sensitive critique of market relations is to read it ahistorically.

36. Showalter claims that if Selden had "jogging shoes and a copy of *The Color Purple* on his coffee table," he would be a perfect 1980s man ("The Death of the Lady (Novelist)," 142); Dimock claims that he hoards his "emotional capital" ("Debasing Exchange," 786); and Lambert calls the republic of the spirit a "vacuous concept" (*"The House of Mirth:* Readers Respond," 75).

37. On the other hand, this notion of valuing someone for themselves rather than for their possessions is exactly how the bourgeois individual, the "domestic woman," was constituted by capitalism, according to Armstrong in *Desire and Domestic Fiction.*

CHAPTER FIVE

1. Painter, in *Standing at Armageddon,* explains in detail how labor conflicts and military and industrial upheaval affected the lives of ordinary people during the Progressive Era.

2. Starr explains that even though the greatest bacteriological advances were made in the late nineteenth century, "it was probably not until the 1910s and 1920s that the momentum they imparted to scientific medicine was clearly evident" (*Social Transformation of American Medicine,* 138).

3. See especially Bannister's chapter on eugenics, "A Pigeon Fancier's Polity," in *Social Darwinism,* 164–79.

4. Ethan's and Mattie's ailments *do* have a specific cause (the sledding accident), but that cause has its origins in weakness and sin.

5. Steele, in *Fashion and Eroticism,* points out that "natural" beauty is a myth; we always have cultural constructions of what counts as "natural." "Natural" beauty in the Progressive Era was often the result of long, sometimes painful, treatments in beauty salons or spas.

6. Ehrenreich and English argue that domestic science was a new move on the part of medical professionals to reinforce the ideology of separate spheres in the aftermath of technological and industrial changes in housework. The industrial production of many goods that had been produced in the home for generations (bread, soap, fabric, and clothing, for example) and the introduction of electrical appliances had drastically reduced the amount of work to be done in

the home. Coupled with women's increased education and political/social activism, the forces of "progress" threatened to remove women from the home altogether (*For Her Own Good*).

7. The fate of Martin Arrowsmith's wife, in *Arrowsmith*, Sinclair Lewis's 1925 novel about a hero-bacteriologist, exemplifies the attitude that women's illnesses are a result of their lack of vigilance. Against Martin's advice, Leora Arrowsmith follows her husband to a Caribbean island, where he is attempting to study and treat a bacteriological plague. When he leaves her alone for a few days in a place "as safe as any place on the island" (383), she forgets to give herself a vaccination and smokes a cigarette she finds in Martin's lab. Unfortunately, plague germs have been spilled from a test tube onto the cigarette (by a black maid), and Leora dies within forty-eight hours (390–92). (Martin is nonetheless responsible for stopping the plague.)

8. For a detailed account of Edith and Teddy Wharton's disputes, see R. W. B. Lewis, *Edith Wharton: A Biography*, 267–313 passim.

9. Wershoven also describes Mattie as an "intruder," but in her view, the intruders in Wharton's novels offer the one hope for a healthy life. As Wershoven reads *Ethan Frome*, "Zeena is a living symbol of Starkfield and its paralysis" (*Female Intruder*, 21), while Mattie represents "a living alternative to the suffocation around her" (22).

10. Ammons's reading offers convincing evidence that "*Ethan Frome* is designed to read like a fairy tale. It draws on the archetypes of the genre—the witch, the silvery maiden [Mattie *Silver*], the honest woodcutter—and brings them to life in the landscape and social structure of rural New England" (*Edith Wharton's Argument with America*, 61).

11. Zeena's "miraculous" recovery after Ethan's and Mattie's "smash-up" also leads to an assumption that echoes Freud's assertion that women who thus use illness are not really ill; Zeena sounds like the women Freud described in the "Dora" case who could get out of bed if they were really needed.

12. My analysis of *Ethan Frome* owes much to Bauer's study of Wharton's later works. Her "Edith Wharton's 'Roman Fever': A Rune of History" analyzes female-to-female violence in the context of the increasing strength of fascism in the 1930s and the "violence women have engaged in to force a place for themselves in society, a violence resident at the center of Western civilization" (687). Bauer argues that "competition [is] forced upon women as a means of escaping their identical status as signs" (688).

13. Zeena's complaint that she is "much sicker" than anyone thinks recalls Milly Theale's predicament in James's *Wings of the Dove* (1902). Like Milly, Zeena has to be "much sicker" in order to get anyone to take her illness seriously.

14. One of the parallels between Wharton's life and the novel is that at the time Wharton was writing this novel, Teddy was making exorbitant demands on her for money as Zeena does on Ethan (R. W. B. Lewis, *Edith Wharton: A Biography*, 304–7).

15. Gilbert and Gubar discuss *Ethan Frome* only briefly and *Barren Ground*

not at all. Of *Ethan Frome*, Gilbert and Gubar claim that Zenobia is a mark that "for Wharton the glamorous and threatening strength of Hawthorne's Zenobia was as unrealistic as the public and private bonding of women that her mentor Henry James explored in *The Bostonians*." They assert that *Ethan Frome* does not explicitly deal with feminist issues but "implicitly points to an issue which concerned many of her contemporaries: the issue of what women could realistically expect to attain and at what cost." They read the novel as a woman-authored story of "violent defeat" (*No Man's Land*, 80–81).

16. In *Tradition Counter Tradition*, Boone describes and illustrates the traditional marriage plot of the novel and then examines late nineteenth- and early twentieth-century attempts to find alternatives to that plot. He cites novels like Virginia Woolf's *To the Lighthouse* and Henry James's *The Golden Bowl* as examples of texts in which the narrative does not end with a happily-ever-after marriage but goes on to explore the ways marriage can be a lifelong mortal battle. He argues that these texts are left open-ended to imply the unceasing nature of the struggle. He does not mention *Ethan Frome* or *Barren Ground*, nor does he explore the female battling that goes on in *The Golden Bowl*, except to note briefly that Charlotte and Maggie are rivals.

17. Glasgow's awareness of and attitude toward race is ambiguous in *Barren Ground*. On the one hand, Fluvanna is Dorinda's only friend, and a black conjure woman her only confidante; the black families in the novel are discussed as being more hardworking and honest than the "poor whites," who are the subjects of much scorn. On the other, Dorinda always holds herself apart from the blacks in the novel; Fluvanna, though Dorinda's closest friend, is nonetheless always treated as her servant. Glasgow does not create fully human black characters; her vision of their lives is restricted to the extent that they can be useful to white characters.

18. In *Ellen Glasgow's American Dream*, Santos disputes the notion that Dorinda accomplishes her success through money. She argues that Dorinda's victory is based "only on her 'approach to life' " (144). Such a view certainly maintains a faith in romantic individualism, but it overlooks the evidence that, in order for Dorinda to renovate her farm, she had to have, first, inherited land, and, second, rich friends in New York who would lend her money.

19. Glasgow's background was Scotch-Irish Calvinist, and although she consciously rejected that religion, its ideology nonetheless informs much of her evaluation of characters and events.

20. In *No Man's Land*, Gilbert and Gubar discuss wounded and maimed men in modernist literature at length, but their focus is on the global political arena. My focus, on the other hand, is domestic—that is, exclusively American and directed at fiction about "home life."

21. In *The Wings of the Dove*, Merton Densher does not become an invalid, but one of the questions the novel raises about his worthiness as the object of female competition is his lack of a successful career.

22. The effects of the war were so pervasive that even characters who did not fight end up wounded by it: Dick Diver is symbolically unmanned after the war,

and Faulkner's Joe Christmas is physically castrated, while his attacker, Percy Grimm, is similarly psychically maimed. For these men, *not* fighting, or not being given the chance to fight, questions their manhood. But as we will see in chapter 6, the war is only one factor contributing to Dick Diver's "invalidism"; in fact, he closely follows the pattern of Ethan Frome and Jason Greylock.

In "Soldier's Heart: Literary Men, Literary Women, and the Great War," Gilbert contends that much hostility between the sexes after World War I was the result of tensions created when men had to go to the front to protect the women who stayed at home. The unprecedented freedom women enjoyed during the war, Gilbert argues, caused them to resent its end; men, on the other hand, resented the comparative safety women had enjoyed while they risked life and limb.

23. Weak and injured men appear elsewhere in Wharton's and Glasgow's work. See Glasgow's short story "Jordan's End," about the death of a weak man, and Wharton's *Custom of the Country*, in which Ralph Marvell commits suicide because of the weakness of his class. Elizabeth Stuart Phelps is an interesting exception; her invalid men—in *Doctor Zay* and *Walled In*—become injured as a result of accidents (a horse and buggy and an automobile) and both recover. *Walled In* has much in common with male modernist texts (compare it, for example, to *The Great Gatsby* or *Lady Chatterley's Lover*): the strong, well-liked man is injured as a result of contact with modern technology—the car—and is then betrayed by his faithless wife.

24. There were numerous representations of the miseries of farm life for women between 1890 and 1925. Mary E. Wilkins Freeman's "The Revolt of Mother" (1891), Susan Glaspell's "A Jury of Her Peers" (1916), and even Willa Cather's *My Antonia* (1918) depict the harshness and loneliness of farm life for women. In Gilman's *Women and Economics,* the only specific women's illness mentioned is the madness to which farm women are driven by loneliness: "On wide Western prairies, or anywhere in lonely farm houses, the women of to-day, confined absolutely to this strangling cradle of the race, go mad by scores and hundreds. Our asylums show a greater proportion of insane women among farmers' wives than in any other class. In the cities, where there is less 'home life,' people seem to stand it better" (267).

25. The trope of battling nature recalls Kolodny's study, *The Lay of the Land,* and returns us to the romantic paradox of conquering nature that I discuss in relation to Poe's and Hawthorne's invalid women (see chapter 3).

26. The "battle" between winter and the inhabitants of Starkfield again is described in military terms.

CHAPTER SIX

1. Critics have praised Hawthorne's and James's "dark" and "light" ladies for years, while, at the same time, condemning women writers for "flat" or "stereotyped" characterization.

2. There are other, smaller similarities between the novels: James adopts Southworth's device of making all the women in the novel motherless and all the family situations rife with conflict, exploitation, and tragedy. Milly, like Hester, delights in buying small presents for her beautiful but poor friend, a friend whose nationality is different from her own. Further, the similarity of the men's names—Ernest Dent, Merton Densher—seems more than coincidental.

3. For a very interesting recent discussion of the Hawthorne/James association, see Rowe's chapter on the literary influences on James in *The Theoretical Dimensions of Henry James* (30–57). There, Rowe argues that James "invented" Hawthorne as an influence to react against.

4. F. W. Dupee has called James "the great feminine novelist of a feminine age of letters" (quoted in Fowler, *Henry James's American Girl*, 5). Veeder, who has done the most extensive comparison of James and popular writers, claims that despite ample evidence that James outright adopted many popular modes, James "transforms these materials into great art" (*Henry James: The Lessons of the Master*, 1).

5. Baym notes that Southworth was one of only three writers in the nineteenth century whose individuality of style was cited as a strong point (*Novels, Readers, and Reviewers*, 134–35). Veeder, who nonetheless believes Henry James's style is "great art," finds through computer analysis of style that, compared to several works of nineteenth-century popular fiction, James's early style is as "extravagant" as any of the popular writers (*Henry James: The Lessons of the Master*, 24–31).

6. We should take James's preface with a good deal of skepticism since, as he reminds us, "one's plan, alas, is one thing and one's result another" (9).

7. For a discussion of James's obscurity, see White's *The Uses of Obscurity*, in which he argues that "in James's novels . . . he associates, at some deep level, the idea of obscurity of information with purity. . . . Overt representation becomes a source of moral danger" (21).

8. James's acceptance of his homosexuality may well play a part in the gender reversal that occurs in his representation of the writer here; the female novelist could be an example of Jamesian "cross-dressing." But we should also note, as Karcher does in "Male Vision and Female Revision," that Densher is also a writer, and a professional one at that, whose "story" ultimately is the controlling one.

9. The term "reciprocal obligation" is Habegger's, although I am using it somewhat differently than he does ("Reciprocity and the Market Place"). He recognizes an absolute difference between Milly's economic transactions and others in the novel that I do not.

10. I cite volume, book, chapter, and page numbers for *Wings of the Dove*; for example, "I, 1, i, 23" means "volume I, Book First, chapter i, page 23."

11. Even Susan Shepherd Stringham, who could be regarded as the most caring character in the text and the least interested in personal aggrandizement, frequently describes her relation to Milly Theale in economic terms. She tells Densher, "With her, at her court . . . it does pay" (II, 8, iii, 300). James also

describes Susan's relation to Milly as a financial one; he writes, "Our couple [Susan and Milly] had at all events effected an exchange; the elder friend had been as consciously intellectual as possible, and the younger, abounding in personal revelation, had been as unconsciously distinguished" (I, 3, i, 80).

12. Habegger maintains that even though the sacrifices in James's fiction resemble marketplace contracts, there is nonetheless an "absolute and un-bridgeable" gap between them ("Reciprocity and the Market Place," 463). I disagree, as does Allen, who points out that James resists moral absolutes (*Woman's Place*, 153–54). But Vernon, in "Labor and Leisure," suggests that Densher may become an English Eugenio, a view supported by the notion that Milly "pays" him for his "kindness" (192).

13. In his chapter on *The Aspern Papers* in *The Theoretical Dimensions of Henry James*, Rowe describes the various critical interpretations of Juliana's eyeshade: it has been associated with "blindness to the outside world" or "the veil of original sin that James might have borrowed from Hawthorne's 'Minis-ter's Black Veil.'" Rowe suggests its similarity to "the veils worn by Muslim women to prevent their violation by the eye of the public" (111). None seem to have associated it with the green accountant's eyeshade commonly worn in the nineteenth century.

14. In his notebook, James's original idea for Milly's situation emphasizes her love of life, like his cousin Minny Temple's: "She learns that she has but a short time to live, and she rebels, she is terrified, she cries out in her anguish" (*Notebooks*, 169)—acts that do not accord very well with the text's calm Milly Theale.

15. Sontag accepts that Milly has tuberculosis, as did Minny Temple (*Illness as Metaphor*, 21), despite Kate's explicit denial that Milly suffers from this disease. Densher asks Kate, "Is it a bad case of lungs?," to which she replies, "Not lungs, I think. Isn't consumption, taken in time, now curable?" (II, 6, iv, 214). In "'Love by the Doctor's Direction,'" McLean suggests that Milly is suffering from sexual psychosis. In "'Consumption, Heart-Disease, or Whatever,'" Mercer and Wangensteen, using medical case histories, have diagnosed Milly's illness as "green sickness," or chlorosis, an often-diagnosed disease at the turn of the century for which the most commonly prescribed cure was marriage. "Love sickness," as it had also been called since the fifteenth century, was probably a form of anemia and was only rarely fatal, but diagnoses had reached an all-time high in the 1895–1905 period. In 1901–2, it accounted for 8 percent of doctor visits in many clinics, and medical journals of the 1890s were full of stories about deaths from chlorosis.

16. Other characters, too, make romance of Milly's illness, especially Maud Lowder and Merton Densher. In one exchange after Milly's death, Maud com-ments, "The mere *money* of her," which Densher understands "as fairly giving poetry to the life Milly clung to: a view of what 'might have been.'" In a "cold moment," Densher describes the case to Mrs. Lowder as exemplifying the "highest heroism": "Milly had held with passion to her dream of a future, and she was separated from it, not shrieking indeed, but grimly, awfully silent, as

one might imagine some noble young victim of the scaffold, in the French Revolution." For himself, he "for that matter took in the scene again at moments as from the page of a book" (II, 10, ii, 369).

17. Fetterley, in "Who Killed Dick Diver?," explores the ramifications of the biographical impulses of this novel and its reaction against women. She argues that Fitzgerald's guilt over Zelda's breakdown and his fear that his social-sexual superiority was not guaranteed provide the impetus for the novel and that Fitzgerald's blaming American women for all of the problems of the American man makes this a dishonest, "self-serving book."

18. In chapter 1, we saw that a woman's lack of control over her life, the necessity of her bending to a husband's or father's will in matters of life-style, is understood as one of the primary causes of nineteenth-century hysteria.

19. Fitzgerald's condemnation of working for money here contrasts rather dramatically with his own habit of writing stories purely for financial gain.

20. Fitzgerald's choice of diagnosis for this woman is interesting in two ways. First, eczema was one of Zelda's most painful and persistent symptoms during her 1931 breakdown and hospitalization and was one of the illnesses to which Scott had, as his biographer calls it, "a sympathetic reaction" (Mellow, *Invented Lives*, 371)—after Zelda had eczema, Scott thought he did, too. Second, the woman artist's illness is also interesting because it parallels one Freud cites in the "Dora" case, in which a woman who had been treated unsuccessfully for years for hysteria was found after her death to have had tabes (tertiary, or inherited, syphilis).

21. We can compare Dick Diver and Hawthorne's Aylmer from "The Birth-mark," too. Like Aylmer, he finds that he can neither maintain the emotional detachment expected of the scientist nor sort out his passion for his work from his passion for a woman. Dick, like Aylmer, devotes his life's work to making his wife "well" again; he eventually gives up all of his other aspirations to devote himself to her and her "case." Dick makes Nicole the "work" of his life; he tries to "perfect" her.

Berman, in *The Talking Cure*, notes that Dr. Diver's care for his wife—which eventually ruins his health—directly contrasts with that given by yet another husband-doctor we have encountered, the one in "The Yellow Wallpaper": "Just as the husband is responsible for the heroine's isolation and madness in 'The Yellow Wallpaper,' so does the wife seem responsible for the hero's self-destruction in *Tender Is the Night*" (85). The conflict apparent in Berman's claim, that Nicole is held responsible for Dick's *self*-destruction, is a conflict apparent in the novel itself.

Bibliography

Adlam, Diana, and Couze Venn. "Women's Exile: Interview with Irigaray." *Ideology and Consciousness* 2 (1978): 74.

Agnew, Jean-Christophe. "The Consuming Vision of Henry James." In *The Culture of Consumption*, edited by Richard Fox and T. J. Jackson Lears, 65–100. New York: Pantheon, 1983.

Alcott, Louisa May. *Little Women*. 1868. Reprint. New York: New American Library, 1983.

Allen, Elizabeth. *A Woman's Place in the Novels of Henry James*. New York: St. Martin's Press, 1984.

Althusser, Louis. *Lenin and Philosophy, and Other Essays*. London: New Left Books, 1971.

Ammons, Elizabeth. *Edith Wharton's Argument with America*. Athens: University of Georgia Press, 1980.

Anderson, Olive. *Suicide in Victorian and Edwardian England*. Oxford: Clarendon Press, 1987.

Ardener, Edwin. "Belief and the Problem of Woman." In *Perceiving Women*, edited by Shirley Ardener, 1–28. New York: Wiley, 1975.

Armstrong, Nancy. *Desire and Domestic Fiction: A Political History of the Novel*. New York: Oxford University Press, 1987.

Atwan, Robert, Donald McQuade, and John Wright. *Edsels, Luckies, and Frigidaires: Advertising the American Way*. Foreword by George Lois. New York: Dell Publishing Company, 1979.

Atwood, Margaret. *Bodily Harm*. New York: Simon and Schuster, 1983.

———. *The Handmaid's Tale*. Toronto: McClelland and Stewart, 1985.

Bakhtin, M. M. *The Dialogic Imagination: Four Essays*. Edited by Michael Holquist; translated by Caryl Emerson and Michael Holquist. Austin: University of Texas Press, 1981.

Banner, Lois W. *American Beauty*. New York: Alfred A. Knopf, 1983.

Bannister, Robert. *Social Darwinism: Science and Myth in Anglo-American Thought*. Philadelphia: Temple University Press, 1979.

Banta, Martha. *Imaging American Women: Idea and Ideals in Cultural History*. New York: Columbia University Press, 1987.

Bardes, Barbara, and Suzanne Gossett. *Declarations of Independence: Women and Political Power in Nineteenth-Century American Fiction*. New Brunswick, N.J.: Rutgers University Press, 1990.

Barker-Benfield, G. J. *The Horrors of the Half-Known Life: Male Attitudes toward Women and Sexuality in Nineteenth-Century America*. New York: Harper and Row, 1976.

Barrett, Michèle. "Ideology and the Cultural Production of Gender." In *Feminist Criticism and Social Change*, edited by Judith Newton and Deborah Rosenfelt, 65–85. New York: Methuen, 1985.

———. "The Place of Aesthetics in Marxist Criticism." In *Marxism and the In-*

terpretation of Culture, edited by Cary Nelson and Lawrence Grossberg, 697–714. Urbana: University of Illinois Press, 1988.

———. *Women's Oppression Today: Problems in Marxist Feminist Analysis*. London: Villiers Publications, 1980.

Barthes, Roland. *A Lover's Discourse: Fragments*. Translated by Richard Howard. New York: Hill and Wang, 1978.

———. *Mythologies*. Translated by Annette Lavers. New York: Hill and Wang, 1972.

———. *S/Z*. Translated by Richard Miller. New York: Hill and Wang, 1974.

Bartlett, Elizabeth Ann. "Liberty, Equality, Sorority: Origins and Interpretations of American Feminist Thought—Frances Wright, Margaret Fuller, and Sarah Grimké." Ph.D. dissertation, University of Minnesota, 1981.

Bauer, Dale. "Edith Wharton's 'Roman Fever': A Rune of History." *College English* 50.6 (1988): 681–93.

———. *Feminist Dialogics: A Theory of Failed Community*. Albany: State University of New York Press, 1988.

Baym, Nina. "Hawthorne's Women: The Tyranny of Social Myths." *Centennial Review* 15 (1971): 250–72.

———. *Novels, Readers, and Reviewers: Responses to Fiction in Antebellum America*. Ithaca, N.Y.: Cornell University Press, 1984.

———. *The Shape of Hawthorne's Career*. Ithaca, N.Y.: Cornell University Press, 1976.

———. "Thwarted Nature: Nathaniel Hawthorne as Feminist." In *American Novelists Revisited: Essays in Feminist Criticism*, edited by Fritz Fleischmann, 58–77. Boston: G. K. Hall and Company, 1982.

———. *Woman's Fiction: A Guide to Novels by and about Women in America, 1820–1870*. Ithaca, N.Y.: Cornell University Press, 1978.

Bazin, Nancy Topping. "The Destruction of Lily Bart: Capitalism, Christianity, and Male Chauvinism." *Denver Quarterly* 17.4 (1983): 97–108.

Beecher, Catharine. *Letters to the People on Health and Happiness*. New York: Harper and Brothers, 1855.

Bell, Millicent. "The Dream of Being Possessed and Possessing: Henry James's *The Wings of the Dove*." *Massachusetts Review* 10 (1969): 97–114.

Belsey, Catherine. "Constructing the Subject, Deconstructing the Text." In *Feminist Criticism and Social Change*, edited by Judith Newton and Deborah Rosenfelt, 43–64. New York: Methuen, 1985.

Berlant, Jeffrey L. *Profession and Monopoly: A Study of Medicine in the United States and Great Britain*. Berkeley: University of California Press, 1975.

Berlant, Lauren. "Fantasies of Utopia in *The Blithedale Romance*." *American Literary History* 1.1 (1989): 30–62.

Berman, Jeffrey. *The Talking Cure: Literary Representations of Psychoanalysis*. New York: New York University Press, 1985.

Biasin, Gian-Paolo. *Literary Diseases: Theme and Metaphor in the Italian Novel*. Austin: University of Texas Press, 1975.

Birdsall, Virginia Ogden. "Hawthorne's Fair-Haired Maidens: The Fading Light." *PMLA* 75 (1960): 250–56.

Bonapart, Marie. *The Life and Works of Edgar Allan Poe: A Psychoanalytic Interpretation.* Translated by John Rodken. London: Imago Publishing Company, 1949.

Boone, Joseph Allen. *Tradition Counter Tradition: Love and the Form of Fiction.* Chicago: University of Chicago Press, 1987.

Boston Women's Health Book Collective. *Our Bodies, Ourselves.* New York: Simon and Schuster, 1984.

Boydston, Jeanne, Mary Kelley, and Anne Margolis. *The Limits of Sisterhood: The Beecher Sisters on Women's Rights and Woman's Sphere.* Chapel Hill: University of North Carolina Press, 1988.

Braden, Charles S. *Spirits in Rebellion: The Rise and Development of New Thought.* Dallas: Southern Methodist University Press, 1963.

Brooks, Cleanth, R. W. B. Lewis, and Robert Penn Warren. *American Literature: The Makers and the Making.* Vol. 1. New York: St. Martin's Press, 1973.

Brown, Gillian. *Domestic Individualism: Imagining Self in Nineteenth-Century America.* Berkeley: University of California Press, 1990.

Brown, Herbert R. *The Sentimental Novel in America, 1789–1860.* Durham, N.C.: Duke University Press, 1940.

Brown, Joanne. " 'Take Me to the River': The Water-Cure in America." *Medical Humanities Review* 1.2 (1987): 29–34.

Brownstein, Rachel. *Becoming a Heroine: Reading about Women in Novels.* New York: Viking Press, 1982.

Bullard, Laura Curtis. *Christine: A Woman's Trials and Triumphs.* New York: De Witt and Davenport, 1856.

Bullough, Vern, and Martha Voght. "Women, Menstruation, and Nineteenth-Century Medicine." In *Women and Health in America,* edited by Judith Walzer Leavitt, 28–38. Madison: University of Wisconsin Press, 1984.

Burke, Kenneth. *The Philosophy of Literary Form.* Berkeley: University of California Press, 1973.

Cady Stanton, Elizabeth, Susan B. Anthony, and Matilda Joslyn Gage, eds. *History of Woman Suffrage.* Vol. 1. Rochester, N.Y.: Charles Mann, 1881.

Carpenter, Frederic I. "Puritans Preferred Blondes: The Heroines of Melville and Hawthorne." *New England Quarterly* 9 (1936): 262–64.

Cayleff, Susan E. *Wash and Be Healed: The Water-Cure Movement and Women's Health.* Philadelphia: Temple University Press, 1987.

Chambers, John Whiteclay. *The Tyranny of Change: America in the Progressive Era, 1900–1917.* New York: St. Martin's Press, 1980.

Chesler, Phyllis. *Women and Madness.* Garden City, N.Y.: Doubleday, 1972.

Cixous, Hélène. "Portrait of Dora." *Diacritics* 13.1 (1983): 2–32.

Clinton, Catherine. *The Other Civil War: American Women in the Nineteenth Century.* New York: Hill and Wang, 1984.

Cogan, Frances B. *All-American Girl: The Ideal of Real Womanhood in Mid-Nineteenth-Century America.* Athens: University of Georgia Press, 1989.

Conn, Peter. *The Divided Mind: Ideology and Imagination in America, 1898–1917*. Cambridge: Cambridge University Press, 1983.

Coward, R., and J. Ellis. *Language and Materialism*. London: Routledge and Kegan Paul, 1977.

Crews, Frederick. *The Sins of the Fathers*. New York: Oxford University Press, 1968.

Culler, Jonathan. *On Deconstruction*. Ithaca, N.Y.: Cornell University Press, 1982.

———. "Story and Discourse in the Analysis of Narrative." In *Pursuit of Signs*, 167–87. Ithaca, N.Y.: Cornell University Press, 1981.

Dark Victory. Directed by Edmund Bourke. Warner Brothers Studio, 1939.

David, Deirdre. *Intellectual Women and Victorian Patriarchy: Harriett Martineau, Elizabeth Barrett Browning, and George Eliot*. Ithaca, N.Y.: Cornell University Press, 1987.

Davidson, Cathy N. *Revolution and the Word: The Rise of the Novel in America*. New York: Oxford University Press, 1986.

Dayan, Joan. *Fables of Mind: An Inquiry into Poe's Fiction*. New York: Oxford University Press, 1987.

Degler, Carl N. "What Ought to Be and What Was: Women's Sexuality in the Nineteenth Century." *American Historical Review* 89 (1974): 1467–90.

Delmar, Rosalind. "What Is Feminism?" In *What Is Feminism?*, edited by Juliet Mitchell and Ann Oakley, 8–33. New York: Pantheon, 1986.

Derrida, Jacques. "Freud and the Scene of Writing." In *Writing and Difference*, 196–231. Chicago: University of Chicago Press, 1979.

———. *Of Grammatology*. Translated by Gayatri Spivak. Baltimore: Johns Hopkins University Press, 1976.

———. "Plato's Pharmacy." In *Dissemination*, translated by Barbara Johnson, 61–172. Chicago: University of Chicago Press, 1982.

Dijkstra, Bram. *Idols of Perversity: Fantasies of Feminine Evil in Fin-de-Siècle Culture*. New York: Oxford University Press, 1986.

Dimock, Wai-Chee. "Debasing Exchange: Edith Wharton's *The House of Mirth*." *PMLA* 100.5 (1985): 783–92.

Dixon, E. H. *Woman and Her Diseases, from the Cradle to the Grave: Adapted Exclusively to Her Instruction in the Physiology of her System, and All the Diseases of Her Critical Periods*. 10th ed. New York: A. Ranney, 1855.

Doane, Mary Ann. "The Clinical Eye." In *The Female Body in Western Culture*, edited by Susan Suleiman, 152–73. Cambridge: Harvard University Press, 1985.

Donaldson, Scott. "The Crisis of Fitzgerald's 'Crack-Up.'" *Twentieth-Century Literature* 26.2 (1980): 171–88.

Donegan, Jane. *"Hydropathic Highway to Health": Women and Water-Cure in Antebellum America*. New York: Greenwood Press, 1986.

———. "'Safe Delivered' but by Whom?" In *Women and Health in America*, edited by Judith Walzer Leavitt, 302–17. Madison: University of Wisconsin Press, 1984.

Donovan, Josephine. *Feminist Theory: The Intellectual Traditions of American Feminism.* New York: Continuum, 1988.

———. "The Silence Is Broken." In *Women and Language in Literature and Society,* edited by Sally McConnel-Ginet, Ruth Borker, and Nelly Furman, 205–18. New York: Praeger, 1980.

Douglas, Ann. *The Feminization of American Culture.* New York: Alfred A. Knopf, 1977.

Douglas Wood, Ann. " 'The Fashionable Diseases': Women's Complaints and Their Treatment in Nineteenth-Century America." *Journal of Interdisciplinary History* 4.1 (1973): 25–52.

DuBois, Ellen Carol, ed. *Elizabeth Cady Stanton, Susan B. Anthony: Correspondence, Writings, Speeches.* New York: Schocken Books, 1981.

———. *Feminism and Suffrage: The Emergence of an Independent Women's Movement in America, 1848–1869.* Ithaca, N.Y.: Cornell University Press, 1978.

Duffin, Lorna. "The Conspicuous Consumptive: Woman as Invalid." In *The Nineteenth-Century Woman: Her Culture and Physical World,* edited by Sara Delamont and Lorna Duffin, 26–56. New York: Barnes and Noble Books, 1978.

Ecob, Helen Gilbert. *The Well-Dressed Woman: A Study in the Practical Application to Dress of the Laws of Health, Art, and Morals.* New York: Fowler and Wells Company, 1892.

Edel, Leon. *Henry James: A Life.* New York: Harper and Row, 1985.

Ehrenreich, Barbara, and Deirdre English. *Complaints and Disorders: The Sexual Politics of Sickness.* Old Westbury, N.Y.: Feminist Press, 1973.

———. *For Her Own Good: 150 Years of the Experts' Advice to Women.* New York: Anchor Press, 1978.

Emerson, Ralph Waldo. "The Transcendentalist." In *Selections from Ralph Waldo Emerson,* edited by Stephen E. Whicher, 192–206. Boston: Houghton Mifflin, 1957.

Epstein, Barbara L. *The Politics of Domesticity: Women, Evangelism, and Temperance in Nineteenth-Century America.* Middletown, Conn.: Wesleyan University Press, 1981.

Faust, Langdon Lynne. *American Women Writers: A Critical Reference Guide from Colonial Times to the Present.* New York: Frederick Ungar, 1983.

Felman, Shoshana. "The Critical Phallacy." *Diacritics* 5.4 (1975): 2–10.

Fetterley, Judith. *The Resisting Reader: A Feminist Approach to American Fiction.* Bloomington: Indiana University Press, 1977.

———. "Who Killed Dick Diver?: The Sexual Politics of *Tender Is the Night.*" *Mosaic* 17.1 (1983): 111–28.

Fitzgerald, F. Scott. *Tender Is the Night.* New York: Scribner's, 1934.

Fitzgerald, Zelda. *Save Me the Waltz.* New York: Scribner's, 1932.

Flexner, Eleanor. *Century of Struggle: The Woman's Rights Movement in the United States.* Rev. ed. Cambridge: Harvard University Press, 1975.

Foucault, Michel. *The Birth of the Clinic: An Archaeology of Medical Perception*. Translated by A. M. Sheridan. New York: Vintage Books, 1975.

———. *Discipline and Punish*. Translated by Alan Sheridan. New York: Vintage Books, 1979.

———. *History of Sexuality*. Vol. 1, *An Introduction*. Translated by Robert Hurley. New York: Pantheon, 1978.

———. *Madness and Civilization*. Translated by Richard Howard. New York: Vintage Books, 1973.

———. *Power/Knowledge: Selected Interviews and Other Writings, 1972–77*. Edited and translated by Colin Gordon. New York: Pantheon, 1980.

———. "What Is an Author?" In *Textual Strategies*, edited by Josué V. Harari, 141–60. Ithaca, N.Y.: Cornell University Press, 1979.

Fowler, Virginia C. *Henry James's American Girl: The Embroidery on the Canvas*. Madison: University of Wisconsin Press, 1984.

Frederick, J. T. "Hawthorne's Scribbling Women." *New England Quarterly* 48 (1975): 231–40.

Freud, Sigmund. *Complete Psychological Works*. 24 vols. Translated by James Strachey. London: Hogarth, 1953–74.

Fryer, Judith. *The Faces of Eve: Women in the Nineteenth-Century American Novel*. New York: Oxford University Press, 1976.

Gallop, Jane. *The Daughter's Seduction: Feminism and Psychoanalysis*. Ithaca, N.Y.: Cornell University Press, 1982.

———. "Snatches of Conversation." In *Women and Language in Literature and Society*, edited by Sally McConnell-Ginet, Ruth Borker, and Nelly Furman, 274–83. New York: Praeger, 1980.

Gates, Barbara. *Victorian Suicide: Mad Crimes and Sad Histories*. Princeton, N.J.: Princeton University Press, 1988.

Gay, Peter. *The Education of the Senses*. New York: Oxford University Press, 1984.

Geertz, Clifford. *The Interpretation of Cultures*. New York: Basic Books, 1973.

Genette, Gerard. *Figures of Literary Discourse*. Translated by Alan Sheridan. New York: Columbia University Press, 1982.

Gervais, Ronald. "The Socialist and the Silk Stockings: Fitzgerald's Double Allegiance." *Mosaic* 15.2 (1981): 79–92.

Gilbert, Sandra. "Soldier's Heart: Literary Men, Literary Women, and the Great War." *Signs* 8.3 (1983): 422–50.

Gilbert, Sandra, and Susan Gubar. *The Madwoman in the Attic: The Woman Writer and the Nineteenth-Century Literary Imagination*. New Haven: Yale University Press, 1979.

———. "The Man on the Dump versus the United Dames of America; or, What Does Frank Lentricchia Want?" *Critical Inquiry* 14.2 (1988): 386–406.

———. *No Man's Land: The Place of the Woman Writer in the Twentieth Century*. Vol. 1, *The War of the Words*. New Haven: Yale University Press, 1988.

Gilman, Charlotte Perkins. *The Living of Charlotte Perkins Gilman: An Autobiography*. New York: D. Appleton-Century Company, 1935.

———. "Why I Wrote 'The Yellow Wallpaper'?" In *The Charlotte Perkins Gilman Reader*, edited by Ann J. Lane, 19–20. New York: Pantheon Books, 1980.

———. *Women and Economics*. Boston: Small, Maynard, and Company, 1899.

———. "The Yellow Wallpaper." 1891. Reprinted in *The Charlotte Perkins Gilman Reader*, edited by Ann J. Lane, 1–19. New York: Pantheon Books, 1980.

Gilman, Sander. *Difference and Pathology: Stereotypes of Race, Gender, and Madness*. Ithaca, N.Y.: Cornell University Press, 1985.

———. *Disease and Representation: Images of Illness from Madness to AIDS*. Ithaca, N.Y.: Cornell University Press, 1988.

———. *Seeing the Insane*. New York: John Wiley and Sons, 1982.

Glasgow, Ellen. *Barren Ground*. 1925. Reprint. New York: Hill and Wang, 1957.

———. *The Woman Within*. New York: Harcourt, Brace and Company, 1954.

Godden, Richard. "Money Makes Manners Make Man Make Woman: *Tender Is the Night*, a Familiar Romance?" *Literature and History* 12.1 (1986): 16–37.

Gordon, Linda. "Voluntary Motherhood: The Beginnings of Feminist Birth Control Ideas in the United States." In *Women and Health in America*, edited by Judith Walzer Leavitt, 104–16. Madison: University of Wisconsin Press, 1984.

Greene, Gayle. "Feminist and Marxist Criticism: An Argument for Alliances." *Women's Studies: An Interdisciplinary Journal* 9 (1981): 29–45.

Greene, Gayle, and Coppélia Kahn. *Making a Difference: Feminist Literary Criticism*. New York: Methuen, 1985.

Greene, Theodore P. *America's Heroes: The Changing Models of Success in American Magazines*. New York: Oxford University Press, 1970.

Griffin, Susan. *Woman and Nature*. New York: Harper Colophon Books, 1978.

Griffith, Elisabeth. *In Her Own Right: The Life of Elizabeth Cady Stanton*. New York: Oxford University Press, 1984.

Gross, Seymour. " 'Rappaccini's Daughter' and the Nineteenth-Century Physician." In *Ruined Eden of the Present: Hawthorne, Melville, and Poe*, edited by G. R. Thompson and Virgil Lokke, 129–42. West Lafayette, Ind.: Purdue University Press, 1981.

Gubar, Susan. " 'The Blank Page' and the Issues of Female Creativity." *Critical Inquiry* 9 (1981): 243–63.

Habegger, Alfred. "Reciprocity and the Market Place in *The Wings of the Dove* and *What Maisie Knew*." *Nineteenth-Century Fiction* 25 (1971): 455–73.

Hale, Nathan G., Jr. *Freud and the Americans: The Beginnings of Psychoanalysis in the United States, 1876–1917*. New York: Oxford University Press, 1971.

Hale, Sarah Josepha. *The Lecturess, or Woman's Sphere*. Boston: Whipple and Damrell, 1839.

Hall, Stuart. "Cultural Studies: Two Paradigms." *Media, Culture, and Society* 2 (1980): 57–72.

Haller, John S., and Robin M. Haller. *The Physician and Sexuality in Victorian America*. New York: W. W. Norton, 1974.

Hallissy, Margaret. "Hawthorne's Venomous Beatrice." *Studies in Short Fiction* 19.3 (1982): 231–39.

Harris, Barbara J. *Beyond Her Sphere: Women and the Professions in American History*. Westport, Conn.: Greenwood Press, 1978.

Harris, Susan K. *Nineteenth-Century American Women's Novels: Interpretive Strategies*. Cambridge: Cambridge University Press, 1990.

Hawthorne, Nathaniel. *The American Notebooks of Nathaniel Hawthorne*. Edited by Randall Stewart. New Haven: Yale University Press, 1932.

———. *The Complete Novels and Selected Tales of Nathaniel Hawthorne*. New York: Modern Library, 1937.

Heilman, Robert. "Hawthorne's 'The Birthmark': Science as Religion." *South Atlantic Quarterly* 48 (1949): 575–83.

Helsinger, Elizabeth K. *The Woman Question: Society and Literature in Britain and America, 1837–83*. New York: Garland, 1983.

Hollander, Anne. "Women and Fashion." In *Women, the Arts, and the 1920's in Paris and New York*, edited by Kenneth Wheeler and Virginia Lee Lussier, 109–25. New Brunswick, N.J.: Transaction Books, 1982.

Holmes, Oliver Wendell. *Elsie Venner: A Romance of Destiny*. Boston: Ticknor and Fields, 1861.

Holmes, Stewart W. "Phineas Parkhurst Quimby: Scientist of Transcendentalism." *New England Quarterly* 17 (1944): 356–80.

Homans, Margaret. *Bearing the Word: Language and Female Experience in Nineteenth-Century Women's Writing*. Chicago: University of Chicago Press, 1986.

Hull, Ramona E. " 'Scribbling Females' and Serious Males." *Nathaniel Hawthorne Journal* 5 (1975): 35–59.

Hunter, Dianne. "Hysteria, Psychoanalysis, and Feminism: The Case of Anna O." *Feminist Studies* 9.3 (1983): 464–88.

Irigaray, Luce. *Speculum of the Other Woman*. Translated by Gillian C. Gill. Ithaca, N.Y.: Cornell University Press, 1985.

———. "This Sex Which Is Not One." In *This Sex Which Is Not One*, translated by Catherine Porter and Carolyn Burke, 23–33. Ithaca, N.Y.: Cornell University Press, 1985.

———. "Women on the Market." In *This Sex Which Is Not One*, translated by Catherine Porter and Carolyn Burke, 170–91. Ithaca, N.Y.: Cornell University Press, 1985.

Irving, Washington. *Biography and Poetical Remains of the Late Margaret Miller Davidson*. 2d ed. Philadelphia: Lea and Blanchard, 1841.

Irwin, John T. *American Hieroglyphics*. New Haven: Yale University Press, 1980.

Jacobus, Mary, ed. *Women Writing and Writing about Women*. London: Croom and Helm, 1979.

James, Alice. *The Diary of Alice James*. Edited by Leon Edel. 1934. Reprint. New York: Penguin American Library, 1982.

James, Henry. *The Aspern Papers*. 1888. Reprinted in *The Turn of the Screw and Other Short Novels*, edited by Willard Thorp, 153–251. New York: New American Library, 1962.

———. "The Beast in the Jungle." 1903. Reprinted in *The Turn of the Screw and Other Short Novels*, edited by Willard Thorp, 404–51. New York: New American Library, 1962.

———. *Daisy Miller*. 1878. Reprinted in *The Turn of the Screw and Other Short Novels*, edited by Willard Thorp, 93–152. New York: New American Library, 1962.

———. *The Letters of Henry James*. Vol. 1. Edited by Leon Edel. Cambridge: Harvard University Press, 1974.

———. *The Notebooks of Henry James*. Edited by F. O. Matthiessen and Kenneth B. Murdock. New York: Oxford University Press, 1947.

———. *The Wings of the Dove*. Edited by J. Donald Crowley and Richard Hocks. 1902. Reprint. New York: W. W. Norton, 1978.

Jameson, Fredric. *The Political Unconscious: Narrative as Socially Symbolic Act*. Ithaca, N.Y.: Cornell University Press, 1980.

Janeway, Elizabeth. *The Powers of the Weak*. New York: Alfred A. Knopf, 1980.

Jehlen, Myra. *American Incarnation: The Individual, the Nation, and the Continent*. Cambridge: Harvard University Press, 1986.

———. "Archimedes and the Paradox of Feminist Criticism." *Signs* 6.4 (1981): 575–601.

———. "The Family Militant: Domesticity versus Slavery in *Uncle Tom's Cabin*." *Criticism* 31 (1989): 383–400.

Jewett, Sarah Orne. *A Country Doctor*. 1884. Reprint. New York: New American Library, 1986.

Johnson, Barbara. *The Critical Difference: Essays in the Contemporary Rhetoric of Reading*. Baltimore: Johns Hopkins University Press, 1980.

———. *A World of Difference*. Baltimore: Johns Hopkins University Press, 1987.

Johnson, Richard. "What Is Cultural Studies Anyway?" *Social Text* 6.1 (1987): 38–80.

Jones, Edgar R. *Those Were the Good Old Days: A Happy Look at American Advertising, 1880–1930*. New York: Simon and Schuster, 1959.

Jordan, Cynthia. *Second Stories: The Politics of Language, Form, and Gender in Early American Fictions*. Chapel Hill: University of North Carolina Press, 1989.

Kamuf, Peggy. "Writing Like a Woman." In *Women and Language in Literature and Society*, edited by Sally McConnell-Ginet, Ruth Borker, and Nelly Furman, 284–99. New York: Praeger, 1980.

Kaplan, Cora. "Pandora's Box: Subjectivity, Class, and Sexuality in Socialist Feminist Criticism." In *Making a Difference: Feminist Literary Criticism*, edited by Gayle Greene and Coppélia Kahn, 146–76. New York: Methuen, 1985.

Karcher, Carolyn. "Male Vision and Female Revision in James's *The Wings of the Dove* and Wharton's *The House of Mirth*." *Women's Studies* 10 (1984): 227–44.

Kasson, Joy. *Marble Queens and Captives: Women in Nineteenth-Century American Sculpture*. New Haven: Yale University Press, 1990.

———. "Power and Powerlessness in Nineteenth-Century Sculpture." Lecture, University of North Carolina, Chapel Hill, 1987.

Kaston, Carren. *Imagination and Desire in the Novels of Henry James*. New Brunswick, N.J.: Rutgers University Press, 1984.

Kelley, Mary. *Private Woman, Public Stage: Literary Domesticity in Nineteenth-Century America*. New York: Oxford University Press, 1984.

———. "The Sentimentalists: Promise and Betrayal in the Home." *Signs* 4.3 (1979): 434–46.

Kelly, Howard, and Walter L. Barrage. "E. H. Dixon." In *Dictionary of American Medical Biography*. New York: D. Appleton and Company, 1928.

Kleinman, Arthur. *Patients and Healers in the Context of Culture*. Berkeley: University of California Press, 1980.

Kolodny, Annette. *The Lay of the Land: Metaphor as Experience and History in American Life and Letters*. Chapel Hill: University of North Carolina Press, 1975.

———. "A Map for Rereading: Or, Gender and the Interpretation of Literary Texts." *New Literary History* 11 (1980): 451–67.

———. "Reply to Commentaries: Women Writers, Literary History, and Martian Readers." *New Literary History* 11 (1980): 587–92.

Kristeva, Julia. "Women's Time." *Signs* 7.1 (1981): 13–35.

Kunzle, David. *Fashion and Fetishism: A Social History of the Corset, Tight-Lacing, and Other Forms of Body Sculpture in the West*. Totowa, N.J.: Rowman and Littlefield, 1982.

Kushner, Howard. *Self-Destruction in the Promised Land: A Psychocultural Biology of American Suicide*. New Brunswick, N.J.: Rutgers University Press, 1989.

Lacan, Jacques. *Ecrits: A Selection*. Translated by Alan Sheridan. New York: W. W. Norton, 1977.

Lambert, Deborah G. "*The House of Mirth*: Readers Respond." *Tulsa Studies in Women's Literature* 3.1–2 (1984): 69–82.

Lamphere, Louise, and Michelle Zimbalist Rosaldo, eds. *Women, Culture, and Society*. Stanford: Stanford University Press, 1974.

Lears, T. J. Jackson. "From Salvation to Self-Realization: Advertising and the Therapeutic Roots of the Consumer Culture, 1880–1930." In *The Culture of Consumption: Critical Essays in American History, 1880–1980*, edited by T. J. Jackson Lears and Richard Wightman Fox, 1–38. New York: Pantheon Books, 1983.

———. *No Place of Grace: Antimodernism and the Transformation of American Culture, 1880–1920*. New York: Pantheon Books, 1981.

Leavitt, Judith Walzer. *Brought to Bed: Childbearing in America, 1750–1950.*
New York: Oxford University Press, 1986.

———. " 'Science' Enters the Birthing Room: Obstetrics in America since the
Eighteenth Century." *Journal of American History* 70 (1983): 281–304.

———, ed. *Women and Health in America.* Madison: University of Wisconsin
Press, 1984.

Lefcowitz, Barbara F., and Allan B. Lefcowitz. "Some Rents in the Veil: New
Light on Priscilla and Zenobia." *Nineteenth-Century Fiction* 21 (1966): 263–
75.

Lentricchia, Frank. *Criticism and Social Change.* Chicago: University of Chicago Press, 1985.

———. "Patriarchy Against Itself: The Young Manhood of Wallace Stevens."
Critical Inquiry 13.4 (1987): 742–86.

Lesage, Julia. "Women's Rage." In *Marxism and the Interpretation of Culture,*
edited by Cary Nelson and Lawrence Grossberg, 419–28. Urbana: University of Illinois Press, 1988.

Lewis, Myrna. "Older Women and Health: An Overview." *Women and Health*
10 (1985): 1–16.

Lewis, R. W. B. *Edith Wharton: A Biography.* New York: Harper and Row,
1975.

Lewis, Sinclair. *Arrowsmith.* New York: Harcourt, Brace and Company, 1925.

Lutz, Tom. *American Nervousness, 1903: An Anecdotal History.* Ithaca, N.Y.:
Cornell University Press, 1991.

McCormack, Peggy. "The Semiotic of Economic Language in James's Fiction."
American Literature 58.4 (1986): 540–56.

Macherey, Pierre. *A Theory of Literary Production.* Translated by Geoffrey
Wall. London: Routledge and Kegan Paul, 1978.

MacKinnon, Catherine. "Desire and Power: A Feminist Perspective." In *Marxism and the Interpretation of Culture,* edited by Cary Nelson and Lawrence
Grossberg, 117–36. Urbana: University of Illinois Press, 1988.

———. "Feminism, Marxism, Method, and the State." *Signs* 7.3 (1982): 515–
44.

McLean, Robert C. " 'Love by the Doctor's Direction': Disease and Death in
The Wings of the Dove." *Papers on Language and Literature* 8, supplement
(1972): 128–48.

MacLelland, Bruce. *Prosperity through Thought and Force.* New York: Elizabeth Towne, 1907.

Marchand, Roland. *Advertising the American Dream: Making Way for Modernity, 1920–40.* Berkeley: University of California Press, 1985.

Matthiessen, F. O. *American Renaissance: Art and Expression in the Age of
Emerson and Whitman.* New York: Oxford University Press, 1941.

Mellow, James. *Invented Lives: F. Scott and Zelda Fitzgerald.* Boston:
Houghton Mifflin, 1984.

Mendelsohn, Robert S. *Mal(e)practice: How Doctors Manipulate Women.*
Chicago: Contemporary Books, 1981.

Mercer, Caroline, and Sarah Wangensteen. " 'Consumption, Heart-Disease, or Whatever': Chlorosis, a Heroine's Disease in *The Wings of the Dove*." *Journal of the History of Medicine* 40.3 (1985): 259–85.

Michaels, Walter Benn. *The Gold Standard and the Logic of Naturalism: American Literature at the Turn of the Century*. Berkeley: University of California Press, 1987.

Michie, Helena. *The Flesh Made Word: Female Figures and Women's Bodies*. New York: Oxford University Press, 1987.

Milani, Laura. "Women in Waiting." *The New Physician*. 40 (March 1991): 21–25.

Miller, Nancy K., ed. *The Poetics of Gender*. New York: Columbia University Press, 1986.

Mitchell, Juliet. *Psychoanalysis and Feminism*. New York: Random House, 1975.

Mitchell, S. Weir. *A Comedy of Conscience*. New York: Century, 1903.

———. *Doctor and Patient*. Philadelphia: J. B. Lippincott, 1888.

Montrelay, Michèle. "Of Femininity." *M/F* 1 (1978): 83–101.

Moore, Rayburn S. "The Magazine and the Short Story in the Ante-Bellum Period." *South Atlantic Bulletin* 38 (1973): 44–51.

Morantz, Regina M. "The Perils of Feminist History." In *Women and Health in America*, edited by Judith Walzer Leavitt, 239–45. Madison: University of Wisconsin Press, 1984.

Morantz-Sanchez, Regina M. "So Honoured, So Loved?: The Decline of the Female Physician, 1900–1920." In *Send Us a Lady Physician: Women Doctors in America, 1835–1920*, edited by Ruth J. Abram. New York: W. W. Norton, 1985.

———. *Sympathy and Science: Women Physicians in American Medicine*. New York: Oxford University Press, 1985.

Mosher, Clelia. *Health and the Woman Movement*. 1915. Reprint. New York: The Woman's Press, 1918.

Myerson, Abraham. *The Nervous Housewife*. 1920. Reprint. Boston: Little, Brown, 1927.

Newton, Judith Lowder. *Women, Power, and Subversion: Social Strategies in British Fiction, 1778–1860*. Athens: University of Georgia Press, 1981.

Newton, Judith Lowder, and Deborah Rosenfelt, eds. *Feminist Criticism and Social Change*. New York: Methuen, 1985.

Nichter, Mark. "Negotiation of the Illness Experience: Ayurvedic Therapy and the Psychosocial Dimension of Illness." *Culture, Medicine, and Psychiatry* 5 (1981): 5–24.

Ohmann, Richard. "The Shaping of an American Canon, 1960–1975." In *Politics of Letters*, 68–91. Middletown, Conn.: Wesleyan University Press, 1987.

Olsen, Tillie. *Yonnondio: From the Thirties*. New York: Dell Publishing Company, 1974.

Ortner, Sherry. "Is Female to Male as Nature Is to Culture?" In *Women, Culture, and Society*, edited by Michelle Zimbalist Rosaldo and Louise Lamphere, 67–88. Stanford: Stanford University Press, 1974.

Painter, Nell Irvin. *Standing at Armageddon: The United States, 1877–1919.* New York: W. W. Norton, 1987.

Papashvily, Helen W. *All the Happy Endings: A Study of the Domestic Novel in America, the Women Who Wrote It, the Women Who Read It, in the Nineteenth Century.* New York: Harper and Brothers, 1956.

Parker, Gail T. "Mary Baker Eddy and Sentimental Womanhood." *New England Quarterly* 43 (1970): 3–18.

———. *Mind Cure in New England: From the Civil War to World War I.* Hanover, N.H.: University Press of New England, 1973.

———, ed. *The Oven Birds: American Women on Womanhood, 1820–1920.* New York: Doubleday, 1972.

Person, Leland. *Aesthetic Headaches: Women and a Masculinist Poetics in Poe, Melville, and Hawthorne.* Athens: University of Georgia Press, 1988.

Phelps, Elizabeth Stuart. *Doctor Zay.* 1882. Reprint. New York: Feminist Press, 1987.

———. *Walled In.* New York: Harper and Brothers, 1907.

Plato. *The Phaedrus.* In *Euthyphro, Apology, Crito, Phaedo, Phaedrus,* translated by Harold N. Fowler. London: Loeb Library, 1971.

Poe, Edgar Allan. *The Complete Tales and Poems of Edgar Allan Poe.* Edited by Hervey Allen. New York: Modern Library, 1938.

———. *Essays and Reviews.* New York: Library of America, 1984.

———. Review of *The Biography . . . of Margaret Miller Davidson,* by Washington Irving. *Graham's Magazine* 19 (August 1841): 93–94.

Poirier, Suzanne. "The Weir Mitchell Rest Cure: Doctors and Patients." *Women's Studies* 10 (1983): 15–40.

Poovey, Mary. "Cultural Criticism: Past and Present." *College English* 52.6 (1990): 615–25.

———. *Uneven Developments: The Ideological Work of Gender in Mid-Victorian England.* Chicago: University of Chicago Press, 1988.

Price Herndl, Diane. "The Dilemmas of a Feminine Dialogic." In *Feminism and the Dialogic,* edited by Dale M. Bauer and Susan Jaret McKinstry, 7–24. Albany: State University of New York Press, 1991.

———. " 'The Writing Cure': Charlotte Perkins Gilman, Anna O., and 'Hysterical Writing.' " *NWSA Journal* 1.1 (1988): 57–79.

Prigozy, Ruth. "From Griffith's Girls to *Daddy's Girl*: The Masks of Innocence in *Tender Is the Night.*" *Twentieth-Century Literature* 26.2 (1980): 189–221.

Purvis, Andrew. "A Perilous Gap." *Time* 136 (1990): 66–67.

Rahv, Philip. "The Dark Lady of Salem." *Partisan Review* 8 (1941): 362–81.

Raper, Julius. *From the Sunken Garden.* Baton Rouge: Louisiana State University Press, 1980.

Reed, James. "Doctors, Birth Control, and Social Values, 1830–1970." In *Women and Health in America,* edited by Judith Walzer Leavitt, 124–40. Madison: University of Wisconsin Press, 1984.

"Review of *Retribution.*" *American Whig Review* 10 (1849): 376–86.

Reynolds, David S. *Beneath the American Renaissance: The Subversive Imagi-*

nation in the Age of Emerson and Melville. New York: Alfred A. Knopf, 1988.

Riley, Glenda. *Inventing the American Woman: A Perspective on Women's History, 1865 to the Present*. Arlington Heights, Ill.: Harlan Davidson, 1986.

Romero, Lora. "Bio-Political Resistance in Domestic Ideology and *Uncle Tom's Cabin*." *American Literary History* 1.4 (1989): 715–34.

Rosaldo, Michelle Zimbalist. "The Use and Abuse of Anthropology: Reflections on Feminism and Cross-Cultural Understanding." *Signs* 4.3 (1979): 497–513.

———. "Women, Culture, and Society: A Theoretical Overview." In *Women, Culture, and Society*, edited by Michelle Zimbalist Rosaldo and Louise Lamphere, 17–42. Stanford: Stanford University Press, 1974.

Rose, Jacqueline. *Sexuality in the Field of Vision*. London: Verso, 1986.

Rosenberg, Charles E. "Sexuality, Class, and Role in Nineteenth-Century America." *American Quarterly* 25.2 (1973): 131–53.

Rothstein, William. *American Physicians in the Nineteenth Century: From Sects to Science*. Baltimore: Johns Hopkins University Press, 1972.

Rowe, John Carlos. *The Theoretical Dimensions of Henry James*. Madison: University of Wisconsin Press, 1984.

Rowson, Susanna. *Charlotte Temple*. Edited by Ann Douglas. 1794. Reprint. New York: Penguin Books, 1991.

Rubin, Gayle. "The Traffic in Women." In *Toward an Anthropology of Women*, edited by Rayna Reiter, 157–210. New York: Monthly Review, 1975.

Ryan, Michael. "The Politics of Film: Discourse, Psychoanalysis, Ideology." In *Marxism and the Interpretation of Culture*, edited by Cary Nelson and Lawrence Grossberg, 477–86. Urbana: University of Illinois Press, 1988.

Salk, Hilary, et al. "The Politics of Women's Health." In Boston Women's Health Book Collective, *Our Bodies, Ourselves*. New York: Simon and Schuster, 1984.

Santos, Joan Foster. *Ellen Glasgow's American Dream*. Charlottesville: University of Virginia Press, 1965.

Satterwhite, Joseph N. "The Tremulous Formula: Form and Technique in *Godey's* Fiction." *American Quarterly* 8 (1956): 99–113.

Scarry, Elaine. *The Body in Pain*. New York: Oxford University Press, 1985.

———. Introduction to *Literature and the Body: Essays on Populations and Persons*, edited by Elaine Scarry, vii–xx. Selected Papers from the English Institute, 1986. Baltimore: Johns Hopkins University Press, 1988.

Schopp-Schilling, Beate. " 'The Yellow Wallpaper': A Rediscovered 'Realistic' Story." *American Literary Realism* 8 (1975): 284–86.

Schriber, Mary. "Justice to Zenobia." *New England Quarterly* 55 (1982): 61–78.

Schweikart, Patrocinio, and Elizabeth Flynn. *Gender and Reading*. Baltimore: Johns Hopkins University Press, 1986.

Sedgwick, Eve Kosofsky. *Between Men: English Literature and Male Homosocial Desire*. New York: Columbia University Press, 1985.

Shorter, Edward. *A History of Women's Bodies*. New York: Basic Books, 1982.

Showalter, Elaine. "The Death of the Lady (Novelist): Wharton's *House of Mirth.*" *Representations* 9 (1985): 133–49.

———. *The Female Malady: Women, Madness, and English Culture, 1830–1980*. New York: Pantheon, 1985.

Shulman, Robert. "Divided Selves and the Market Society: Politics and Psychology in *The House of Mirth.*" *Perspectives on Contemporary Literature* 11 (1985): 10–19.

Smith, Barbara Herrnstein. *Contingencies of Value: Alternative Perspectives for Critical Theory*. Cambridge: Harvard University Press, 1988.

Smith, Henry Nash. "The Scribbling Women and the Cosmic Success Story." *Critical Inquiry* 1 (1974): 47–70.

Smith, Page. *Daughters of the Promised Land: Women in American History*. Boston: Little, Brown, 1970.

Smith-Rosenberg, Carroll. *Disorderly Conduct: Visions of Gender in Victorian America*. New York: Oxford University Press, 1985.

Smith-Rosenberg, Carroll, and Charles Rosenberg. "The Female Animal: Medical and Biological Views of Woman and Her Role in Nineteenth-Century America." In *Women and Health in America*, edited by Judith Walzer Leavitt, 12–27. Madison: University of Wisconsin Press, 1984.

Sontag, Susan. *Illness as Metaphor*. New York: Farrar, Straus, Giroux, 1978.

Southworth, E. D. E. N. *Retribution*. Chicago: M. A. Donahue and Company, 1849.

Spiller, Robert E., Willard Thorp, Thomas H. Johnson, and Henry Seidel Canby. *Literary History of the United States*. Vol. 1. New York: Macmillan, 1948.

Spillers, Hortense. "Changing the Letter: The Yokes, the Jokes of Discourse: Or, Mrs. Stowe, Mr. Reed." In *Slavery and the Literary Imagination*, edited by Deborah E. McDowell and Arnold Rampersad, 25–61. Baltimore: Johns Hopkins University Press, 1989.

Stage, Sarah. *Female Complaints: Lydia Pinkham and the Business of Women's Medicine*. New York: W. W. Norton, 1979.

Starr, Paul. *The Social Transformation of American Medicine*. New York: Basic Books, 1982.

Steele, Valerie. *Fashion and Eroticism: Ideals of Feminine Beauty from the Victorian Era to the Jazz Age*. New York: Oxford University Press, 1985.

Stein, Gertrude. *Three Lives*. 1909. Reprint. New York: Modern Library, 1933.

Stowe, Harriet Beecher. *Pink and White Tyranny: A Society Novel*. Boston: Roberts Brothers, 1871.

———. *Uncle Tom's Cabin; or, Life Among the Lowly*. Edited by Ann Douglas. 1852. Reprint. New York: Penguin American Library, 1981.

Stowe, Harriet Beecher, and Catharine Beecher. *The American Woman's Home: or, Principles of Domestic Science; Being a Guide to the Formation and Maintenance of Economical, Healthful, Beautiful, and Christian Homes*. New York: J. B. Ford and Company, 1869.

Strouse, Jean. *Alice James: A Biography*. Boston: Houghton Mifflin, 1980.

Suleiman, Susan, ed. *The Female Body in Western Culture*. Cambridge: Harvard University Press, 1985.

Tims, Margaret. *Mary Wollstonecraft: A Social Pioneer*. London: Millington, 1976.

Tompkins, Jane. "Highbrow-Lowbrow Revisited: The Revival of Mass-Culture Criticism." Paper presented at Modern Language Association Convention, San Francisco, 28 December 1987.

———. *Sensational Designs: The Cultural Work of American Fiction*. New York: Oxford University Press, 1985.

Treichler, Paula. "Escaping the Sentence: Diagnosis and Discourse in 'The Yellow Wallpaper.' " *Tulsa Studies in Women and Literature* 3.1–2 (1984): 61–77.

Turkle, Sherry. *Psychoanalytic Politics: Freud's French Revolution*. New York: Basic Books, 1978.

Uroff, M. D. "The Doctors in 'Rappaccini's Daughter.' " *Nineteenth-Century Fiction* 27 (1972): 61–70.

Veblen, Thorstein. *The Theory of the Leisure Class: An Economic Study of Institutions*. 1899. Reprint. New York: B. W. Huebsch, 1918.

Veeder, William. *Henry James: The Lessons of the Master—Popular Fiction and Personal Style in the Nineteenth Century*. Chicago: University of Chicago Press, 1975.

Verbrugge, Lois. "Gender and Health: An Update on Hypotheses and Evidence." *Journal of Health and Social Behavior* 26 (1985): 156–82.

Verbrugge, Martha. *Able-Bodied Womanhood: Personal Health and Social Change in Nineteenth-Century Boston*. New York: Oxford University Press, 1988.

Vernon, John. "Labor and Leisure: *The Wings of the Dove*." in *Money and Fiction: Literary Realism in the Nineteenth and Early Twentieth Centuries*. Ithaca, N.Y.: Cornell University Press, 1984.

Wagenknecht, Edward. *Eve and Henry James: Portraits of Women and Girls in His Fiction*. Norman: University of Oklahoma Press, 1978.

Wagner, Linda. *Ellen Glasgow: Beyond Convention*. Austin: University of Texas Press, 1982.

Wagner, Vern. "Henry James: Money and Sex." *Sewanee Review* 93.2 (1985): 216–31.

Wakefield, Edward. "The National Disease of America." *McClure's Magazine* 2 (1893): 302–7.

Walsh, Mary Roth. *"Doctors Wanted: No Women Need Apply": Sexual Barriers in the Medical Profession, 1835–1975*. New Haven: Yale University Press, 1977.

Warhol, Robyn. *Gendered Interventions: Narrative Discourse in the Victorian Novel*. New Brunswick, N.J.: Rutgers University Press, 1989.

Wasserstrom, William. *Heiress of All the Ages: Sex and Sentiment in the Genteel Tradition*. Minneapolis: University of Minnesota Press, 1959.

Way, Brian. *F. Scott Fitzgerald and the Art of Social Fiction*. London: Edward Arnold, 1980.

Welter, Barbara. "The Cult of True Womanhood, 1820–1860." *American Quarterly* 18 (1966): 151–74.

———. *Dimity Convictions: The American Woman in the Nineteenth Century*. Athens: Ohio University Press, 1976.

Wershoven, Carol. *The Female Intruder in the Novels of Edith Wharton*. Rutherford, N.J.: Fairleigh Dickinson University Press, 1982.

Wharton, Edith. *Ethan Frome*. New York: Charles Scribner's Sons, 1911.

———. *The House of Mirth*. New York: Charles Scribner's Sons, 1905.

———. "Roman Fever." In *The World Over*. New York: D. Appleton-Century Company, 1936.

White, Allon. *The Uses of Obscurity: The Fiction of Early Modernism*. London: Routledge and Kegan Paul, 1981.

White, Hayden. *Tropics of Discourse: Essays on Cultural Criticism*. Baltimore: Johns Hopkins University Press, 1978.

Williams, Stanley T. *The Life of Washington Irving*. Vol. 2. New York: Oxford University Press, 1935.

Willis, Ellen. "Comment." In *Marxism and the Interpretation of Culture*, edited by Cary Nelson and Lawrence Grossberg, 117–19. Urbana: University of Illinois Press, 1988.

Wolff, Cynthia Griffin. *A Feast of Words: The Triumph of Edith Wharton*. New York: Oxford University Press, 1977.

Wolp, A. M., and A. Kuhn. *Feminism and Materialism*. London: Routledge and Kegan Paul, 1978.

Woolf, Virginia. *Collected Essays*. Vol. 2. New York: Harcourt, Brace and World, 1966.

Woolson, Abba Goold. *Woman in American Society*. Boston: Roberts Brothers, 1873.

Yeazell, Ruth Bernard. Introduction to Alice James, *The Death and Letters of Alice James*. Berkeley: University of California Press, 1981.

Index

112–13, 128, 129, 133–40, 141–49, 152, 171, 178, 185, 208, 216, 217; *Ethan Frome*, 151, 164, 165–72, 175, 178–83, 185, 196, 206–7, 210–11, 215; "Roman Fever," 168–69, 171; *Custom of the Country*, 241 (n. 23)

White, Hayden, 5

Willpower, 54, 92, 94, 140, 189–90; in New Thought, 114, 119; as cause of illness, 151, 198; bequests, 186, 189, 200; failure of, 201

Woman, representations of: as nature, 82, 229 (n. 5); doubled/contradictory, 83–84, 88, 90, 98–99, 104–5, 109, 197, 217; as natural invalid, 85, 86; as object, 63, 89, 98, 104, 125, 132, 134, 135–38, 195, 206; "dark" versus "light," 93, 100, 233 (n. 33), 241 (n. 1); as child, 130

Womanhood: contradictory models of, 25, 38, 39, 41, 49, 100, 115; defined as invalidism, 30

Wood, Ann Douglas, 7, 21, 22, 24, 224 (n. 3). *See also* Douglas, Ann

Woolf, Virginia, 137

Woolson, Abba Goold, 7, 110–11, 122

Work, 185; as sickening, 78; as healthful, 143–44, 174–75; woman's, 189, 194; in consumer economy, 194, 197; idealization in *Tender Is the Night*, 203, 205

Yeazell, Ruth Bernard, 126

Zola, Emile, 136, 237 (n. 25)